Through
GREAT CENTRAL
England

Through GREAT CENTRAL *England*

A railway journey
by trackbed and train from
Nottingham to London

DAVID ABLITT

Drawings by Bill Vincent

• RAILWAY HERITAGE •
from
The NOSTALGIA *Collection*

First published in 2009
Reprinted 2009

British Library Cataloguing in Publication Data

A catalogue record for this book is available from the British Library.

ISBN 978 1 85794 317 7

Silver Link Publishing Ltd
The Trundle
Ringstead Road
Great Addington
Kettering
Northants NN14 4BW

Tel/Fax: 01536 330588
email: sales@nostalgiacollection.com
Website: www.nostalgiacollection.com

Printed and bound in the Czech Republic

Note: Every effort has been made to trace the owners of the copyright of photographs used in this book; however, if any reader is aware of any error in this respect please contact the author via the publisher.

The extract from *Great Central, Sheffield Victoria to Banbury* by John Betjeman on page 28 is reproduced by kind permission of John Murray (Publishers) Ltd.

Wherever possible, published sources have been mentioned in the text. However, there were two books that served as my constant companions on the journey: *Great Central* by George Dow, the most authoritative history of that railway company, and relevant volumes of *The King's England* by Arthur Mee.

Readers wishing to explore the course of a disused railway are advised to respect the law relating to trespass and always seek permission before entering private land.

CONTENTS

ACKNOWLEDGEMENTS

I received an immense amount of help from a large number of people when writing *Through Great Central England*. First, I am indebted to all the interviewees, who shared their memories so generously and without whom the book would of been of much less interest. However, among them, Richard Hardy and the late Jim Anscomb are deserving of special thanks for the vast amount of background information they provided in addition to that which appears in the record of their interviews.

In many instances I have referred to my sources in the body of the text, but feel that my gratitude to the following individuals and organisations should be recorded here.

My good friends Stephen Best and Bill Vincent; Stephen, a retired Nottinghamshire Local Studies Librarian, for commenting on the manuscript, and Bill for providing his excellent drawings and also for checking the text; and both of them for unstinting encouragement.

Ken Grainger, of the Great Central Railway Society, and another good friend, for advice and help with photographs.

Staff in the Local Studies Libraries at Nottingham, Leicester, Rugby and Westminster (Marylebone); Leicester City Museums Service; and the Planning and/or Information Departments at Nottingham, Loughborough, Leicester, Lutterworth, Rugby, Brackley and Aylesbury.

British Railways staff, especially the following, who held the positions mentioned when the book was being written: Malcolm Southgate, General Manager of the London Midland Region, for arranging my journey by empty stock train from Bletchley to Aylesbury; J. Reeks, Nottingham Divisional Manager, for allowing me to walk the operational line from Ruddington to Loughborough; and Steven Hawkes, the Station Manager at Marylebone.

Chiltern Trains for information and photographs; The Great Central Railway, Loughborough; The Buckinghamshire Railway Society; The Bell Foundry Museum, Loughborough; and others too numerous to mention.

Finally Judy, my partner, who has tolerated and encouraged me in my endeavours over many years.

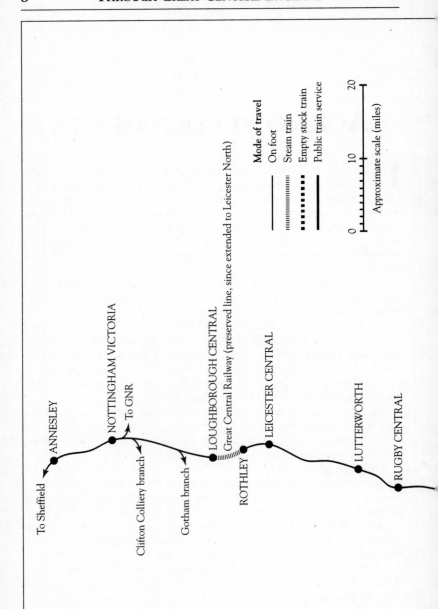

To Sheffield

ANNESLEY

NOTTINGHAM VICTORIA

To GNR

Clifton Colliery branch

Gotham branch

LOUGHBOROUGH CENTRAL

Great Central Railway (preserved line, since extended to Leicester North)

ROTHLEY

LEICESTER CENTRAL

LUTTERWORTH

RUGBY CENTRAL

Mode of travel

On foot

Steam train

Empty stock train

Public train service

Approximate scale (miles)

0   10   20

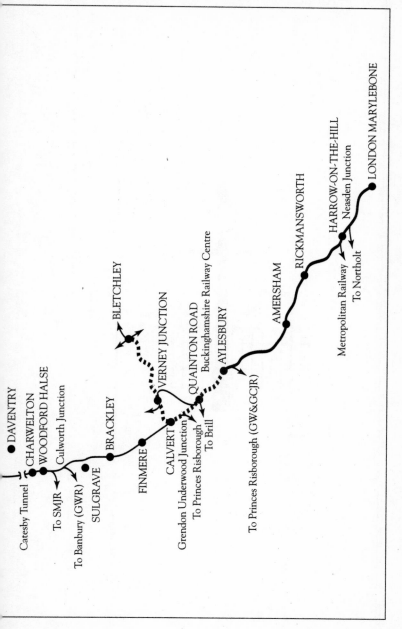

The course of the author's journey along the GCR 'London Extension', showing the principal places visited.

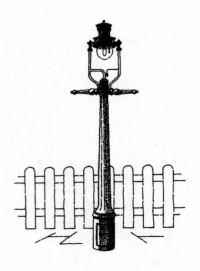

INTRODUCTION

Few books have endured a gestation period as long as that of *Through Great Central England*. The idea of walking the abandoned track of the Great Central Railway, from its start among the coal mines north of Nottingham to the fashionable and affluent Marylebone area of London, was conceived in the 1980s but, although the manuscript was completed before the end of that decade, it was not to be published for almost another twenty years.

With supreme confidence, born of naivety, I was convinced that I could write a book based on the history of a railway, but aimed at a readership with wider interests and one that would be eagerly sought by publishers competing for the honour of introducing it to the waiting world. It was not to be like that. A leading railway publisher of the day commented that it was a very interesting travel book and suggested an approach to a certain reputable travel publisher. The reputable travel publisher remarked that it was a very interesting railway book – and suggested an approach to the railway publisher! The book had fallen through a gap between what were perceived as two separate markets and, with many other things happening in my life at that time, the manuscript was placed on one side.

Time passed by. The engineering industry, which had provided me with a living since leaving school, suffered a severe decline and the site of 'my' factory was soon occupied by the newly thriving finance sector and DIY stores. The Soviet Union collapsed, the Cold War ended and the Berlin Wall came down. Margaret Thatcher was chased from office and, a few years later, the electorate replaced her successor with a New Labour Prime Minister. Privatisation of the nations assets continued. The Channel Tunnel opened. We stopped worrying about the coming Ice Age and became anxious about global warming instead. My children grew up. My hair turned from black to grey and from grey to white. I worried less that the police were a force of oppression and started to feel concern that there were too few of them on the streets. And still the manuscript mouldered on a shelf in a spare room.

Things began to change when an acquaintance from long ago, so long ago that he could no longer remember me, rang to say he had heard of the manuscript and could he read it? A professional author, he was writing about *The Lost Railways of Leicestershire* and his comments on the work prompted a re-evaluation of the manuscript, and the realisation dawned that the book now had a different value. Although written when the 1980s were the present and containing personal recollections of what had gone before, the passage of time had ensured that it was now set entirely in the past – and the journey it described could never be repeated, for so much had changed forever. Most of the people who had been so free with their recollections had moved to a place where they could never again share their experiences with human beings. And much else had changed along the course of my walk. From the start of the journey near Nottingham, to its end at Marylebone, there had been vast changes and the book now stood not only as a record of what the railway had been like in its working days but also of what the country through which it passed had been like in what are now the long-gone days of the 1980s. In these circumstances, it was my good fortune that Will Adams and his colleagues at Silver Link Publishing realised that the book had potential and were willing to explore that space between railway and travel publishing, from which others had shied away.

I trust that Silver Link's confidence will prove well founded and that readers will gain pleasure from the book.

David Ablitt
Thorneywood
Nottingham

1
ANNESLEY

From Robin Hood's Hills, near Annesley in Nottinghamshire, there is a view down the valley of the River Leen – a wide, flat-bottomed valley with low conifer-clad hills rising on either side and a massive, squat slag heap in the middle. At that time, in the mid-1980s, the headstocks of three collieries were spaced out into the distance and a single-track railway snaked northward, to end forlornly at a set of rusting buffer-stops where a few horses grazed at the foot of the hill. I was there to begin a walk through the middle of England, along the track of a disused railway, and it could not have been a more appropriate starting point. Not just because Annesley marked the northern extremity of the Great Central Railway's route to London, but because it lay in the true heart of England, where rolling hills cohabited with colliery spoil heaps and coal miners with farmers, land-owners and estate workers.

Nearby, the homes of two literary giants illustrated this blend of traditions: Newstead Abbey, one-time seat of Lord Byron, lay in magnificent parkland two miles to the south-east, while five miles south-west stood the small town of Eastwood and the house in a humble terrace where D. H. Lawrence was born into a mining family. The spirit of the place remained much as described by Lawrence: green countryside, grey pit-heaps and down-to-earth people. The pits and their spoil heaps were fewer, though larger by that time, and modern housing was beginning to surround some villages, but the local folk and the terraced rows seemed little changed.

Only an hour previously I had been in the company of a man who would have fitted as easily into the lines of one of Lawrence's stories as he did into the public house where we met. We took our drinks outside and sat on a decaying bench to exchange opinions on the weather, local beer and the peaceful situation. In his early thirties and muscular, but with the pallor that typified the younger miner until it eventually gave way to ruddiness caused by a lifetime of scrubbing coal dust from the pores, he seemed to symbolise the area. I wondered how people would change as I journeyed south and whether they would be as frank as this man, who basked in the sunshine and told how he had exaggerated the pain in his back to win a few days away from the mine.

'There is a better life to be had than that down there, crawling around in the dark and filth all day. Take the landlord of this pub; he'd got nowt when he moved in a few years back, and look at him now. That's his car – the Jag. And he's got a cottage in Norfolk and a knock-off in Pinxton, not that he did much to earn either of 'em. So, I reckon I'm entitled at least to a bit of sun and fresh air.'

Moments later, the publican emerged from the doorway and eased his barrel-shaped body into the Jaguar, which the collier dismissed sourly as 'flash'. Comic, in the mismatched attire of the middle-aged newly rich and with his flabby flesh squeezed into undersized clothes in deference to vanity, he looked the archetypal fancy-man. After the car had drawn away, we sat in silence for a few moments, the collier no doubt ruminating on life's inequalities, while I toyed with bizarre images of the overweight publican and his knock-off in Pinxton.

The pub had seemed an ideal place to sit and contemplate what lay ahead on the long southerly walk along the Great Central Railway, but the collier was a sociable man with little inclination to leave others to their inner thoughts. Casting his eye over my map, he was free with advice on local matters, but soon digressed on to scandal. With a couple of hours to spare it would have been fascinating, and the prospect of another pint of beer was tempting but, if any progress was to be made that day, the time had come to search for the remains of the railway.

The idea of walking the course of the Great Central had evolved during a period when its characteristic buildings and great engineering features were fast being destroyed, a disquieting process for one with memories of the 1940s and '50s, when it seemed inconceivable that a main-line railway could ever disappear. In those days the company's vast Nottingham station seemed part of the very fabric of the earth, while even small country stations possessed a reassuring air of permanence. That was a time when, with Britain struggling to regain normality after the Second World War, trains were rarely clean or new, but the faint sulphury, dusty odour of the carriage upholstery was familiar and comforting, even romantic. Like the layers of drifting smoke, pierced by shafts of sunlight in the void beneath its grimy glass roof, the station was associated with the start of a day out, or a family holiday.

Following closure of the line, even when the track had been lifted and the stations demolished, great viaducts, bridges and embankments remained as seemingly permanent reminders of the railway's place in the landscape, until they too fell victim to the drive to clear away the remnants of Britain's industrial past. By the early 1970s some sections of the route had been obliterated by new developments in towns and, by the end of that decade, the process had spread to the countryside. Graceful viaducts were demolished as eyesores and massive embankments, already developing into nature reserves, were carted away to fill equally massive cuttings in a pointless reversal of the work of those who had built the line. So the opportunity to walk the track had to be seized, or be lost forever along with the chance to view the scenes that passengers had once enjoyed, to admire the engineering achievements of its builders and to listen to those who remembered the railway in better days.

The area around Robin Hood's Hills is rich in railway history. Mansfield, visible to the north-west, had, in the 1980s, the dubious distinction of being the largest town in England without a passenger railway. And yet a primitive tramway had first reached there as long ago as 1819, for the local coalfield was a magnet to early railway builders. The line below my viewpoint, meandering along the valley floor to its inglorious terminus amid grazing horses, was the sole survivor of three built by major companies to serve the area. Opened by the Midland Railway in 1848, it tunnelled through the hill to Mansfield and beyond, but that tunnel and another that carried the Great Central line, was filled in during the 1970s, leaving the truncated Midland route as the sole link between the Leen Valley mines and the main rail network at Nottingham. Remarkably, twenty years after closure, the Midland Railway's tunnel was re-excavated and Mansfield was reconnected to the rail network in 1995. But that is another story.

Second on the scene was the Great Northern Railway, in 1882. From Colwick, on the Grantham to Nottingham branch, it sent out an expeditionary line westward into the Midland's home territory of Derbyshire, with a branch striking north into the Leen Valley from Nottingham's outskirts. But it was the arrival of the Manchester, Sheffield & Lincolnshire Railway (MS&LR), forerunner of the Great Central, from the north in 1892 that guaranteed Annesley a place in British railway history. For this was no mere branch line competing for local coal traffic, but part of an ambitious, if unsuccessful, plan to link the Industrial North of England with Europe, via London and a Channel Tunnel.

The scheme involved joining the Manchester, Sheffield & Lincolnshire Railway to the Metropolitan Railway, which owned a tunnel under the Thames, and the South Eastern Railway, which offered running rights onward to the Kent coast. Work started in 1894, and by 1899 ninety-two miles of track had been laid between the

MS&LR's southern extremity at Annesley and a junction with the Metropolitan near Aylesbury. From the moment of its birth the new line was forced to fight for survival against well-established rivals, a fight that resulted in its services becoming famous for speed and efficiency, while engendering a loyalty among passengers and staff that lived on long after the line's death. As a recognisable entity the Great Central survived integration into the London & North Eastern Railway in 1923, and later absorption by British Railways, only to meet a miserable fate of run-down and closure as a result of the infamous Beeching Report in the 1960s. By the 1980s, what had been probably the best-engineered railway in Britain merited no more representation on Ordnance Survey maps than a faint dotted line, extending from the Nottinghamshire Coalfield to the Home Counties.

2
THE JOURNEY BEGINS

George Dow, a lifelong professional railwayman who was fascinated by the Great Central, wrote in his monumental history of the GCR that the start of its London Extension was at Annesley North Junction, 'about a quarter of a mile beyond the south portal of Annesley Tunnel which pierced the Robin Hood Hills.'

A walk down the hillside revealed no evidence of the tunnel, and only a mound of earth marked the course of its infilled approach cutting. Gone forever was the scene described by Dow:

> 'South of the junction were laid extensive sidings for coal traffic. These were arranged for the marshalling of loaded wagons for the south and the sorting of empties for the various collieries. They had a total holding capacity of 1,665 and additional land had been taken to lay sidings for 2,040 more wagons when needed. At the south end of the yard was built a locomotive depot for thirty locomotives ... supplemented by a wagon repair shop and electricity generating plant.'

All had disappeared and the site lay buried beneath a massive colliery slag heap, on which crawled seemingly miniscule, yellow-painted earthmovers.

Two workmen, servicing a colliery pump-house that stood in a field, told me that the only practical route south was along the surviving railway towards the coal mine and assured me that, with the pit closed for the annual holiday, I would not be prosecuted for trespass. And so began the first part of my Great Central Railway trek. It was an inauspicious start, for the railway along which I had for so long planned to walk was mostly buried beneath slag heaps, while unevenly spaced sleepers and roughly heaped ballast on the track that I was forced to follow made progress slow and uncomfortable.

A few hundred yards along the line a solitary railwayman busied himself removing equipment from a redundant signal box. He was as friendly as the collier I had met earlier, more interested in welcoming a visitor than challenging a trespasser, and talked affectionately of the Great Central, although confessing that he was unable to point out exactly where it had been since British Coal had rearranged the landscape. A Midland Railway man himself, with fond memories of his time spent working on that company's Mansfield Station, his manner only betrayed bitterness when he looked towards the filled-in tunnel.

'It was criminal what they did, killing the railway. We often had ten-coach trains full of shoppers and factory girls coming into Mansfield, so don't believe them when they tell you the trains were empty.'

Behind us, a moonscape of spoil from Annesley Colliery rose skyward. At its foot, grey slurry had dried to form a barren surface where nothing grew, except for a ruby-red rose near a patch of asphalt. He told me it was all that remained of Annesley's Midland Station.

After passing between slag mountains, the track widened and hundreds of coal wagons stood in sidings. This was Newstead Colliery, the second pit in little over a mile, and the railway, now double-track, appeared more purposeful. On one side stood the pit, on the other miners' terraced cottages, which took on a warm glow as their mellow red brickwork absorbed and softened the sun's harsh light.

A path meandered across the deserted grey wasteland of the pit yard, passed beneath a cast-iron bridge that had once carried the Great Northern's tracks, and grew into a lane leading to Newstead Abbey. Now owned by Nottingham City Council, Newstead is justifiably famous for its house and grounds, ornamental lakes, Japanese garden and the tomb of Byron's dog 'Boatswain' – with its remarkable eulogy to a canine at the expense of humanity. The house remained an important seat of power even when the Great Central was being built, obliging the company to cross its drive by an unusually ornate bridge and to build the adjacent signal box of stone, instead of the usual brick and timber. Only a dip in the ground, where the lane once passed beneath the bridge, remained as evidence of the course of the railway and, immediately to the south, the trackbed lay buried under yet another slag heap, this one grassed over and grazed by sheep.

From this point the abandoned trackbed of the Great Northern offered the best route, even though the surface of lorry-rutted slurry had been baked hard by the sun. At first sight the dry grey mud of that unearthly trackway appeared completely barren, but nature was already fighting the abuse of her territory. No grass had yet appeared but, like the poppies that rose from the mud of Flanders, wild flowers were raising their colourful heads from the crusted surface, while butterflies danced above in the shimmering heat. Alongside, a corrugated-iron

tunnel stretched into the distance like a giant caterpillar and concealed a conveyor built to transport waste the couple of miles between Linby Colliery and the slag heap on the site of Annesley Marshalling Yard.

About a mile further on, after crossing a small bridge over the conveyor where it lay in a shallow cutting, the view eastwards across a cornfield revealed a low embankment emerging from the grassed-over slag heap. This was my first sighting of the remains of the Great Central Railway – a forlorn and uninspiring embankment broken by gaps left by demolished bridges.

Half a mile after joining the railway I entered the village of Linby, part chocolate-box picturesque and part industrial. Streams flowed on both sides of the village green, which extended almost the length of the main street, and at each end stood a stone cross. In the old part of the village, immaculately kept houses with rustic nameboards and a surfeit of door-side carriage lamps indicated gentrification. Except for the distant sound of a motorised lawnmower, the place was silent.

A road bridge over the course of the Great Northern track led to a different world: eastward the old village and its church, to the west the colliery estate of 1940s council-type houses in a country setting. In a neighbouring field stood the platform of the Midland Railway's station, closed in 1964. Since abandonment, the once lovingly tended garden had grown wild and red rose blooms cascaded over decaying palings into the pasture below. Nearby, a neat little timber signal box guarded a level crossing and added interest to the peaceful scene. However, only a few yards to the south the slag heaps and headstocks of Linby Colliery loomed large. This village had lived with industry and its excesses since the first days of the Industrial Revolution, when water-powered textile mills prospered here before coal and steam were of much consequence. In the churchyard the graves of London orphans, forty-two recorded and many more unmarked, who were sent here by their Board of Guardians and worked to death by a local mill-owner, serve as a grim reminder of that unhappy period.

Leaving the village on an embankment that formed a barrier

between slag heaps rising high on the left and colliers' houses below on the right, the Great Central began to show its character. While the other two railways were content to follow a falling gradient, similar to that of the river, before skirting around the high ground on which Nottingham was built, the Great Central was already high above them as it manoeuvred into position for a frontal assault on that city, still some eight miles distant. In a sense, the methods used by Great Central engineers were reminiscent of those employed by Roman road builders so many centuries before, and the line was remarkable for the way it traversed hilly terrain with few curves or severe gradients. Throughout the ninety-two miles between Annesley and Aylesbury there were few sections steeper than 1 in 176, and these were confined to the short stretch north of Nottingham, while curves of less than a mile in radius and level crossings were avoided entirely; even farm tracks were carried over or under the line. Such features gave the railway its characteristically massive earthworks and contributed to its tremendous cost, but also provided a railway racetrack that, had it survived, would have been perfect for modern high-speed trains.

The grand concept seemed distant on entering the small town of Hucknall, along a scruffy cutting where a lorry was tipping rubble against a filled-in bridge. Beyond, the railway had disappeared, its trackbed claimed for garden extensions by the owners of neighbouring houses, making inevitable a tedious detour through streets of between-the-wars housing. Hucknall was once a mining and textile town abounding with Nonconformist chapels, and was, understandably, proud of its associations with Byron, whose remains lie in the parish church adjacent to the Market Place. Even the facade of the Co-op sported his statue, and the cinema and bingo hall bore his name.

Eventually, I was to regain the trackbed slightly west of the town, where it had once passed through a deep cutting. George Dow's book told me that 270,000 cubic yards of limestone had been excavated from here by the Great Central's builders, which, in more recent times, Nottinghamshire County Council had replaced with a similar amount of rubbish. But it was here that a girder bridge, carrying a road over the man-made ravine, still stood. The space beneath had not been completely filled, leaving on view the first Great Central structure to be seen intact since leaving Annesley. Regrettably, the County Council had not shared the railway's concern to provide proper drainage, and a pool of stinking water had formed in the hollow under the bridge. Treading gingerly through this quagmire I was to experience one of the less predictable hazards of walking a disused railway. Two boxes of grass cuttings flew over the parapet to splash down among the half-submerged mattresses and supermarket trolleys, as an unseen gardener demonstrated indifference to his natural environment.

Hucknall Central, the first true station south of Annesley, where only halts had been provided for golfers and workmen, had been situated at the southern end of the cutting, where it widened out and became shallower. In common with almost all stations on the line it had a single island platform, in this case with access from a small red-brick booking hall standing on the east side of an overbridge. The bridge survived, but with earth packed beneath and only the blue-brick parapets visible. This part of the cutting had been untidily filled to a level slightly higher than the surrounding land, a sad sight that revived memories of a neat little station, of the booking hall and its solitary ticket window, and the elevated glazed timber passageway leading to the platforms that echoed noisily to generations of footfalls on its bare boards. A cedar-like odour had lingered in that passage, developed from dust and smoke absorbed by its timbers over their sixty-odd years of use. There were memories of the platform scene too: the tiny waiting room, with its welcoming fire on a winter evening, and the sight and sound of a train rounding the curve in the rock cutting as it rattled down the grade towards Nottingham.

Alongside a bridge to the south of the station a sign read: 'Nottinghamshire County Council – Hucknall Great Central Railway Reclamation Scheme – Grant Aided by the Department of the Environment.' Reclamation? Well, maybe even the barbarians could have boasted they had reclaimed a way of life when they sacked Rome. What's more, they managed to do the job without a Government grant!

A short walk through a nearby park led to the local cemetery, where a small urn marked the grave of my grandparents and the unmarried aunt who sacrificed so much to care for them in old age. Their life had been centred on this railway. Originating in Lancashire, they had moved their home up and down the line as work demanded and spent their last days at Hucknall, close to Annesley and its marshalling yard. It was here, in 1927, that they had set themselves up for retirement, buying a plot of land and erecting a wooden bungalow that they purchased in kit form from a mail order catalogue. Still standing, the bungalow's railway connections were betrayed by the Victorian guard's van converted into an outhouse, and the family link by the name 'Tilba Cottage', an anagram of their surname, engraved on a plate fixed to the front gate.

Immediately south of Hucknall the trackbed had been landscaped to the point of blandness, smooth new grass making it difficult to believe that a railway had ever passed by. Barbed wire barred the route, but local children had made a gap wide enough to squeeze through. Later, nearer the city, fences were to become more numerous and, on a number of occasions, progress was only possible due to the determination of children to reach their chosen play areas. But soon the scene was again that of an abandoned railway, with the trackbed skirting an airfield. Devoid of aircraft, other than a few that belonged to a flying club, nothing was visible to betray Hucknall Aerodrome's place in aviation history. Between 1934 and 1972 this was the principal Rolls-Royce Flight Testing Establishment, and many developments in aviation technology first took to the air at Hucknall.

In 1935 the Merlin engine, later to play such an important role in the Second World War, made its first flight from here. And it was here that the slow and underpowered American-built Mustang fighter was developed into one of the deadliest aircraft of the war, able to escort Allied bombers all the way to Berlin and back. Early turbo-jets were test-flown from the airfield, including one mounted in the tail of a Wellington bomber. Local people may have grown accustomed to such strange sights, but more than a few passengers on this railway would have been mystified by the ungainly machine that trundled around the sky with stationary propellers, heralding the birth of the jet age by emitting a deafening roar from a pipe that protruded from its rear end.

In 1945 another Hucknall hybrid made history. A Meteor jet fighter was fitted with propellers driven by gas turbines, to become the world's first turbo-prop aeroplane and the forerunner of the many successful aircraft powered by engines of this type, especially civil airliners, which travelled the world's air lanes from the 1950s onwards. Strangely, although it was developed later, the turbo-prop system had occurred to the inventor of the jet engine even before he conceived the idea of the turbo-jet, back in 1929. Perhaps even stranger was the apparently coincidental link between the Great Central Railway and the development of the jet engine, the line passing all of the principal development sites, including the first factories at Whetstone, Lutterworth and Rugby.

It was at Hucknall, in 1953, that engineers took another radical step forward, with one of the strangest looking aircraft ever built. The 'Flying Bedstead' was a wingless contraption, standing on four spindly legs that supported a pair of massive downward-thrusting jet engines and a mass of exposed pipework. The ultimate touch of ridicule was added by the pilot sitting on top on what looked from a distance like a dining chair! Never rising more than a few feet above the ground and consuming fuel at an alarming twenty-five gallons per minute, the Bedstead was, nonetheless, the ancestor of modern vertical-take-off aircraft, and an example is preserved by the Science Museum.

The Hucknall flight testing establishment was to continue its work until the early 1970s, when it became a victim of the Rolls-Royce financial collapse. By the time I walked by, the glamour of test flying was long gone, but the company still retained a factory on the airfield.

Eastward from the embankment was a long view across the Leen Valley, with the massive red-brick engine house of the defunct Bestwood Colliery in the middle distance, while beyond the raw new buildings of Nottingham's outer fringe confronted green fields. Next, the track passed a park and golf course, on what were once the grounds of Bulwell Hall and which had been for many years in the ownership of Nottingham Corporation. Before demolition in the early 1950s, the hall had suffered a varied existence, in the 'twenties and 'thirties housing a school and hospital for tubercular children – the innocent victims of nature's microbes and man's poor living conditions. Between 1909 and 1931 the railway maintained a halt here for the convenience of golfers, but no trace remained when I passed by.

This was a pleasant section of embankment, where wild flowers grew in profusion and attracted an impressive display of butterflies. Even the proximity of an estate of council houses posed no threat; they had co-existed for long enough and only the pathway betrayed recent human involvement in the scene. An unusually sympathetic approach, especially for one emanating from a local authority, had given access to the public while allowing nature its freedom. I wondered how long it could last, those in positions of authority so often being obsessed with control of the natural world. They prune trees that do not need to be pruned, make unnecessary asphalt paths to separate our feet from Mother Earth and build car parks in isolated places to encourage the idle to descend in multitudes and so destroy the peace they profess to seek.

About three hundred yards short of Bulwell Viaduct, the path ended where the embankment had been removed to leave a broad expanse of barren earth. As I walked on, the pleasure of seeing children enjoying themselves in an open-air swimming pool offered a little relief from the discomfort of the hot afternoon sun. But the viaduct that dominated the scene, towering over rooftops and shimmering in the heat, was too daunting a challenge to explore at the end of a tiring walk, so was left until the following day.

3
APPROACHING NOTTINGHAM

Bulwell Viaduct, which carried the railway across the Leen Valley, was the first major engineering work after the line left Annesley. Already severed at its northern end, as part of a road-widening scheme, it lacked some of the grace it had once possessed, but the hard blue brickwork was in perfect condition and the majestic lines of the structure made it hard to accept that the authorities could see no further use for it. Twenty-six arches spanned 420 yards, about forty-five feet above ground level and the track of the Midland Railway, which hugged the river bank below. Constructed of six and a half million bricks, reinforced with local stone, it took a mere twelve months to build and, like so many Victorian structures, survived as a monument to quality in an age of architectural mediocrity. Unfortunately, access to the viaduct, from the surviving embankment linked to its southern end, was barred by tall railings and a tangled mass of razor wire, which denied me the chance to revisit a view I had once enjoyed from a carriage window.

A little to the south the trackbed passed Bulwell Common, a municipal park mainly occupied by a golf course. There was once a complicated series of junctions here, linking the Great Central's tracks to the Nottingham-Derby line and the Leen Valley lines of the Great Northern Railway. Nowadays, the flyover and underpass are commonly thought of as inventions of motorway engineers but before the turn of the 19th century these two railways had built their own modest precursor to Spaghetti Junction, which allowed trains to cross over or join other lines without fouling up traffic in the process. A few years previously this area had been a fascinating maze of railway earthworks; but when I passed only a great scar of raw earth, where embankments had been removed and cuttings filled, betrayed the course of the railway. Cramped groups of modern little houses with mock-Tudor

porches obstructed the way and more were being built on the site of the
cutting that had once contained Bulwell Common Station. As at
Hucknall, only an underfilled road bridge remained as a locator to the
station site. Maybe passers-by could have recollected the scene but,
except for the children who played ball games on the Common, they
seemed silent, careworn and unapproachable as they took their dogs to
foul the nearby football pitch.

South of the station site, a few fragments of cuttings and
embankments remained. One section played host to a car-breaker's
yard, where a horde of men and youths pawed over rusting wrecks in
search of transplant organs for their motorised sacred cows. From the
brow of a hill, at one time sliced through by a cutting, the railway's
straight path into Nottingham stood out clearly as an undulating tract
of open land crossing terrain restored mostly to the contours that had
faced the line's builders ninety years previously. Below, to the west, a
short section of the Great Northern's sandstone cutting remained
intact, but modern warehousing was rising on the site of that company's
Basford North Station. A group of tinkers was camped nearby. What
seemed to be hoards of unruly children played with hungry-looking
dogs among luxurious caravans and ramshackle lorries, while weather-
beaten women sat around a fire amid scrap cars and other rubbish.

Shortly, the Nottingham ring road came into view from the top of a
vast embankment, which had recently been reduced in height to
expose a desert-like expanse of sandy sub-soil. No grass was to be seen,
but wild flowers and self-set lupins had already begun to thrive. Ahead,
the embankment and bridge over the road had been removed, revealing
a cross-section of the earthwork that must have been 200 yards wide at
its base and forty feet high. I scrambled down the steeply sloping end,
where rainwater had already cut gullies six feet deep in the year or so
since the earthmovers had done their work. South of the ring road it
was impossible to follow the trackbed, its filled-in cutting taken over by
neighbouring households. Next came steeply sloping streets, quiet as
middle class ones usually are, leading over the hill and down to the site
of New Basford Station, perhaps the most atmospheric place so far. A
few yards north of here had been a carriage shed and works that made
gas for carriage lighting, but modern industrial buildings and a timber
yard had taken their place.

New Basford Station, unlike Hucknall and Bulwell Common, had
been built on an embankment, to a pattern typical of the high-level
stations along the line. Passengers had entered at street level, through
an arch in the bridge abutment, and climbed steps to the island
platform. Here at Basford one abutment remained, with the outline of
the bricked-up archway clearly discernible. Other railway buildings

survived here too; the Station Master's house was lived in, while the adjoining goods yard eked out its days as a coal depot. An office stood inside the gateway, near an attractive, though decrepit, little weighbridge. Around the yard, coal dumps, partitioned off with ramshackle fencing consisting largely of old doors and sleepers, gave an air of neglect – with a little colour added by the occasional enamel advert, which had somehow evaded the eyes of antique collectors and bric-a-brac dealers.

A short section of platform remained, made colourful by flowers from the abandoned garden. Beyond the goods shed, four square and substantial, the trackbed entered a sandstone cutting leading to Sherwood Rise Tunnel. This, the first of a line of tunnels under Nottingham, had been bricked up for use as a store by an electrical contractor. I set out to walk over the hill.

A short deviation from the railway's route led through two vividly contrasting areas of high-density housing. It is one of life's ironies that housing developments tend to be named in memory of the countryside destroyed to accommodate them; this was Forest Fields, an estate of several thousand tightly packed terraces built for the better-off elements of the Edwardian working class. It was not unattractive; even though its streets were laid out in a grid-iron pattern they possessed a certain neatness, while the uniformity of the millions of bricks was relieved with decorative courses and carved stonework over windows and porches. It was easy to visualise these streets in Edwardian days and, even if the majority of shops were now owned by Asian families, there had been little visual change over the years.

Nottingham brick, with its mellow red hue, is particularly attractive and until recently most of the city, apart from some imposing stone structures in the central area, was built of it; but now it only predominated in older districts. The city was once a brickmaking centre of some consequence, clay being quarried around the town and brickworks set up to satisfy the voracious needs of the building boom of the 19th and early 20th centuries. And production must have far exceeded local demand, for it was Nottingham that supplied fifty-five million bricks for the construction of the Midland Railway's station at St Pancras, surely one of the nation's most imposing buildings.

The scene changed abruptly on entering an estate of council-owned flats, where drab, brooding concrete blocks were reminiscent of wartime fortifications. When I visited, the days were numbered for this crime and vice-ridden ghetto, which had gained notoriety in the inner-city riots of 1981, but it was still living up to its reputation. Even in the late afternoon, with streets almost deserted, there was an ominous atmosphere. A prostitute, one of a small group, called out an invitation from across the road. Probably sixteen years of age, undersized and anaemic-looking, she had a complexion pale as sliced white bread. In this sordid place, it was difficult not to think of and admire the majority of residents who were quietly going about the business of trying to live decent lives surrounded by vice and graffiti-scarred concrete. Fortunately for everyone, the local authority decided to sweep away the mess and the estate was demolished within two decades of its building.

4

BENEATH THE CITY

'Through cuttings deep in Nottingham
Precariously we wound;
The swallowing tunnel made the train
Seem London's underground.'

Great Central, Sheffield Victoria to Banbury
John Betjeman

The old city of Nottingham was built on sandstone hills, eroded on their southern slopes to form cliffs overlooking the Trent Valley. On the most spectacular of these outcrops stands the famous castle, actually a mansion bearing no resemblance to the Hollywood version of the building and probably a great disappointment to its many visitors. It was almost in the shadow of the castle and those cliffs that the Midland Railway built the city's first station in 1839, when it opened a line that crawled along the valley floor from Derby. Fifty years later the Great Central's engineers came on the scene with more ambitious plans and cut straight through the city from north to south. First piercing the hills at New Basford, the line passed through Sherwood Rise and Mansfield Road Tunnels, 665 and 1,189 yards long respectively and separated by a short length of open cutting containing Carrington Station. In another deep cutting near the city's centre they built the vast Victoria Station, before continuing the line through the 393-yard-long Victoria Street Tunnel to emerge on to a viaduct to cross the city's southern environs.

After closure, this section of railway, including the tunnels, had been purchased by Nottingham City Council, but its officers were kind enough to grant permission for me to explore it. The letter authorising me to walk through the Mansfield Road Tunnel caused a perceptible raising of eyebrows when I collected the key to the Carrington Station site from the newsagent whose shop occupied the old booking hall, but then grovelling around in a dark and sooty hole is hardly the most conventional way to spend a summer afternoon.

Carrington Station closed in 1928, as a result of competition from municipal buses and trams, but the station house and booking hall had been kept in good repair. The last remaining example of a Great Central station entrance in Nottinghamshire, it had previously housed a poodle-grooming parlour, and the arrival of a newsagency was to impart some welcome dignity. In common with Arkwright Street and Rushcliffe Halt, the station had side platforms, an unusual feature on the Great Central's London Extension. The area they occupied, approached down a sloping pathway, had become isolated and overgrown. Weeds, wild flowers and young trees grew in profusion, while on that afternoon butterflies fluttered around in the hot sun and the sound of crickets almost drowned the noise of traffic on surrounding roads. Rubbish abounded, and a handsome stone cornice from a demolished building lay among other debris – computer-generated spreadsheets, a supermarket trolley and rusty bicycle frames. In both directions, the dark, sullen tunnel mouths dominated the scene.

Mansfield Road Tunnel, leading south to Victoria Station, remained open and its size was impressive, the arched portal rising twenty-five feet above ground level and its blue-brick construction still sound and true. No light was visible through the bore, only impenetrable darkness, and within a few yards the air became chill, but the ballast was level and easy underfoot. The builders must have thought themselves fortunate to be boring through Bunter Sandstone – soft yet stable – so only the roof required to be reinforced with a brick lining. In the years since the last train had passed, dampness had eased soot from the walls to expose patches of clean sandstone that contrasted with the remaining steam-age grime.

Walking on, the small patch of daylight to the rear soon disappeared, obscured by distance and the slight curvature of the bore. Gradually, the chilliness increased until the torch beam illuminated a mist, formed by the reaction between the warm air from outside and the damp subterranean coolness. Near the middle of the tunnel, standing perfectly still in the all-enveloping darkness, it was just possible to detect the distant rumble of traffic, a tenuous link with the surface one hundred and twenty feet above. Few railway artefacts remained – wooden troughs used to protect signal wires, wooden rail keys left behind when the track was lifted, and alcoves in the sandstone walls to provide refuge for permanent way men.

I remembered looking from the window of a slowly moving train and seeing men in those alcoves – dark figures, misshapen and distorted by shadows, grotesquely illuminated by their own hand lamps and the light from the carriage windows. For them, in the smoke-laden darkness, it must have been awe-inspiring . Exhaust beats, amplified by the confined space of the tunnel, roaring ahead of the train, hissing steam and clanking connecting rods preceding the hellfire glow of the firebox and the shuddering, crunching of the ground as the locomotive passed. It would have been quieter as the coaches slipped by, with passengers peering from the windows high above. Now only the tunnel and its alcoves were left as a reminder of generations of work and sacrifice, like the mute earthworks of an extinct civilisation.

A few larger rooms, about eight feet square, were cut into the walls and seemed to have contained racks and lockers. Possibly they had been provided as messrooms for platelayers; not an ideal arrangement, but the company did sometimes expect men to spend their working days in conditions of unhealthy discomfort. At one period they even built a signal box deep inside the notoriously foul Woodhead Tunnel, on the Manchester to Sheffield line. But, whatever the real purpose of these rooms, the rusting iron bedstead in one of them bore witness to a mysterious use the company could not have intended.

Near the southern portal the corroded remains of two signals remained, fixed high on the walls, one either side. The tunnel mouth was plugged with an advertisement hoarding, but daylight streamed in around its edges and through a partly open door. The floor was littered with a tangle of steel cable, possibly dumped as scrap or maybe the proceeds of a theft from a building site, hidden and forgotten.

Emerging from the doorway into the warm outside air gave the sensation of being wrapped around with a heated blanket; and to be down at the level of Victoria Station's platforms again after so many years was a strange, melancholy experience. The ground had been bulldozed flat, but vegetation had already become established. While ferns and willow herb were colonising the great blue-brick retaining

walls, a buddleia in full bloom was further decorated by a multitude of richly coloured butterflies. Some basked and others fluttered, a silent argument for this inner-city wilderness, more important to our wellbeing than the vast concrete bunker full of shops, competing to sell nearly identical goods at nearly identical prices, which had invaded the southern end of the cutting.

Nottingham Victoria was the largest station on the Great Central's route to London, although its tremendous cost, in excess of £1 million at 1900 prices, was shared by the Great Northern Railway, which had lines running from Grantham and Derby. During construction the companies were unable to agree on a station name and, while the dispute simmered, it was known as the Nottingham Joint Station. However, a last-minute appeal to patriotism by the Town Clerk proved irresistible and the station was named in honour of the Queen, opening on her birthday in 1900.

The impact of the building work on Nottingham was traumatic; clearance of the twelve-acre site in the city's heartland involved the demolition of the workhouse, 1,300 houses and twenty pubs. Whole streets disappeared, to be replaced by a gigantic sandstone cutting 650 yards long, 100 yards wide and varying from forty to fifty feet in depth. The station's interior was palatial, contrasting strongly with the confined murkiness of the tunnels at either end. Two massive island platforms, almost a quarter of a mile long and with double bays at each end, provided no fewer that twelve platform faces, all sheltered by an elegant glass and steel roof standing forty-two feet above platform level.

The street frontage was handsome, described as being of Renaissance style, built of Darley Dale stone and Nottingham pressed brick. To one side stood the hotel and, centrally, an ornate clock tower rose more than 100 feet above street level. There was a large booking hall with a first-floor gallery, and a wide footbridge gave access to the platforms, while parcels, luggage and services to the refreshment rooms travelled by lifts and subways to avoid cluttering the public areas.

Victoria Station served Nottingham well. The journey time to Sheffield remains unbeaten by present-day trains using the Midland Railway route, and even the advent of High Speed Trains on the Midland line only succeeded in cutting two minutes from the Great Central's best time to Leicester. There were fast services to London and Manchester, and the very useful York to Bournemouth trains called here, while through expresses ran onto the Great Western system near Banbury to form a north-east to south-west service. After being taken over by British Railways' London Midland Region in 1958, the run-down of the Great Central began, accelerated in the 1960s, and the station was closed as part of the Beeching Plan in 1967. An alliance of property developers and the local authority ensured that one of Europe's ugliest shopping centres and flats complexes would occupy the main part of the site, with only the hotel and clock tower allowed to remain. Some years after I passed by, a standard utilitarian concrete car park was planted in the remaining part of the cutting, destroying the inner-city nature reserve and hiding the retaining walls and tunnel mouth.

Down near the tunnel, among the tall grass, part of a platform and the outline of a rubble-filled turntable pit could still be seen. 'The Hole', as the local media then called the surviving cutting, may only have covered about a quarter of the station site, but it was still vast. Huge retaining walls and man-made sandstone cliffs stood testimony to 19th-century enterprise and as a reminder of the Victorians' confident view of the future. In the tunnel mouth, that ridiculous advertisement, showing a toy-like train in bright, childish, primary colours, added a tawdry element to the scene, while ahead the Victoria Centre, which was once claimed to be the largest shopping centre in Europe, appeared a puny impostor sitting in the hole that the Victorians had dug. The ugly lines of the multi-storey car park were topped by the crudely designed bus station and, beyond, tall slab-sided flats. Incongruously, the copper cupola of the old station clock tower poked skyward among the concrete slabs to form a singular decorative feature in the harsh townscape. High above the cutting, youths shouted abuse from the bus station, their loutishness at one with their environment.

There was only one route out of the station site and that involved retreading the path through the tunnel. Leaving Carrington Station at rush hour was like entering bedlam, and treading the narrow pavement, sandwiched between an urban racetrack and the railings of a Victorian cemetery, bizarre. On one side granite monuments and marble angels crowded the hillside, on the other man and his motor car rushed insanely onward. Somehow the neglected tunnel and station cutting seemed preferable for their tranquillity and man's absence, and the purpose of the rusty iron bed, in its room far below, perhaps a little less mysterious.

I followed the streets above the tunnel back to the Victoria Centre. The view of the centre from the cutting had been akin to peering up the skirts of an old hag; that from the street was little better. The massive conglomeration, out of scale and character with its surroundings, was the sort of place architects of the 1960s described as 'exciting'. Most people have probably accepted it now. After all, there is more than one generation of Nottingham people who can't remember the station, who have no recollection of boarding a train there for London, or some distant South Coast resort, and do not remember when the hotel accommodated the well-heeled patrons of a proud railway. Most are unaware that the clock, in its ornate tower, now standing so inappropriately among high-rise blocks, once instilled a sense of urgent anxiety into countless travellers as they hurried to buy their tickets. But to those who did know the station, the memories of its golden years are indelible, as are those of its subsequent decline.

5
MEMORIES OF NOTTINGHAM VICTORIA

I met several local people with memories of Nottingham Victoria and it was typical that their own lives were of equal interest to anything to be learned of the station. No attempt was made to limit our conversations to purely railway matters, for the real pleasure of this journey lay in its diversity – not just diversity of scenery and environment, but of people and their backgrounds. The oldest I interviewed was George Fox. Born in 1889, he was perhaps the only survivor of that multitude evicted to make way for the coming of the Great Central, and even remembered watching the building of the station. Despite great age and failing eyesight, he was a vigorous and lively man who threw open the door to welcome me into his home on the outskirts of the city.

His first words were not about the station, or old Nottingham, but about his recent stay in the 'sheltered accommodation for the elderly', situated across the road from where we sat. He had stayed there for a few weeks while the council replaced his 1940s prefab with a new bungalow, and considered it an experience not to be repeated at any cost, the need to get his view of the matter off his chest obscuring all other items of conversation. Apparently the problem stemmed from his independent spirit, which had little in common with the other residents who occupied the diminishing number of their days on earth with a tedious routine of eating, sleeping and pill-taking. Such a life was not to George's liking and he had taken to rising early and going for long walks to escape the overheated atmosphere and the company of those bereft of hope, in some cases thirty years his junior! What annoyed him even more was that, despite his determined efforts to spend as much time as possible outside the place, he still caught diarrhoea and influenza during that brief stay – his first illnesses for many years. Lest his disapproval of institutionalised living be interpreted as disapproval of the welfare state, George added that he had much to thank the welfare system for. But he was so adamant about not returning to the home that he suspected that a trap was being set when the matron was kind enough to invite him back for dinner.

George Fox entered this world in a house on Charlotte Street, one of the main thoroughfares that crossed the site of Victoria Station, and although that house had been demolished when he was six years old he continued to live in the area until the turn of the 19th century. It was a time when conditions were so different from those we know today that, as he spoke, it seemed as if his long life had been a journey from a distant world.

With the building of the station, the railway company had been proud to boast of the destruction of an unpleasant and insanitary slum, but George explained that many of the residents had not viewed it in that light.

'You see, we had completely different standards; life in those conditions was quite normal to us. You'd have a row of houses with a row of tub-closets across the passage and quite often there would only be one closet to two or three houses. In fact, when you come to consider, it's a wonder that we survived.

'So many things were different then. For example, people today think that we were all scared of the railway navvies, but to us children they were just working men doing their job. Most people around there were manual workers. My dad worked in a little factory on Sherwood Street owned by Boots' [the chemists] and I often used to take his dinner in a basin wrapped in a large red and white spotted handkerchief, just like people imagine the navvies doing.'

But if the navvies did not attract his attention, some of their machinery certainly did. The building of the Great Central brought 'steam-navvies', excavators usually built by the Lincoln firm of Ruston's, to Nottingham, and George remembered peeping through a gap in the fence to watch these impressive machines working in the cutting that was to house the station. And I considered myself privileged to hear an impression of the sound they made – as described by one of the diminishing band who had witnessed them at work.

By the time the station was open to traffic George had moved to another part of the city and took little interest in it in subsequent years, but our conversation continued to roam the fascinating world of his childhood. He told of his first sighting of an elephant.

'Not on television, of course, as children see them now. These elephants belonged to an American circus called Barnum and Bailey's but, as I stood near the corner of Glasshouse Street, I knew nothing of that. I just saw these great things coming along Parliament Street. I couldn't believe my eyes and, as they came lumbering on, turned and ran up Glasshouse Street as if the devil himself were after me.'

He also spoke of the time when, at the age of eleven, he was chosen to be one of four choirboys who would sing at a memorial service following the death of Queen Victoria, held in Nottingham's Albert Hall. 'We stood behind a projection screen and, as the film showed the Queen's coffin being carried down the steps of St Paul's, we sang her favourite hymn.' And more than eighty years later, he sang for me a few bars of 'Lead Kindly Light'.

In Edwardian times the station offered a wide range of services to the traveller. In addition to those already mentioned, many local communities benefited, not only along the Great Central line but also on the routes of the Great Northern and the Nottingham Suburban Railway. Great Northern passengers in particular must have welcomed the opportunity to use the new station, at the heart of the city, instead of the old terminus, which was in an out-of-the-way quarter and hemmed in between a municipal gas works and the tracks of the Midland Railway.

For many people those days prior to the Great War were happy, and they enjoyed themselves travelling. Cheap day excursions were enthusiastically supported by citizens able to broaden their horizons by using the new facilities, and it was common for local firms to charter special trains for works outings. Examples of destinations and return fares on offer at that time ranged from Liverpool for 4s 9d to Bristol for 6s 6d, or Chard in Somerset for 8s 6d.

When, in 1914, the developed world embarked on one of its bouts of criminal insanity the station played its part in the scheme of things, first dispatching willing, optimistic volunteers and later less enthusiastic conscripts to be torn apart by explosives or tortured with poisonous gas in war-racked Europe. Whole young men departed from here, often to return pathetically injured, and the station saw distraught relatives cling to departing soldiers as their carriages drew away. And throughout the period it witnessed long trains of munitions and industrial raw materials rumbling relentlessly through its cavernous interior, as the railway demonstrated its efficiency in moving the immense volume of equipment and supplies to sustain the world's first global war.

The 1920s saw the railway recovering from the war, only to be hit again by economic recession that struck hardest in the industrial areas that provided its bread and butter. One who remembered that period well was Bob Sharp, a retired guard who worked from Victoria for many years and who still lived in a neatly kept terraced house on Watkin Street. Built by the company, which named the street after the man

who was its chairman for thirty of its formative years, the house was a stone's throw from the station site.

Bob started on the railway as a 'lad porter' in 1921, with the Great Northern at Humberstone, and served at eleven locations, including Nottingham Victoria, before becoming a guard twenty-two years later.

'You had to move around to get any promotion in those days; people were always being set-back or made redundant. Times were hard and a great deal of misery was sometimes involved. I can remember when some passenger guards were made redundant at Leicester and they sent one of them to be a shunter here at the Vic. Well, he must have been the weakest shunter on the railway, being so small, and throwing shackles and couplings around all day must have been killing for the poor bugger. I was fourteen years old when I started, and I got my first guard's job, at Woodford, when I was thirty-six. I often think that people can walk in off the street and become a guard today, while at that time we spent years chasing promotion and learning the rule book. But I suppose we at least had a bit of status at the end of it.'

Bob was very impressed with Nottingham Victoria when he first arrived there in 1927.

'I'd never seen a better station – never seen anything like it. And I've never seen anything better since! It was well constructed and laid out, but I must admit there was one fault. Although it had that system of lifts and subways to separate passengers from the goods traffic, all the parcels had to be taken round from the office and through the booking hall to the lift. If the lift man was at the bottom, they were sometimes left unattended – and that's how parcels get knocked off. So, in that particular respect, it was not good for security. But it was a grand place and I had many pleasant times there.

'It seems amazing now, but when I first worked at the Vic it had only been open for twenty-seven years and some of the staff had been there from the start. In fact, my first tunic was older than the station itself, though, strangely enough, I didn't acquire it in Nottingham. When I first started as a porter I was classed as temporary; and you did not get a uniform until you were permanent. One day a relief signalman, whose home was in Nottingham, brought me an old tunic to wear. I wish I'd kept it now because it was embroidered with the letters N.J.S., which also appeared on the buttons – it stood for Nottingham Joint Station, the name the Vic was known by before it was opened.'

Bob Sharp remembered the gleaming engines that hauled the crack expresses of the 1930s, but it was the arrival at the station of a different type of train that he described when talking to me. From its beginning the Great Central was a large-scale carrier of fish, especially from Grimsby where the docks had largely been built by the company. Nowadays, when fish rarely travels by rail, it is difficult to imagine the importance once attached to the traffic in this highly perishable and potentially obnoxious commodity. The heavily laden trains were often hauled by special locomotives and were given a priority second only to the most important expresses. Two such trains passed through Victoria each day, one from Hull in the morning and the other from Grimsby in the afternoon.

'The Grimsby fish was due in at 3.38pm, usually three passenger coaches and twenty-two fish wagons – one of which was uncoupled here. It always had the same engine, unless it was in the works, a 4-6-0 named *Valour*. She was always immaculate!'

Clearly, the sight of the Great Central Railway's mobile memorial to its employees killed during the Great War had left a deep impression on Bob.

Another local man with memories of the station was John Wilson, a founder member and one-time chairman of the Nottingham branch of the Railway Correspondence & Travel Society. A telephone call resulted in an immediate invitation to visit his home and we were soon talking over tea and cakes provided by Mrs Wilson. The tastefully chosen prints hanging in the lounge did little to betray the presence of a railway historian and photographer of fifty years' standing. His lifelong interest in railways was not something he boasted of and it was some time before he mentioned the Victoria Station bench in his back garden, or the ticket window in the conservatory – still bearing the gilt-painted legend 'Great Central'.

He had already sorted out a collection of photographs, crystal-clear black and white shots of a bygone era – shots of the station in its prime, spacious, noble and airy, playing host to handsome Great Central 'Atlantic' engines and 4-6-0s, including *Valour* so beloved by Bob Sharp. The later LNER locomotives of the 1930s contrasted with venerable old engines dating from somewhere near the middle of the last half of the 19th century, living out their final years on light duties. They were all there, paper images of people long dead and machines since recycled into anything from lamp posts to razor blades, photographed in an environment since crushed beneath the foundations of modern Nottingham's monument to greed and poor taste.

John Wilson's first memories of the station went back to the 1920s.

'But I developed a keen interest in the mid-thirties. Of course, like most railway enthusiasts my great interest was in the locomotives themselves and it was only in later years that I began to take much notice of railway architecture, when it became threatened I suppose.

'Victoria handled an immense amount of excursion traffic: Aintree and Doncaster for racing and the East Coast resorts via the Great Northern line. Literally hundreds of people flocked to the Skegness and Mablethorpe excursion trains, which often ran in duplicate, or even triplicate. Then, on summer evenings there were the half-crown (2s 6d) evening trips to Skegness, which were so popular that they ran in up to six portions, all leaving within one and a half or two hours and consisting of all the old stock that could be raked up. People usually had about four hours at the coast and arrived back in the small hours of the following morning. Then there were the London excursions, starting out about eleven o'clock on a Saturday morning and 10.00am on Sundays. They were always well patronised, starting back from Marylebone about midnight to arrive home about 3.00am. I don't suppose it mattered much, arriving at 3.00am on a Sunday – but Monday morning must have been another thing entirely!

'One of the most impressive memories I have is of the time the Gresley "Pacifics" began working some of the principal expresses into the station. The old Great Central engines were not exactly small, but these new "Pacifics" were absolutely massive – they seemed to fill the station. I can remember the first time I heard one coasting in; you had the 'clinketty-clonketty-clink' of the coupling rods, followed by their habit of blowing off steam through the cylinder drain cocks. So when they came to a halt you had this great hiss of escaping steam, not always appreciated by me because it obscured the front of the locomotive and made photography difficult. And they always seemed to slip when restarting, the exhaust shooting up into the sky. They made a very dramatic sight and these are the sort of things I remember, along with the old Great Central 2-8-0 mineral engines with their long, heavy coal trains, full ones going south and the returning empties heading north. Sometimes they would be halted in the station and when they got under way again there was a lot of snatching of couplings and clashing of buffers. That was a familiar sound in Victoria, and with the station being in a deep cutting covered with that great glass roof, the sound was magnified and echoed all around.'

Another vision of the station imprinted vividly in John Wilson's mind was of a scene he sometimes witnessed when standing at the north end, with the tall sandstone cliffs rising on either side and in front, where they were pierced by Mansfield Road Tunnel. 'There was this odd phenomenon of a plume of smoke and steam issuing from the tunnel mouth whenever the north wind blew, which I always found fascinating and rather mysterious.'

John Wilson lost contact with the station for a time during the Second World War.

'In the first place, the climate turned against railway photography. It was all right until Dunkirk, but then attitudes changed and anyone foolish enough to point a camera at anything that could be considered "sensitive" was likely to be marched off to the nearest police station. And, after that, I was away in the RAF most of the time. Of course, no one could have failed to notice the removal of the glass from the ends and top of the roof. Although the roof was reglazed after the war the ends were clad in corrugated iron, which robbed the station of one of its most distinguishing characteristics.'

It seems to be true that measures designed to protect the station from Nazi bombers did more damage than any action instigated by Hitler. Bob Sharp remembered the removal of the glazing. 'It was all supposed to be taken to Derby for storage, but it ended up being buried in a hole they dug near the northern turntable – I suppose it is still there now!' According to his memory the station was uninjured by the Luftwaffe, despite some severe damage to nearby buildings, and nobody knew the origin of the machine-gun bullets that chipped the brickwork of the retaining wall at the south-east corner.

Someone who treasured affectionate memories of Victoria Station in the early post-war period was Barbara Loin, a large jovial woman, well known and liked in the inner-city district where she made her home. She had arrived in Nottingham four years after starting a journey that began with the German invasion of her Polish homeland, having fled with her mother and father, a Polish Air Force officer, first to Rumania then France. But that had been only a brief respite and a further Nazi victory resulted in their arrival in Britain, where her father resumed his air force role and her mother found work as an RAF cook.

Barbara had learned her new language quickly, as the young tend to, and after completing a course in English and Polish shorthand became secretary to a wing-commander. Barbara arrived in Nottingham in 1944, the bride of a Polish airman, and her son was born the following year. The tragedy of being widowed in 1946 was to lead to her first encounter with Victoria Station when, three years later, she took the difficult decision to send her young son to boarding school while she trained for a career in nursing. She used the station at the beginning and end of every school term from 1949 to 1956 and remembers the period well.

Boarding fees were a heavy burden, so she recouped some of the travel costs by sharing expenses with two other parents, whose sons she accompanied on the journey. At the beginning of term she would deliver the boys to Paddington, from where the school assumed responsibility, and at the end of term she would repeat the journey to collect them. The Great Central route, with its terminus at Marylebone, offered the most convenient service and she used it exclusively.

'I can remember how it was even now, after thirty years, the sadness of the farewells and the joy of the greetings. Sometimes I would arrive at Victoria early and go to the refreshment room for a cup of coffee. There always seemed to be a lot of people in there because the food was good and the room clean and nicely furnished. And the train always seemed to arrive from Sheffield dead on time whenever I used it. It was named "The Master Cutler" and maybe it would be eight or ten minutes late in a thick winter fog, but it was usually ready to leave at 8.43. I always used "The Master Cutler" and I'll remember the departure time – 8.43 – for ever.

'If there was not time for a drink at the station, I would use the restaurant car on the train and have a good cup of coffee before we drew into Leicester. And everyone was so friendly. I remember one gentleman, a businessman who worked in a bank, always used to say "Oh, so we meet again – after another three months!" He always remembered me. Of course, there were many businessmen on the train and a lot seemed to use it to travel to Leicester.

'When I arrived in London, I would collect the children and have a meal before catching the train back, soon after three o'clock, which got into Nottingham about 5.30. I was the happiest woman on earth riding those trains; it was wonderful, speeding along through such lovely countryside. I loved steam trains, with their sounds and smells, but I don't care much for these diesels – they are just not the same.'

Barbara Loin thought the Great Central was wonderful in the 'forties and early 'fifties, but she had been a young girl in Eastern Europe when the line was at its best. Although, in a sense, she was right – it was wonderful how the men who ran the railway had fought to regain the standards that prevailed before the system had been debilitated by war.

John Wilson recalled: 'Up to the mid-'fifties there was a very strong attempt to get back to pre-war standards. But there were awful problems at that time, coal was in short supply and of poor quality, while the track was in a pretty poor state. However, by the mid-'fifties a lot had been achieved: "The Master Cutler" service had been reintroduced and named, "The South Yorkshireman" had been introduced too and things were looking up. I used the 3.20 down from Marylebone a few times during that period and it was always a well-patronised train of eleven or twelve coaches. There was a lot of commuting on the Great Central between Sheffield, Chesterfield, Nottingham, Loughborough and

Leicester. You have got to remember that you were in Loughborough in sixteen or seventeen minutes and Leicester in twenty-five. I know the private car was partly to blame, but I also think the Great Central was deliberately run down to some extent.'

And run down it certainly was. The Conservative Government of the late 'fifties and early 'sixties had no love of publicly owned railways and helped to create the climate in which they became the butt of every second-rate comedian's bad joke. British Railways was vilified as the personification of the country's industrial backwardness and the opportunity to simultaneously discredit public ownership was avidly seized. The legacy of wartime neglect was forgotten; the difficulties caused by years of under-investment dismissed; the experience of European countries that treasured their railways and treated them as a national asset was ignored. A draconian plan to transfer much of the railway's traffic to the predominantly privately owned road haulage companies was hatched and executed. The effect on the quality of our lives has been markedly detrimental, with ever larger lorries intimidating the inhabitants of previously quiet residential streets, but the effect on Victoria Station and the Great Central Railway's route to London was fatal.

The anti-rail climate was well established by 1958, when the Great Central Section of British Railways' Eastern Region was placed under the control of the descendants of its old adversary – the London Midland Region. In the summer of 1957 eighty-six trains left the station each weekday; by 1962, when the results of the Beeching Plan were beginning to bite, the number had fallen to seventy. The London expresses had become 'semi-fast' and by 1966 the number of departures had dropped to twenty-one. And so, in the autumn of 1967, it fell to a Midland Region driver, George Chambers, to perform the sad task of driving the last passenger train out of the station. By that time, the only trains using Nottingham Victoria were diesel multiple units that operated a service to Rugby, but the developers were so anxious to begin demolition that this service was transferred to the temporarily reopened Arkwright Street Station, about half a mile to the south.

Although retired from the railway, George Chambers, at that time Chairman of Nottinghamshire County Council, was easy to locate. The railway workers' tradition of civic involvement was not difficult to see in Nottingham for, in addition to George being Chairman of the County Council, the City of Nottingham's Sheriff was a retired railway clerk and the Deputy Lord Mayor was the daughter of a former Great Central guard. And Nottingham was never thought of as a railway town!

George was a railwayman to the core, although he would not have been if he had obeyed his mother's wishes. The family lived in the

Northamptonshire village of Pipewell and George's mother was determined that he should avoid agricultural work by becoming a butler! As we sat talking, it was hard to imagine him in his first job, as a fourteen-year-old pantry-lad at the local manor house. The idea of being in service for the rest of his life did not appeal very much to George, so in 1924 he took himself off to the nearby town of Kettering and got a job as an engine cleaner on the London Midland & Scottish Railway. Memories of that first day were still clear to him, especially of his mother's tears at the sight of her grime-caked son returning home in the evening. As he put it, 'She had got used to me coming home in a clean white shirt and bow tie.' It seemed a pity that she did not live to see him as Chairman of the County Council, well able to mix with visiting Royalty, his old railway mates and neighbours on the pleasant estate of council houses where he lived.

He talked at length about his past, starting with village life before gentrification set in.

'We were poor, but lived well. Not only was there game to be poached, but my father always kept two pigs. He would buy them as piglets to fatten up and, when they were slaughtered, would sell one to the butcher, to cover costs, and the other would be our profit. There was always a lot of work involved when we killed a pig. It had to be cut up, salted and the fat rendered down into lard – there was enough of that to ensure that we never had to buy any from a shop – and there were scratchings, sausages and ham. We used to wrap the ham in white linen and hang it in the kitchen, cutting a slice as we needed it. It lasted for ages. That really was ham! You know, I often tell my wife that you just can't get real ham any more.'

Perhaps it was just another old man's memory of those days when summers were warmer and all Christmases were white, but I had a feeling that he was correct.

George arrived in Nottingham in 1927 as a 'passed cleaner', an engine-cleaner allowed to take turns as a fireman when the work was available. In those days, that was quite an achievement for an eighteen-year-old. But, like Bob Sharp, he suffered in the Depression and was not promoted to become a driver until 1945. During the intervening years he was forced by redundancy to leave the locomotive department to work as a station porter, and it was an incident at that time that persuaded him of the need for a strong trade union.

'I was working on Nottingham Midland Station when, one Saturday morning, I was given orders to report for work at Watford at 8am on the Monday. I was incensed at the harshness and injustice of it; how could I keep a wife, child and two homes on £2 a week? After the first week I came home and wrote a letter to the General Manager of the London

Midland & Scottish Railway, setting out the injustices of my treatment, and I won the right to return to work in Nottingham.'

Soon he was to become immersed in the union and the Labour Party, running three successful election campaigns for a local MP, and in 1949 he was elected to the National Executive of his union. Despite a rule of the National Union of Railwaymen that stated that an Executive Council member could only serve three years before having to return to his old railway job for at least a further three, George Chambers served three terms on the Executive and became National President, shortly before retirement, in 1969.

It was shortly before his election to the presidency that he was transferred to the Great Central Section to work from Nottingham Victoria.

'I did not know the Great Central well, having served all of my forty-three years on the Midland, and the two systems were always viewed as completely separate entities. One day, when I first went down on Victoria Station, I was waiting to take over a train when I went into one of the signal boxes. All the old timetables, instructions, working schedules and rule books were there as well as the bell system, which had fallen into disrepair. As I stood looking along the platforms at the dereliction in the vastness of that place where a hive of activity had once been, I thought what a tragedy it had been, allowing it to fall into that state.'

The station was within six months of closure and only the service to Rugby remained, although heavy freight trains still rumbled through the otherwise silent emptiness. George found it to be a miserable job driving trains through the closed-down stations, lifeless and dismal, with only the principal ones, at East Leake, Loughborough, Leicester, Ashby Magna and Rugby, remaining open. But even in that depressed condition he described it as 'a lovely, picturesque line.' As the last train prepared to leave at 5.34pm on 2 September 1967, George told the local press that the closure was a tragedy and that Nottingham and Leicester councils should have invested in the line as a link between the two cities. His train returned at 8.04pm, shortly before the station gates were closed for the last time and Victoria Station died as it was born – without ceremony.

The immense shopping centre, topped by flats, took over the site and is now accepted by the present-day population of the city. But few will remember that, when permission was being sought for the centre's building, citizens were told that it would contain not only shops but a thousand-seat cinema, theatre, concert hall, assembly rooms, bowling alley, swimming pool and five acres of roof gardens. The citizens were short-changed.

6
LEAVING VICTORIA

The railway's southern exit from the station had been through a short, vertical-sided cutting and into the 393-yard Victoria Street Tunnel, but the cutting had been blocked by the foundations of a supermarket and a walk through the streets was again necessary. The massive bridge that carried Parliament Street, once the city's main thoroughfare, over the station's south end and offered an alternative access to the platforms, remained in position but was no longer recognisable. Gone were the parapets, which once permitted a view down into the vast station, replaced by the mundane facade of the shopping centre. However, across the road a public house that predated the railway's construction survived largely in its original form. The Old Dog and Partridge still offered 'traditional ales drawn from the cask' – presumably similar to the stuff the navvies had in mind when they took a break from digging the cutting to burrow into the cellar! Sadly for them, they only got their hands on the landlord's stock of ginger beer, although better luck was experienced further along the line of the tunnel, when they made an underground entrance into The Cross Keys. Contemporary reports imply the construction of Victoria Street Tunnel to have been a particularly invasive project; not only were the two pubs entered, but the crown of the bore even broke into the strong room of a bank.

This part of Nottingham retained much of its late-19th-century character and some fine buildings. The former Westminster Bank, sitting above the tunnel on Thurland Street, was one of the best examples of the work of the local architect Watson Fothergill, whose ideas had a great impact on the city in the late 19th and early 20th centuries. The design of the bank, said to have been influenced by Manchester Town Hall, included a profusion of intricate decoration, including a frieze depicting the trades of the area. Also visible to those with keen eyesight was the architect's little joke – a carving of a monkey in chains – dating from the time when a monkey was a nickname for a mortgage. A few yards away, above the plastic-veneered shop front that spoiled the ground floor of an attractive gothic-style building, a bronze plaque told that J. M. Barrie, author of *Peter Pan*, had once worked there on the staff of a local newspaper.

A hundred yards or so from the route stands Nottingham's Council House, a massive and imposing building of Portland Stone topped by a great dome, looking over the spacious Market Square. A bold project at the time of its building in the depressed days of the 1920s, when it provided work for the local unemployed, the classical style and grand scale of the Council House continue to exude a confidence and pride befitting a city that calls itself the Queen of the Midlands.

Following, as nearly as possible, the line of the tunnel along a bustling street, once a medieval thoroughfare but now pedestrianised, gave the feeling of a lively and vibrant place. Bridlesmith Gate, with its small shops and human-scale buildings, seemed a world away from the vulgarity of the Victoria Centre, yet it was only a couple of hundred yards distant. Streets such as this were spared from demolition in the late 1970s by the groundswell of opinion against the ravages of the wholesale redevelopments of the previous decade. Sadly, in more recent years, planning controls have been relaxed in the city's headlong rush to convert itself into a regional capital of leisure-shopping and, at ground level, much of the character of this and other streets has now been destroyed. This rampant commercialism, which has led to the pursuit of fulfilment through material gain, might also explain the many unhappy and harassed faces to be seen among the crowd.

Victoria Street Tunnel broke out into a cutting that I reached by climbing over the wall of a small park, only to be faced by railings across its portal, but the gate was hanging ajar and I was able to follow the track's underground course back towards the station. This bore had an atmosphere totally different from the one north of the station, being so close to the surface that most of its length had been dug by the 'cut and cover' method. Lined entirely with blue brick, it was warmer too, thanks to the pipes that passed through and linked the shopping centre to a district heating scheme. At the northern end the passage widened out into the station cutting, now roofed over for a few yards, before being blocked by the yellow brick wall of the supermarket. Walking back, light streamed through the tunnel mouth to reveal an array of litter on the barren ground. Polythene bags, discarded by glue-sniffers, were spread around mingled with hundreds of dirty, discarded handbills advertising 'Jennie's Sandwich Bar – the nicest shop in town'.

Leaving the tunnel, the line passed abruptly onto a viaduct, which divided as the Great Northern's tracks curved away eastward towards Grantham. A signal box bearing the name Weekday Cross once guarded this aerial junction, a reminder of the days prior to the 19th century when the town's weekday market was held here. Standing among brambles and buddleia, overshadowed by a road on concrete stilts and the blank concrete walls of yet another shopping centre, any link with ancient times seemed remote, although an older, quieter area standing on rising ground to the east invited exploration. But first I wandered along the viaduct to the junction, where the heating pipes, cocooned in dented aluminium cladding, emerged from the ground via a small brick and concrete building that resembled a wartime air raid shelter. Peering through the doorless opening and down a vertical shaft where the pipes and an iron ladder disappeared into the gloom, I heard the distorted mumbling of voices far below and caught the sickly odour of chemical solvents.

The area on the hill to the east of the line is the edge of a district known as the Lace Market, deceivingly named for it was never a market in the usual sense, but the centre of Nottingham's lace industry. A fascinating place standing on a rock outcrop overlooking the Trent valley, the site is a modest version of a similar one, half a mile to the west, where the Normans built their castle. The history of this area is as old as that of the town itself. On this easily defended hill Nottingham was founded by the Angles in the 6th century. In the 9th century it became a regional headquarters of the Danish army and the Danes' influence survives in the many street names that end in 'gate', derived from the Nordic word 'gata', meaning street.

Following the conquest, the Normans built their castle on a hill about half a mile to the west of the old town and a market gradually became established in the valley between, but the area now known as the Lace Market remained the administrative centre. The Shire Hall, once the seat of government for all Nottinghamshire, still stands as the Galleries of Justice Museum, but the old Guildhall was a casualty of the building of the Great Central. It was here that, as navvies dug the tunnel approach through sandstone below the Hall's foundations, they revealed the oppressive nature of Medieval government. Caves and underground cells were exposed, including one awful dungeon still containing shackles and leg-irons.

This area was where public executions used to take place and is notorious as the scene of a hanging in 1844 that led to the death of more than just the hapless victim of public revenge. A stampede occurred among the huge crowd gathered to watch the killing of William Saville, possibly caused by pickpockets who worked among the crowd, undeterred by the draconian punishments of the day, or by those at the rear pushing forward for a better view. The resulting crush left twelve people dead, seven of them under fifteen years of age, and more than a hundred seriously injured, of whom five died later. The last public execution here occurred in 1864, after which hanging took place in private. But the spirit of that mob lived on as long as capital punishment itself and for the next hundred years their descendants would fight like bargain-hunters at a West End sale to get a glimpse of an execution notice pinned on the gates of a prison after a hanging.

During the 17th century the old settlement became a desirable residential area, but its fine houses and gardens were soon to succumb to the pressures of industrial development. The Nottingham area contributed greatly to the Industrial Revolution, and it was as early as the 16th century that William Lee, of nearby Calverton, invented a stocking-knitting frame. This was to form the basis of a domestic hosiery industry, but in the late 18th century Lee's design was modified to produce lace and its further development led to the town becoming a major centre of lace and lace machine manufacture. Meanwhile, Richard Arkwright improved on the design of Hargreave's 'Spinning Jenny', another local invention, and this man, who figured so prominently in Britain's industrial development, had his first cotton mill built in the Lace Market. Dating from 1770, what is believed to be the shell of the building survives as a public house.

Turbulent times followed, as industry and the factory system took hold of Nottingham. New developments, industrial growth, population expansion and economic exploitation combined to turn a handsome town into a slum, but the revolution also brought some fine buildings in its wake. As industry prospered, the manufacturers commissioned the best architects to design factories and warehouses on a grand scale, in a style befitting their status, and the Lace Market took on the appearance it largely retains today. Great warehouses, some displaying lavish ornamentation, still crowd over narrow streets that retain their medieval pattern. And central to it all, the 15th-century church of St Mary rises above the green oasis of its churchyard with the majesty of a small cathedral.

This part of the city survived the attentions of railway builders, attacks by Nazi bombers and the decline of its industry, only to be threatened with further desecration by a particularly pernicious 1960s road scheme, but by the 1980s it had the protection that comes with being designated as an Outstanding Conservation Area. Although dereliction remained evident, the city was by then pursuing a policy that it described as progressive conservation – renovating and encouraging new uses for old buildings. An imaginative little park had been created on a small patch of derelict land and a new housing estate, designed in a sympathetic style, had helped reintroduce people and life.

Regrettably, in 2006 the park was destroyed and its site given over to a concrete cube housing a 'conceptual' art centre.

A remarkable view from the Lace Market was of a windmill in the adjacent suburb of Sneinton. It could be seen from the viaduct too, but no traveller on the Great Central ever watched its sails turn, for the mill was already a ruin when the railway was built and was not restored until long after its demise. Now the mill stands on a green hilltop not a mile from the city centre, its white-painted ogee-style cap and sails prominent against a background of distant trees and framed between multi-storey buildings.

Sneinton windmill was restored as a memorial to its one-time owner, who combined the occupation of milling with a spare-time passion for mathematics and physics. George Green was a self-taught genius whose true contribution to science was only realised in the 20th century, long after his death. Spending most of his forty-seven years (1793-1841) in his native town and working in a room at the top of the mill, Green evolved theories that were to earn him the title of the father of modern English mathematical physics. His achievements included the first expression of electrical potential and the development of a method of analysis later used in solid state and nuclear physics. He went on to correct Newton's Law on wave motion, lay the basis for the theory of elasticity and to produce a means of understanding the behaviour of ultrasonic sound, now of great value in medical and engineering fields. Prior to the 1980s restoration of Sneinton windmill, Green had no memorial other than his grave in the local churchyard.

7
NOTTINGHAM GOODS YARD

The viaduct continued for a hundred yards or so to an abutment that had once supported a girder bridge spanning Canal Street. Fifty or sixty yards eastward a similar bridge had carried the Great Northern Railway's Grantham line over the same street, but that had also been removed. Ahead lay a fifty-yard gap in the viaduct, but the fine, slightly skewed blue-brick arch that carried the Great Central over the Nottingham Canal was in good condition and probably a source of wonderment to any modern-day bricklayer who may have cared to examine it.

Retracing my steps and leaving the truncated viaduct, I followed the course of the railway through an area where it had been largely obliterated by redevelopment. The remaining arches, their ends partitioned off and decorated with a mural of country scenes and a steam train, were occupied by small businesses in an unusually tidy fashion. Overall, the effect was cheerful and bright, but superficial and irreverent to the viaduct. South of the canal a few arches survived, adjacent to an abutment that had supported a three-span bridge over the six platforms of Nottingham Midland Station. This gigantic structure had consisted of a fifty-foot section, which bridged a road to rest on steel columns within the station's boundary, followed by a 170-foot span that crossed the entire station to connect with a further span of 104 feet over adjacent sidings and another road. At the centre of the longest section, the bowstring girders had been almost twenty feet deep.

Another short length of viaduct, curving slightly westward, still survived to the south of the Midland Railway's tracks and had once led to Arkwright Street Station. Although the bridge abutment remained, on the east side of Arkwright Street all trace of the station, which had been built with a street-level booking hall and side-platforms above, had been swept away by redevelopment work in the early 1970s, together with the following 1,100-yard viaduct of fifty-three arches and twelve steel bridges. Fortunately, the Midland Station remained to symbolise the great age of railways in a city that had suffered greatly as a result of Dr Beeching's policies, although it was not the same station that the Great Central had originally bridged. That had been untidy and ramshackle – easily put to shame when Victoria Station opened. But the Midland, not prepared to be outdone, commissioned the same architect who had designed Victoria Station to upgrade theirs and the present building, with its frontage on a bridge where the lines were crossed by one of the main roads into the city, opened in 1904. It is a skilful blend of architecture; a grand façade of ornately detailed terracotta fronting a lofty carriage entrance and a palatial parquet-floored booking hall. Yet the red-brick buildings down at platform level are unpretentious and homely. The survival of Nottingham's Midland Station, even in a neglected state, should be a cause for celebration, for it welcomes travellers in a style that could never be equalled by a johnny-come-lately coach park or airport.

This was the fringe of a part of Nottingham known as The Meadows. Situated on the flood plain of the River Trent, it had been packed with terraced houses during the town's 19th-century expansion in a way that belied its rural name, and few who addressed letters to Crocus, Briar or Hawthorne Street, The Meadows, would have guessed their urban destination. The poorer parts could never have provided a pleasant environment for living, but for many years it supported an industrious and cheerful community. The new Meadows, crowded with jagged-roofed houses of insipid yellow brick, probably has less self-respect than the old and was not a welcoming place. Even the house windows were narrow mean slits; defensive – like arrow slots in a castle wall – they peered suspiciously onto litter-strewn walkways that had probably looked beautiful on the drawing-board. Children seemed wan-faced and adults worried or preoccupied. These were the people of a ghetto – not a racial ghetto, but one created by those politicians who stigmatised council-house living. This was the lower layer of a divided society, where lives were lived secret from the affluent suburbs, for outsiders need not visit this place, which has few shops, entertainment or through routes.

But the estate was an improvement of sorts, built a decade after the Hyson Green flats that I had passed in the north of the city. Prostitutes did not ply these pathways and most residents lived near ground level, while even spiky roofs and yellow bricks were preferable to grey concrete blocks. And it did have its more pleasant parts, such as that where the offices of the Great Central goods yard still stood. Now used as a community centre, it is a good-looking building of red brick, stone and grey slate, facing onto an avenue of mature trees left over from a thoroughfare of the old Meadows. Solidly built to a height of three storeys, its well-proportioned lines exhibit modest ornamentation while offering a purposeful and dignified image to the street. The rear wall was covered by yet another mysterious mural, this time of blue sky and white clouds.

The thirty-three-acre Nottingham goods yard had been situated on an embankment behind this building. The main running lines approached from the north on the viaduct and from the south over the River Trent, to cut through the middle of the yard on an embankment substantially higher than the sidings that flanked them. For the whole length of the yard and across the river, loop lines ran parallel to the main ones so that trains could stand clear of through traffic while wagons were detached, often to descend into the yard by gravity. East of the main lines were carriage and engine sheds; to the west were a goods warehouse, timber, coal and mineral yards, offices and a power station for generating electricity and hydraulic power. From the south-west corner a line branched off to Clifton Colliery, less than a mile distant. Almost the whole area was now filled with houses, but the embankment, offices and several terraces of company houses, each named after a town served by the Great Central, remained – as did the river bridge, until demolished by Nottingham City Council in the winter of 1985-86.

My grandfather, after travelling the railway as a goods guard, settled in the Meadows in 1907 following promotion to the position of traffic inspector at the yard. It was a period my father remembered well.

'Often, my mother would prepare a dinner for him which was delivered to the yard by my eldest brother, but when Aubrey started work, at fourteen, the job was mine. I'd be twelve years old at that time and so it would be 1917. I had been aware of the yard before that and remember how older children had scared me by saying that the suffragettes would come and set fire to the timber stacks.'

Surprisingly, despite his tender years, he was entrusted with a gate key.

'They seemed huge gates, but often they did not need opening because they served as the exit for the colliery line, which crossed the road at that point. I'd take his dinner to the mess hut, next to his office, which had a coal-burning range on which most of the men reheated their food, although some took the ingredients to fry a meal. But I soon learned that shunters and inspectors were always in demand and if a train arrived it had to be worked. I've often seen him put aside the dinner I'd taken and go out to deal with some problem in the yard.'

At that inquisitive age my father was in an ideal position to observe the workings of the place. He watched the antics of the flagman, trying to stop child cyclists dodging across the path of the colliery train on its daily trip across the road. On another occasion he stood for half a day to watch an entire trainload of racing pigeons being released, a basketful at a time, to find their way back to Newcastle. He viewed the 'Goliath' electric travelling crane – an immense machine spanning sixty-six feet, standing twenty-five feet high and able to lift twenty-five-ton loads – as an everyday sight. Yet when installed, only seventeen years previously, it had been, together with its sisters at Leicester and Marylebone, the first of its kind in the country. He watched it unloading tree trunks, which were then stacked for seasoning, and drums of tobacco leaf for John Player's cigarette factory. Each autumn, when Goose Fair, that great funfair that figures so large in the lives of Nottingham children, was due, he would be excited by the sight of the crane unloading brightly painted fairground equipment from trains of flat trucks.

At that time of the year a distinguished visitor would arrive in the yard.

'Pat Collins was one of the really big showmen and Mr Jakes, from the top office, used to bring him to meet my father. He looked very showy to me in his short coat, slightly flared at the bottom, and a "billy-cock" hat in the same light colour. They'd shake hands and have a talk, and I'm sure it was worth it for him, the railway and my father. Goose Fair only lasted three days and it was important to see that the equipment was unloaded promptly and, afterwards, dispatched quickly to its next destination. So Pat Collins always attended to that part of the business personally.

'I saw a lot of the crane, because my father had a garden nearby – but more of that later. It had a crew of six men who operated from an old guard's van that had been set on the ground. They had a fire in there, which always had a mash-can on the go, and I often went in for a warm on a winter's day.'

Apparently, the crane was expensive to hire and he recollected one occasion when a customer refused to pay the fee.

'There was this brand new Lancashire boiler, about eight feet in diameter, thirty feet long and weighing the earth, to be unloaded for transport to the General Hospital. My father said the contractor had refused to pay the twenty-pound crane fee, which was a ton of money in those days, and intended to do the job himself. About half-a-dozen men arrived with a horse-drawn drug, which they positioned alongside the well-wagon carrying the boiler. After bridging the gap with timbers, they gradually jacked up the load and eased it across onto the drug, using winches that they had spragged to the ground.'

It was a difficult and dangerous operation, but in those days of cheap labour less costly than the crane.

My father never saw inside the power station, although he would dearly liked to have done, nor did he visit the engine or carriage sheds across the main lines. But he was able to describe how hydraulic power was used in the main warehouse.

'A rope would be hitched onto a wagon and given a turn or two round one of the capstans, which were set in the ground alongside the tracks. When a foot pedal was pressed down, the capstan would slowly revolve until it had pulled the wagon level with itself. This made it unnecessary to bring a shunting engine into the warehouse and, probably because they were so slow-moving, I never heard of an accident with a capstan.

'The timber yards were of special interest to me because my father had a goat, which I used to take to graze among them. So, by that time he had a decent-sized garden near his office, with a hut and two greenhouses about twelve feet by eight, which he had built from old window frames, and a goat. There was quite a lot of grass in the timber yard, which my dad's goat shared with the local wildlife, rabbits, rats and birds. The timber was stacked in piles as high as a house and it was by asking questions, as I took that goat to pasture, that I learned the importance of wood being seasoned.'

My father did not know the official attitude to his father's horticultural sideline, but it must have been tolerated at a fairly high level, as was another of his eccentricities.

'The time even arrived, my father being the man he was, when he took the liberty of wearing a trilby hat at work. He was supplied with a peaked cap with a GCR badge, but was convinced that its hard top, rubbing against the crown of his head, was the cause of his baldness. It's true that the trilby allowed his hair to grow again, but very sparsely, and one could always see the top of that wise old pate, which could manage a goods yard, workmen, accidents, emergencies, a garden and a big family.'

But the garden did fit into the scheme of things rather better than people today might realise. It made tolerable a life of long working hours when there was precious little money for leisure activity and, from the company's viewpoint, made him available in emergencies. Many was the time that a day's relaxation would be interrupted while he gave unpaid help or advice in the yard.

Working conditions have changed greatly since those days, not least in the way of toilet facilities. At that time the only lavatory available to my grandfather and the other men was a wooden hut over a hole, which had been dug in the soil of the embankment. This little hut was equipped with carrying handles and, periodically, would be picked up and moved a few yards to be placed over another freshly dug hole. Apparently, grandfather's ingenuity was taxed for a time in the First World War by the arrival of two women shunters – sent to replace a man who had been conscripted into the Army, on the basis that two women equalled one man! That little hut hardly offered proper facilities, but he did improve matters by having the bottom sawn off the door, which at least permitted occupancy to be betrayed by the sight of a pair of ankles. Unfortunately, it also permitted the icy winter winds, which swept mercilessly over that exposed place, to gain entry just when the occupant was least protected.

Another great change since the days of my father's childhood was the disappearance of the working horse, which hauled virtually all road traffic at that time. The Great Central kept its own horses to pull the drays that transhipped goods between the rail yard and the customer.

'I don't think they were shires, but a similar type of heavy horse, and practically all were mares. They were stabled in the arches of the viaduct, off Blackstone Street, and, surprisingly to me, they even bred them there to ensure a supply for the future.

'At the end of the day, each drayman would walk his horse from the yard through the streets to the stables, and that could be like a scene from a comic opera! In theory, he would unshackle his horse from the cart, loop the traces over its back, and lead it quietly round to the stable. But the horses always knew when the day's work was over and had strong feelings on the matter. I've seen a drayman hanging on to the wrong end of his horse as it dragged him back to the stable. And sometimes they would break away completely to trot home alone, the noise of their iron shoes and the jangling of their chains on the granite

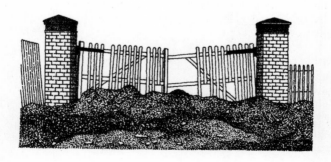

cobblestones sending local women scurrying into the nearest alleyway for refuge. But I never saw one go on the pavement, or heard of an accident.'

Until the mid-1980s a strip of land, where the south end of the yard had been, remained undeveloped. This was the site of the timber stacks and that famous garden. The gates, which had seemed so huge to my father as he struggled to unlock them almost seventy years previously, still stood – although ramshackle and ajar. When I passed by, earth had been piled between their red-brick piers to keep out tinkers and their caravans. But this last remnant of the goods yard has now been built over, and other things have changed too; the trackbed of the Clifton Colliery branch has been buried beneath a road and the colliery itself replaced by warehouses and a pork-pie factory.

8
FROM THE TRENT
TO THE SOAR

Demolition of the girder bridge across the River Trent was completed early in 1986, in the face of half-hearted local opposition. An imposing structure, it was actually a pair of identical bridges standing side by side and each consisting of three 112-foot spans. The downstream bridge carried the passenger tracks and the other the goods lines. Despite a spattering of tasteless graffiti, the bridge remained an impressive sight until the end – especially at close quarters when the strength and neatness of its girder construction could be appreciated. In all, the bridge contained more than two thousand tons of steel and had a total length, including the four-track approach viaducts, exceeding eight hundred feet.

Looking westward from the bridge it was possible to see the topmost towers of Wollaton Hall, an Italianate stately home, standing on the outskirts of Nottingham and marking an important location in railway history. For it was at Wollaton, in 1604 when the hall was new, that coal waggons were first hauled along wooden rails from local mines, the first ever recorded use of a railway. And although the focus of railway development subsequently moved to the North East, this was not the town's only contribution to the development of the railway age. Some two centuries after horse-drawn waggons first rumbled along those crude wooden rails, a local industrialist, with the remarkably mundane name of Sidney Smith, invented the pressure gauge. This ingenious device, when applied to the steam engine, allowed its crew to continuously monitor the behaviour of the boiler, leading to great improvements in efficiency and safety. Today, even after the demise of steam, Smith's invention remains in use whenever it is necessary to measure the pressure of a fluid or gas.

South of the river the track took on more of the appearance of a railway than it had done in the north of the county, a straight section climbing towards the distant, invisible ridge that separates the valleys of the rivers Soar and Trent. After passing the village of Wilford, overshadowed by a derelict power station and almost surrounded by the city, the track crossed a main road where a bridge had been removed, before heading for open country. Within half a mile of crossing the Trent the embankment was giving views across farmland, through gaps in the trackside trees that already reached almost to the tops of the disused telegraph poles. Apple trees, self-set from seeds carried along by passing trains, were weighted with firm-looking fruit, which promised that sharp flavour fondly remembered from childhood. Temptation proved too strong, but it was an unwise impulse. Modern dentistry may preserve teeth into middle age and beyond, but sensitive nerve endings responded painfully and the bitter acidity warned of the prospect of severe indigestion. Disappointed, I threw the half-eaten fruit into some brambles, where it may by now have flourished, and trudged on.

The trackbed continued, punctuated by trenches dug across to discourage travelling folk from settling, past an industrial estate tucked away in an old clay pit, and under a road carried on a modern concrete bridge, possibly the last to be built across the Great Central Railway. Next came a half-mile cutting leased by the Nottinghamshire Wildlife Trust and managed as a nature reserve. In the years since the line had been abandoned, most of the ballast had been removed, drainage channels had silted up and nature had recolonised the land. The Trust had discreetly managed this process and, with a minimum of interference, maintained a balance so that the more successful plants and trees did not exclude the less robust.

There was dry grassland, where kestrels hunted their prey and, according to the Trust's leaflet, the green winged orchid kept company with the wild carrot. On the trackbed damp grassland and a display of wild flowers provided a fine habitat for butterflies and moths that, in turn, attracted birds. On one part of the trackbed pools of water had formed, supporting bulrushes and other water plants, while dense woodland was growing up along one side of the cutting, offering a home to refugees from grubbed-up hedgerows and agricultural chemicals. It was good to see that some people cared enough to spend their leisure time giving nature a helping hand, but sad that they felt the need to guard it with barbed-wire fences and keep-out signs.

From the end of the nature reserve Ruddington village was visible, about half a mile distant across a field where wheat grew over a filled-in section of cutting. Ruddington marked the northern end of a section of the railway that had been retained to serve an Ordnance Depot and the gypsum works at East Leake. A few yards beyond the buffer-stop, at the end of the track, a typical Great Central blue-brick and steel road bridge crossed over the railway at the site of the station. Ruddington, a village expanded over the years to become one of Nottingham's dormitories, has a bustling centre more in keeping with that of a small town, although the station, on the western fringe of the village, presented a desolate scene. All buildings had been razed, with the exception of the Station Master's house, and only dilapidated coal stages remained in the overgrown goods yard.

A family of derelict-railway buffs stood on the platform, examining its crumbled edges and weed-cracked asphalt. It was pleasant to talk and exchange experiences with them, but I soon became irritated by the man's exaggerated enthusiasm and habit of speaking about steam locomotives he was scarcely old enough to remember with a familiarity that implied more than a little footplate experience. Even more tiresome was his repeated reference to his wife and young sons as 'chaps', an unusual habit in those days before it was fashionable to refer to people of both sexes as 'guys'. While he took the children into the remains of the lamp-room, housed in the central pier of the bridge, I walked slowly along the rusting track with his wife. She had an air of melancholia, which matched the surroundings, and shared her husband's affection for these decaying places without sharing his overexuberant manner. And she was good company, a sensible woman who observed the scene and developed her thoughts quietly, leaving him to prattle on. They had come from the South of England, and as we approached an elegantly arched footbridge of lattice steelwork she told of the pleasures of walking the long-abandoned Somerset & Dorset Railway. We talked under a disused signal gantry that had once guarded the junction where a rusted siding led into the closed Ordnance Depot, until her husband and sons returned and I left to continue my journey south.

In 1991, a few years after my visit, part of the Ordnance Depot site was taken over by a group of enthusiasts under the banner of the Great Central Railway Northern Development Group. Their aim was to build a transport heritage centre and link it with the preserved section of the Great Central at Loughborough, bridging the Midland Railway's main line to London in the process. That final, ambitious part of their plan has yet to be achieved, but their efforts have met with much success. They have built their heritage centre on part of the depot land and it is now possible to run trains down the Great Central main line as far as Loughborough. An associated group has constructed a fine miniature railway, and other attractions at the Nottingham Transport Heritage Centre include a historic collection of Great Central carriages, albeit awaiting restoration, and an extensive collection of vintage buses.

Alongside the steel mesh fence of the depot the track entered a long, shallow cutting. Sheltered from the cooling breeze, the pleasantly warm day became humid and oppressive, bringing back the memory of the words of an old platelayer who had told me how his gang had saved non-urgent work in cuttings for the winter and that on breezy embankments for the summer. This was not a particularly beautiful piece of countryside but a spectacular display of butterflies, forty or fifty of them, mainly Peacocks, which fluttered in a great cloud above some giant thistles, brightened things up. And the line had now gained more of the character of the old Great Central. Admittedly, only a little-used single track stretched into the distance, but it was straight as an arrow and spanned by three-arched, blue-brick bridges, so characteristic of this railway.

The atmosphere became fresher on the low embankment that crossed Ruddington Moor, a wide plain of waving wheat undivided by hedgerows. A couple of miles to the west the stubby spire of Gotham's 14th-century church, one of the first stone-built spires in England, stood below a range of low hills that formed the horizon. Towering up behind those hills, the eight gigantic cooling towers, turbine hall and chimney of Ratcliffe-on-Soar power station dwarfed all natural features in the landscape. When completed in 1970, Ratcliffe was the nation's largest power station and the statistics of its operation are staggering. With a generating capacity of 2,000 megawatts, it has a voracious appetite for coal, consuming up to 20,000 tons daily, supplied by trains that discharge their cargo in the power station yard without stopping. By-products of this energy conversion process include vast quantities of ash, transported away by the trainload for use in land reclamation schemes, and steam from the evaporation of the twelve million gallons of river water used each day in the cooling towers. The station's massive bulk stood over the rural landscape, giving the appearance of two worlds somehow mixed but not combined, while an immense cloud of water vapour spread across the summer sky. In this setting the natural world appeared subservient, but time may yet tell a different story.

Soon the line passed close to Gotham, not the fictional city made famous by Batman, the American comic-book hero, but a sleepy village that provided the setting for a collection of tales rooted firmly in English folklore. According to legend, the villagers were alarmed to hear that King John intended to build a hunting lodge in the vicinity, because they believed that wherever the monarch trod must become a right of way. The 'Wise Men of Gotham' set out to persuade the King to build his lodge elsewhere, by subjecting him to a remarkable piece of play-acting in which they portrayed themselves as fools – and undesirable neighbours for a King. They built a fence around a bush to imprison a cuckoo perched in its branches; rolled cheeses down a hill to send them on their own way to Nottingham; burned down a forge to destroy a wasp's nest inside it; and engaged in a catalogue of other ridiculous antics. Over the years the tales have increased in number and been elaborated on, but the story of the cuckoo bush, commemorated by the name of one of the pubs in the village, remains the best known.

Shortly after passing milepost 86, the first to be seen in the 17 miles since leaving Annesley and showing the mileage from Manchester London Road (now Piccadilly) Station, where the GCR had its headquarters when the line was built, the trackbed widened at a point where sidings had been laid. This had been the junction of the Gotham branch, built to serve local mines, but an altogether different type of mine than those to be found north of the Trent. Miners here did not emerge from the ground blackened by coal dust, for they dug gypsum, a white mineral quarried and mined in these parts for centuries and which now appears in products as diverse as cement and toothpaste, but most commonly in plaster.

I tripped over an iron bar concealed in the grass, which turned out to be part of the lever mechanism for a set of non-existent points. There were other relics too, and odds and ends left behind when the track was lifted. A hut, built of tongue-and-groove boarding and still bearing the red and cream colours of British Railways London Midland Region, contained an iron cooking range of oatmeal-coloured enamel. There was a bench with a hinged lid concealing an empty tool chest, and window shutters that still worked. In was not difficult to imagine the scene in this place on a cold, wet day many years ago. Huddled figures of men in heavy serge coats and peaked caps, with black oilcloth tops, crowded around the stove, broad, work-hardened hands clutching thickly sliced bread and mugs of strong tea filled from white enamel mash-cans – a scene from a way of life now long passed into history, as the cabin had passed into the occupancy of children by day and itinerants by night.

Continuing, the track remained perfectly straight, two lines converging in front and behind to vanishing points on each horizon. A rabbit ran madly ahead, receding into the distance on a straight path exactly in the centre of the rails, which must have blinkered its vision. Suddenly, it freed itself from the hypnotic effect of the perpetually converging lines, gave a great heel-kicking leap to the left, and disappeared into dense undergrowth at the side of the track. A set of overhead power lines crossed the railway as it traversed the moor, still on its low embankment, and the crackling, buzzing noise they made was an unwelcome intrusion into the silence. In the two hours since leaving Ruddington I had seen one person, a woman on a horse, about half a mile distant. The map showed large villages, linked by roads that criss-crossed the area, but this once great railway had now become a place of tranquillity.

Once more the track widened, where sidings served the East Leake plasterboard works, said to be the largest in Europe. Here, hundreds of wagons were stored, mostly steel-built twenty-one-tonners in need of a coat of paint. Again, the character of the railway was changing; the rail tops were no longer rusted, and, although the yard was closed for the weekend, it was clearly an important transhipment point for gypsum products. As late as 1981 the daily train from these sidings had moved an annual total of no less than 84,000 tons of crushed gypsum for use in cement manufacture. A signal box of 1950s vintage overlooked the scene, but contained no signalling equipment and was being used as a workmen's mess hut, the yard's reduced signalling needs being met by lineside point levers. A few yards beyond, the remains of Rushcliffe Halt nestled in a cutting beneath a three-arched road bridge. Built to serve the gypsum works and a nearby golfcourse, it was an unusual station for the Great Central, more modern than most, the concrete-edged, tarmac-surfaced platforms having a stark, utilitarian appearance. Except for an overgrown pathway leading down the cutting side from the road, little else remained and I continued my walk towards East Leake.

The railway soon left its cutting for a high embankment and took a gentle curve to the west, its first deviation since crossing the River Trent. Through the trees that grew densely from the embankment sides the spire of East Leake church was visible and, in the hot afternoon sun, the clock confirmed the operation of Sod's Law, which ruled that, in those days of strictly enforced licensing laws, I would arrive in the village just in time to see the pub door being closed.

A solitary concrete signal post guarded the approach to the semi-derelict East Leake goods yard, a little to the north of the old station. There was still a usable siding, a small goods shed and a strange, relatively modern, brick and concrete building with a row of steel doors. The clinker-covered earth was in turn covered by mineral dust, resembling silica, which glistened like gold in the bright sunlight. A lane led past the former Station Master's house and onto a quiet road, with large Victorian houses set among tall trees, which took me into the village.

East Leake was busy that afternoon, and had the feel of a village that had outgrown itself. Modern housing sprawled all around and filled the old farmyards, even at the village centre. A modern shopping area, reminiscent of a housing estate precinct, offered the chance to buy a can of beer from the drinks department of a windowless, fluorescent-lit grocery store. I ate a sandwich and drank my beer while sitting under a tree on the green, looking across the shallow waters of a brook to the ancient church. A strange place this village green, preserved long after the demise of the way of life it once served and now resembling a small park in a middle-class suburb. Yet the cultural conflict was even stranger. Youths on whining little Japanese motorcycles rode up and down the main street, while wedding bells peeled out from the grey-stone church. Arthur Mee, author of *The King's England*, described St Mary's as partly Norman, or even Saxon, with a 15th-century spire atop a 13th-century tower and containing a seven-hundred-year-old font. But what he considered to be its greatest treasure was concealed within, for this was one of only six churches in England that still possessed a tin trumpet 'for making joyful noises to the Lord'. This peculiar instrument, eight feet long and twenty-one inches in diameter at the rim, was last used in the middle of the 19th century, and I could not help thinking it was a custom best not revived.

Rested and fortified with good bread and cheese, though belching quietly from the gassy beer, I returned to the station. The single island platform was intact, although having crumbled before nature's advance to the point where a ten-foot silver birch tree was growing directly from the asphalt. A typical overhead-type station with a stairway, by now filled in, leading up from the road that passed beneath, it stood with its northern end on an embankment and its southern end at the mouth of a cutting. In that half-mile long cutting, impressively wide and deep, the atmosphere became more oppressive and relief only came with the breeze that fanned over the embankment that followed. Here the landscape was changing rapidly and becoming more undulating; there were more trees, smaller fields and diary cattle instead of cereal crops. A short thickly wooded cutting led to the mouth of the ninety-nine-yard-long East Leake Tunnel, situated at the summit of the climb out of Nottingham and on the watershed of the Trent and Soar valleys.

The tunnel, twenty miles south of Annesley, marked the southern extremity of the section of railway built under contract by the firm of Logan & Hemingway. George Dow's history of the Great Central records that the work had occupied two thousand men, fifty horses, twenty locomotives, nine steam-navvies, twelve steam cranes and six hundred wagons. It had included the construction of seventy-five bridges and consumed ten thousand tons of iron and steel. Significantly, this massive undertaking was not administered from a large office block, in the modern way, but from a Georgian house in Nottingham.

The tunnel appeared to be in good condition, although the sides of the approach cutting were overgrown with trees whose roots had begun to penetrate the masonry of the abutment walls. Above the portal, almost hidden by foliage, a stone tablet recorded 1897 as the year of construction, but this tunnel had none of the dark mystery of those in Nottingham, and sufficient light penetrated to show that blue bricks lined its entire length. Near the south portal, alongside a flooded gypsum quarry, were the ruins of a few brick and concrete huts. I spent a little time exploring their vandalised interiors – and wondered why anyone would want to drag out a complete cast iron cooking range, only to abandon it by the lineside.

A little later, another long cutting suddenly opened onto an embankment, some fifty feet above the flood plain of the Soar. Away to the east lay the small, pretty village of Stanford while, immediately below, a widely spaced line of anglers fished a deep and placid stretch of river. A teenaged girl on the far bank called excitedly to her boyfriend that she had a catch, their voices carrying clearly through the silent air, for privacy can be elusive in the countryside. Beyond lay meadows, until Herbert Morris's crane factory and the main line of the Midland Railway marked the outskirts of Loughborough.

A solitary semaphore Distant signal stood at the approach to Loughborough Viaduct. All other signals on the route from Ruddington had been of the more modern colour-light type, long disused, lamps missing, their empty lens sockets giving the look of skulls impaled on steel poles. But this bright yellow semaphore arm was more cheerful, even though the control rods had been disconnected to leave the arm resting permanently in the horizontal position. This signal gave notice that, ahead, stood the Home signal guarding the junction with the Midland main line, where the few remaining freight trains that still used the Great Central never received priority.

Soon I was on the viaduct, crossing the Soar and entering

Leicestershire. Less than half the length of its sister at Bulwell, but equally graceful, the Loughborough Viaduct has eleven arches, the northernmost crossing a road and three of the central ones, skewed at an angle to the remainder, bridging the river. Although adapted to this local need, the structure was built to the same pattern as that at Bulwell, with long-lasting blue brick formed into semicircular arches resting on stone inserts on the piers. There was no sign of recent maintenance and vegetation was making a tentative exploration of the mortar courses, but the basic structure appeared sound. Looking back, after crossing the viaduct, the southern embankment curving gently leftward towards that line of handsome arches, it was difficult not to imagine for a few moments the same scene through the eyes of a footplateman. The evening was conducive to such illusions, until the excruciating whine of an undersized and overstressed motorcycle intruded. Strange how that tiny machine should more offend the senses as it carried its rider to some youthful assignation than the thousand-ton coal train that was speeding along the main line railway not far beyond.

After passing the Brush electrical engineering works, and crossing the Nottingham to Loughborough road on a steel plate bridge, the track curved sharply to the left and descended steeply, along a formation built in 1970 that joined this isolated section of the Great Central to the Midland main line. Ahead, the GCR embankment ended at the abutment of a demolished bridge, which had once carried this brave and ambitious railway over the quadruple tracks of its competitor. Below, a massive diesel-electric locomotive throbbed and growled as it waited to move a London-bound train out of Loughborough Midland Station. Across the tracks, a flock of gulls scavenged a rubbish tip where the Great Central's embankment had been removed, and beyond lay the town. The day's walk was over.

9

LOUGHBOROUGH AND ITS PRESERVED RAILWAY

Superficially, Loughborough has the appearance of any other medium-sized Midland industrial town. Certainly it does not show its best aspect to visitors who approach from the north. Narrowish streets of terraced houses, occasionally dwarfed by red-brick mills, which lack the ornamentation common in larger industrial centres, seem to be the norm. It is the sort of place that those who think of England in terms of stately homes and thatched cottages close their eyes and minds to, but in reality it is a fine little town whose industry has contributed more than its share to the wealth of the nation. Many of the fifty thousand people resident at the time of my visit lived cheek-by-jowl with industry, the murky waters of the Grand Union Canal lying alongside backyards and gardens, while the whirring and clicking of textile machinery could be heard from a mill in a residential street. Through open loading doors, next to terraced houses, engineers' patternmakers could be seen going about their precise and highly skilled craft.

Prior to the Industrial Revolution Loughborough lived by malting and the wool trade but, like Nottingham, became deeply involved in lace manufacture and hosiery in the 19th century. And, as in Nottingham, the presence of these trades led to the birth of a machine-building industry, so that in 1839 it had the distinction of providing a home for the country's first steam-powered mill. One firm with its roots firmly fixed in those far-off days was Bentley Textile Machinery, whose factory in the town remained one of the largest of its type in the world.

In time, the products of Loughborough's engineering industry became more diverse. Herbert Morris set up his factory in 1884, which still employed one thousand people making cranes, hoists and conveyors. Shortly afterwards, in 1889, the Brush Company, later part of the Hawker-Siddeley Group, established its works on the northern fringe of the town. Over the years that factory has produced railway locomotives, tramcars, generators, transformers and other items of heavy electrical engineering equipment. Even in the late 1980s, five thousand people worked at the Loughborough factory making products for both the home market and export. There were newer industries too, a pharmaceutical company and its laboratories, and the printing works of a particularly successful publisher of children's books being but two. And, as an investment in its future, the town plays host to the University of Technology, where more than five thousand students study while maintaining close links with industry. But it is as the home of one of the most traditional industries that Loughborough is perhaps best known.

In 1840 an Oxford bell-founder named John Taylor visited the town to recast the bells of the parish church and found the place so much to his liking that he moved his business there, where it remains – still in the care of the same family. Many famous bells have been cast in Taylor's Foundry on Freehold Street, including 'Great Paul' of St Paul's Cathedral, which, at more than 37,000lb, is the largest bell in the British Commonwealth. The three next largest bells in Britain were also cast there: 'Great George' of Liverpool Cathedral (33,098lb), 'Great Peter' in York Minster (24,270lb), and 'Little John', the hour bell of the Nottingham Council House clock, which weighs 23,211lb. And Loughborough bells ring in the cathedrals of places as distant as Adelaide, Perth and Christchurch.

Another of Taylor's claims to distinction was the rediscovery, in 1896, of the method of casting bells that could be accurately tuned, an art lost for the previous two centuries. They demonstrated their achievement on a carillon specially built at the works, and as a result

Taylor's carillons have been exported even more widely than their single bells. The music of Loughborough-built carillons can be heard as far afield as the Mountain Lake Sanctuary in Florida, at Niagara Falls, at Cape Town, at Yale University, at Sidney in Australia and in the Washington National cathedral.

It is therefore fitting that the principal landmark of Loughborough should be a 150-foot-high carillon tower, completed in 1923 as a memorial to the men of the town killed in the First World War. Standing in the pleasant, if unfashionably formal, Queen's Park, it is a square tower of brick and stone, topped with a heavy-looking copper-

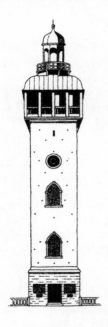

roofed gallery, an unusual and entirely appropriate memorial. In a room half-way up the tower was a small museum, mainly containing personal effects of First World War soldiers, bringing home in a personal way the human tragedy of human conflict. But it is not a mournful place and each Sunday afternoon in the summer recitals are given and the sound of bell music rings out across the town.

There was much more of interest to see in Loughborough, its good-looking Italianate Town Hall dominating the bustling open-air market, scores of busy shops and dozens of small public houses. True, it has a modern indoor shopping centre, but that was almost small enough to ignore. But for many visitors, the main focus of interest is Central Station, headquarters of a group of enthusiasts who have preserved part of the old Great Central. Nearing the station, the company's influence gradually became apparent; first there was Wharncliffe Road, named after the man who was Chairman at the time of the line's building, then the cheerful sound of a steam whistle followed by the sight of a plume of smoke and steam rising above the rooftops. At the corner of Wharncliffe Road and Great Central Road was the entrance to the goods yard, now used by industry but still retaining its typically Great Central appearance. On one side of the gateway stood the office block; fairly small, immaculately maintained and handsome, with Flemish gables topped by terracotta urns. Opposite, the weighbridge attendant's hut was equally well kept while, across the road, the classically railway-style Great Central Hotel stood in unspoilt splendour. Red bricks, cream terracotta mouldings, ornate balustrades and tall, elegant chimneys combined with fine proportions to transform something that could have been modest into something almost grandiose.

Inside the hotel the bar was disappointing. Not that the beer and lunch was anything but pleasant, but it seemed as if a previous owner had been ashamed of the hotel's Victorian associations. Here was comfort without elegance, the furnishings and decor for the tall, high-ceilinged room having been changed to a style more in keeping with a country inn than an Edwardian railway hotel. But it was a popular place, filled with friendly people, and it is they who are the real heart of the English public house.

A neat little booking office, on a bridge spanning the tracks, is the visitors' introduction to one of the finest railway preservation projects in Britain, and it was in the panelled interior of the booking hall that I met Stanford Jacobs, Deputy Commercial Manager of the Great Central Railway (1976) plc. An ebullient man, he lost no time in explaining that he was known as 'Jake' to his friends before leading me down the broad wooden stairway to the platform. In a lull between trains we sat on a bench, talked of the railway's resurrection and met some of the volunteers who had made it all possible: Geoff Hall, a retired schoolmaster, who explained that the brick and concrete building with steel-shuttered windows that had mystified me so much in East Leake goods yard had been a Second World War control office; Graham Oliver, the Company Secretary, who gladly offered the loan of historical documents and a list of contacts; and David Pugh, who had recently succeeded Jake as Commercial Manager and whose wife Carol was manageress of the company's excellent on-train catering service.

The history of the preserved section of the Great Central goes back to the days when the last diesel multiple units were still plying between Nottingham and Rugby. Graham Oliver told how the originator of the scheme had been a man named John Kirby who, at that time back in 1967-68, had worked for BBC Radio Leicester. He also spoke of his own early experience with the railway as Publicity and Sales Manager – 'general dog's body, really.'

'One thing I will always remember, though,' he said, 'are the times I went trudging around traction engine rallies to drum up support for the scheme. There was this chap who always used to stand looking at me, tugging at his braces and saying, "You'll never do it, you'll never do it." Yet we have done it and I often think of him when I stand back and look at our achievements.'

Jake reminded me how, during that period, a total ban on steam locomotives by British Rail had led to a number of over-optimistic schemes for private lines.

'The original plan for this railway was to preserve the section between Leicester and Nottingham as a line where steam locomotives could work over a respectable distance. So they formed the Mainline Preservation Group, rented this station off British Rail and started work. At that time there was still a connection with British Rail, through Abbey Lane sidings at Leicester, and one or two of the first locomotives came in by that route. It would have been a very nice scheme, if it could have been made to work, and a lot of enthusiasm was generated for it. So the next stage was to form the Mainline Steam Trust, and they soon had a service running the two miles between here and Quorn. Some of the first trains consisted of a couple of coaches and a Norwegian 2-6-0 named *King Haakon*, which had distinguished itself in the war by hauling the King's train away from the advancing German Army.

'Things went well, traffic was building up and British Rail allowed us to run trains over the five and a half miles to Rothley. Suddenly they hit us with a bombshell by demanding that we buy the track, which we had been renting at £1,200 a month, for £100,000. They gave us about three months' notice and we could only see one way of raising the cash – so we went public and hurriedly created the Great Central Railway (1976) plc. It was absolutely touch and go whether we could raise the money; meanwhile they gazumped us on the price, first to £150,000 and then £200,000. Apparently it was the Property Board putting the squeeze on us and they never thought we would make it. But we did – by the skin of our teeth and an overdraft that has damn near crippled us ever since. Although you would not think it to look at us, we've got no money whatsoever, we are perpetually in debt and any profit we make has to go towards paying off the overdraft. I know all the best companies have an overdraft, but I often think just how nice it would be to have some money to play with.

'Unfortunately, we could not raise sufficient funds to pay for both tracks to Rothley, or even a single stretch of line south of there. So we ended up with this isolated single-track railway. And then, in July and August 1976 – the busiest part of our season – they hit us again by closing us down while they lifted the track we had been unable to purchase. But we gradually got on our feet and have built up steadily, despite periodic financial crises, ever since.'

If the restoration of the Nottingham to Leicester line was wildly beyond the resources of the volunteers in the 1970s, they never accepted that the situation would last forever. An extension south to Belgrave & Birstall was planned and a feasibility study reported optimistically on a proposal to connect the railway at Loughborough with the British Rail line to Ruddington, so putting the preserved Great Central into the outskirts of both Nottingham and Leicester. It all seemed rather too optimistic, but I was told to 'remember the chap at the traction engine rallies' and to 'wait and see'.

Certainly, their achievements were impressive. The station had changed since George Chambers had driven through and described it as nearly derelict; it had a real purpose again and its volunteer staff had a future to look forward to. The green and cream paintwork shone, the canopy had been repaired and reglazed, and on winter days warming fires burned in the refreshment and waiting rooms. The ladies' waiting room was immaculate; with its gold-lined iron fireplace, parquet floor and beautifully restored pine woodwork. There were other attractive touches around the station too, like the enamel advertisements, such as 'Matchless Metal Polish – Liquid or Paste, According to Taste', not to mention Wills's Woodbines and Bovril.

The station restoration group viewed its work as being similar to that of the well-known painters who used to care for the Forth Bridge. But the task facing the eight regulars in the team must surely have seemed less daunting than it did when they first took over, after years of neglect and vandalism. It is easy for the public to think of a preserved railway only in terms of trains, but these volunteers were doing much more than amusing themselves with an outsize train-set, and much of their work is hard, dirty and unglamorous. Although here, among these enthusiasts, the media-fostered attitude that assumes that everyone 'goes to the office' is reversed. It is easier to get volunteers to do the practical work than it is to involve them in administration, many welcoming relief from a working life separated from physical labour. A regular maintenance team was based at each of the company's three stations and there were departments for administration, signal & telegraph, permanent way, bridges, catering, publicity, and carriage & wagon repair, and a number of independent groups were restoring their own locomotives.

One siding near the station was occupied by a Travelling Post Office (TPO), a train converted into a mobile sorting office and equipped to collect and set down mail while travelling at speed. Although at that time a network of TPOs still covered much of Britain, they were used only for sorting mail while on the move and it was only here on the preserved Great Central Railway that the method of picking up and setting down mail at speed could be seen in operation.

The station yard contained an array of coaching stock and railway equipment, some immaculately restored, some awaiting attention. A coach specially adapted to meet the needs of disabled passengers was the latest to be commissioned. Nearby, a newly acquired diesel multiple unit awaited attention before being declared fit for service. In the early days of railway preservation all efforts had been devoted to saving steam locomotives from the scrap-heap, but, with the first generation of diesels having reached the end of their working lives, some preservationists were turning their attention to them. Some steam buffs may have felt betrayed, but a generation of rail enthusiasts had grown up since the time when the last steam engine was withdrawn from normal service in 1968 and, while many of this younger generation grew to love steam, the diesel could not be ignored. Even Jake, who had started watching trains about 1930, admitted to enjoying travel by diesel multiple unit 'because, for once on the railway, you could actually see where you were going'.

Nearer the engine shed, unrestored relics lay in wait of attention. A dirty tarpaulin covered one of those three-wheeled 'mechanical horses', which were such a familiar part of the 1950s street scene as they hauled railway drays around our cities. Locomotive boilers rested on baulks of timber next to sets of driving wheels. The bridge and other parts of a turntable, recently rescued from Calais with some deeply appreciated help from the citizens of that town, lay in apparent disarray among the grounded box vans, which some of the restoration groups were using as storage sheds.

Stanford Jacobs explained the relationship between the various locomotive restoration groups active on the site, and the railway company.

'They are all independent bodies, but we provide the facilities for their restoration work and, in return, they sign a contract that stipulates that the completed engine will remain on our railway for an agreed period. We contribute to their maintenance fund and have the use of their loco – it's a system that works very well for both parties.'

Loughborough's locomotive stock was impressive at that time and included *Butler-Henderson*, the sole surviving Great Central Railway passenger engine. On loan from the National Railway Museum, it was one of the 'Director' Class engines designed by the company's Chief Locomotive Engineer, John G. Robinson, and had given valuable service from the date of building at the end of the First World War to the last years of British steam. The remaining members of the collection to be seen that day ranged from a diminutive 0-4-0 tank engine, weighing in at little more than twenty tons, to the gigantic 157-ton *Duke of Gloucester*.

The engine shed was more than a home for locomotives – a dark womb-like place where man-made giants crowded together patiently awaiting rebirth. For even those sleek and powerful monsters that are in working order lie dead when their fires are out and their boilers are empty. And there lies the fascination of steam, for it transforms cold machinery into the nearest thing to a living creature that humans have ever created. This was no sanitised or deodorised exhibition hall, but an earthy place where men seemed to have a sort of spiritual connection with these great iron beasts, where cinders crunched underfoot and old odours hinted of steam, soot and oil.

Resting next to the venerable old *Butler-Henderson* was the apple-green-liveried *Mayflower*, a good looking LNER mixed-traffic locomotive from the 1940s, and a powerful-looking old black tank engine that had once hauled suburban trains out of King's Cross. A number of industrial engines and a diesel shunter were also in working order, awaiting their turn on some of the lighter trains. Other engines were still in the course of restoration, some, such as *Duke of Gloucester*, after long years in a scrapyard. Built in 1954, it was British Railways' last steam design, intended to have been the first of a class for hauling heavy Anglo-Scottish expresses. But it was fated to remain unique, its emergence from Crewe Works preceding by only a few months the decision to abandon the use of steam on British Railways. After many years of painstaking voluntary labour, while its owners struggled with technical and financial problems, 'The Duke' was almost complete and its clean-cut lines were accentuated by a coat of grey primer. Other engines nearing completion included the former Great Western Railway's *Witherslack Hall*, which was not so far from home as some would think, for GWR locomotives frequently worked trains onto the Great Central system as far as Leicester and, more occasionally, Nottingham. *Witherslack Hall*, in particular, was no stranger to this part of the world, having spent part of its early life on the Great Central Section during the 1948 Locomotive Exchanges, when the designs of the old companies were evaluated by the different Regions of the newly nationalised British Railways.

But it was one of the least likely looking locomotives that was due to be the next to re-enter service, an old Great Western Railway 2-8-0 tank engine. Its wheels, chassis and coal bunker stood on one set of tracks while the boiler lay on an adjacent well-wagon. A volunteer, crouching inside the smokebox as he expanded the boiler tubes into the front plate, estimated that three months' work would see the engine hauling trains again. I could not help thinking that, after a working life spent dragging thousand-ton coal trains along the valleys of South Wales, the more modest demands of a preserved railway would offer an easy retirement for the old lady.

One restoration group had arrived too late to claim a place in the shed and their charge, a British Rail 9F heavy freight locomotive, stood in the open, partly protected by a temporary building that had been erected around it. The tender was almost complete but the engine, with cab and wheels removed, rested on baulks of timber. The three-sided shed had been built to form such a close fit that it was difficult to walk between the walls and the locomotive. Standing back for a better view, I shuddered to think of the working conditions during bleak, wintry days on that exposed embankment. But such was the dedication of these people to their cause.

10
BY STEAM TRAIN TO ROTHLEY

L oughborough was left behind as the train accelerated away from the station, before settling to the sedate 30mph permitted by the rules of the Light Railway Order, under which the preserved Great Central operated. It caused a vague feeling of melancholia to sit in a main-line coach being hauled along a main-line railway by an express locomotive at such a pedestrian pace, but the feeling did not persist. Politely efficient staff served meals at well-laid tables, a uniformed Inspector checked tickets in a manner businesslike and pleasant, while wisps of steam and smoke drifted past the windows and over the fields.

It was impossible not to feel admiration for the dedicated volunteers whose efforts had saved this part of the line and its way of life. For their railway consisted of much more than five miles of track, three stations, a collection of rolling stock and a group of mildly eccentric people. It had atmosphere and a fascination reaching beyond the adult visitors with their memories to the parties of schoolchildren who, perhaps for the first time, could see a system permeated throughout by orderliness, responsibility and pride – engendered by loyalty rather than financial gain. If it is easy to understand the nostalgia felt by the comfortably off, the undoubted affection of working people for this railway must have a more ambiguous basis, for its heyday was in a time when folk had to know their place and when to touch their cap, and were worn out by long hours of hard work that made men grizzled and women careworn before their time. But there was also a feeling of community and many, particularly on the railway, possessed that dignity born of responsibility of which much of the working class has since been robbed. Perhaps the orderliness of the steam railway represents an age of security that we crave to recapture because, although it was an era when death from disease or war was commonplace, no frail and fallible human being possessed the means of destroying civilisation itself. In that sense it was a secure world.

After a couple of miles we eased to a halt at Quorn & Woodhouse, typical of a Great Central country station with its red-brick buildings well maintained and the cast-iron lamp posts on the island platform decorated with baskets of flowers. The other window of the carriage looked onto a line of restored goods wagons in a siding and, beyond, the goods shed and yard. This was pleasant countryside: grazing cattle, fields of corn interspersed with woodland and, over to the west, the high ridge of the Charnwood Forest Hills. It was all seen at its best as we steamed across Swithland Reservoir on a viaduct giving fine views of mixed woodland that cloaked the hills and reached down to the water's edge. Yet this was an area where natural resources had been exploited for centuries.

Many of the elegantly inscribed 18th-century gravestones to be seen in the churchyards of Nottinghamshire and Leicestershire are of Swithland slate, which also graced the roofs of so many houses with its attractive blue-grey hue. And only a mile eastward lies the village of Mountsorrel, whose quarries supplied the red granite cobblestones to pave thousands of Midland streets. In modern times there is little demand for cobblestones and most of the granite is reduced to chippings, but it still provides work and the village had gained other industries, including a Rolls-Royce Aerospace factory. But possibly the area's greatest natural resource was its water, supplied to the people of Leicester from the reservoirs of Swithland and Cropston since Victorian times.

An overgrown open space and a ruined goods shed betrayed the site of the junction where a branch line had once reached out to the quarries. There were sidings here to accommodate stone trains and a station was planned, but never completed, for the benefit of city folk wishing to visit this pleasant place. Only a bricked-up arch in a bridge abutment, where steps had led up to a platform that was never built, remained as evidence of the aborted plan. Minutes later the train rolled into Rothley Station, at that time the southern terminus of the preserved railway.

Passengers flooded from the carriages to look about themselves while the engine ran round its train to prepare for the return journey. For fifteen minutes the station was a busy place as people milled around, buying refreshments, looking at train departure lists from the 1950s, peering into the waiting room or just standing and staring at the locomotive, now coupled up and ready to leave. The guard's whistle shrieked out several times, for those passengers unaccustomed to the disciplines of public transport and whose organisational skills were tested by the need to board the train at a scheduled time. When all were aboard, the engine whistled in reply and, with a sharp, precise exhaust beat, accelerated its train under the bridge and away towards Loughborough.

I had the feeling of having passed through a time-warp. Along the now deserted platform, short cast-iron lamp posts supported baskets of geraniums and lobelia while, across the goods yard, a light breeze whispered through the trees, gently rustling and turning the silvery undersides of their leaves towards the sun. Enamel signs on red-brick walls extolled the virtues of old and familiar brands of household goods, while a timetable showing departures from Leicester Central in 1957 told of services heading for places as diverse as London, Sheffield, Manchester and Bournemouth throughout the day and night. A porters' barrow, parked at the foot of the steps leading down from the road bridge, carried a bundle of newspapers that turned out to be facsimiles of *The Daily Telegraph* of 26 October 1928, and a young bespectacled booking clerk peered from his ticket-window, alert for approaching custom.

At the open door of the ticket office I asked for the Station Master. He was off duty but his deputy, a local lorry driver named John Saddler, who was leaning against a high Dickensian desk, invited me in. It was a small, comfortable office – crowded with John, a couple of porters, and the efficient-looking ticket clerk. They were as much actors as railwaymen, having subconsciously acquired the attitudes and mannerisms of men who had laboured in an earlier time. Sharing the same environment, uniform, job and dedicated attitude of service to the public, this role-playing was almost inevitable. And certainly desirable.

The office was never without activity; telephone calls about the train's progress were made and received and details of ticket sales noted down, while outside a porter armed with a mop and galvanised bucket went clanking along the platform in the direction of the gents' toilet. When the pace slowed, I sat with John Saddler in the attractively restored waiting room as he told of his involvement with the railway. I learned other things from him as well, about the running of the station and how various members of staff had become involved, but it was for telling me about Madge Sleath that John earned my eternal gratitude.

11
MADGE

It was some time after visiting Rothley that I called on Madge Sleath, a remarkable woman who could claim the distinction not only of belonging to that diminishing group of people who had been on the payroll of the old Great Central Railway Company, but also of working for its present-day successor. She had answered my letter by return and I was soon making the bus ride through pleasant countryside from Loughborough to her home village of Sileby. The place had been industrialised for over a century; making shoes and textiles, sending men to the Mountsorrel quarries and transporting away its products along the quadruple tracks of the Midland Railway, which cut through the village on an impressive line of viaducts and bridges.

The bus stopped at the bottom of the High Street, in the shadow of a former brewery, which had long since fallen victim to Mammon's manipulation of the public's taste-buds. Madge had offered to meet me at the bus stop 'because Sileby is a funny place to get lost in', but she was nowhere to be seen. It was then I realised that one of two women, talking by the parapet of a small bridge, must be her. After all, there could not be many other diminutive, white-haired old ladies going around the village with chrome-plated 'GCR' lapel badges on their best blue coats.

Introductions over, she led the way to the plain-looking block of old people's flats where she lived, carefully re-locking the door after we entered. This security-consciousness seemed out of place with the trusting, confident soul who had straightaway invited me into her home after meeting me for the first time. But as we walked the highly polished, hospital-like corridors she explained how the flats had been attacked by vandals and one resident robbed – viewed as easy meat in these days when the age-old relationship between the young and the very old seems to be breaking down.

Her tiny flat was cosy, with good old furniture, china displayed in glass cabinets and pictures of her twenty-one great grandchildren covering its walls. Plants thrived by the window, which offered a view of a train of oil tanks trundling across the tall red-brick viaduct carrying the Midland main line. Another wall was adorned with her present-day Great Central Railway share certificates, framed and hung alongside a photograph of herself with Prince Philip. How did she come to be in such company?

'Well, I always said my first love was the railway and the second was the Leicestershire Yeomanry, because I married a yeoman when I left the railway in 1919. That picture was taken at one of their functions when the Duke – he's Commander-in-Chief of the regiment – wanted to know why I was the only lady present. My first husband served twenty-six years with the regiment, and when he died they gave him a full military funeral. There were hundreds there and the yeomen made me promise to visit them again. I'm invited to all their reunions – I've not missed one of their memorial services since 1927 and now they say they can't go anywhere without me. It's very nice, even though I'm the only lady there. They all call me Mrs Huddy, you know, because my first husband's name was Hudson.'

The army and the railway had been interlinked in Madge's life and it was because of the First World War that she had become a railway worker.

'I was eighteen when the First World War broke out and living in Ibstock. All the boys volunteered and went off to form a battalion of the King's Royal Rifles and we girls were left behind in a mining village where there was never much for us to do. Well, I'd seen this photograph of a girl working as a porter on one of the London stations and told the other girls that I'd love to work on the railway. A few days later a friend told me that she knew someone whose father was a Station Master who had lost two of his porters, because of the war, and he was willing to take on a girl as a replacement. So I wrote off and got an interview at Rothley.

'He remarked that I wasn't very big, but that I looked tough enough! And so I got the job. Then I had to find lodgings – I couldn't stay at his home because he had a family of ten – but he soon fixed me up with a signalman who lived in one of the railway cottages and had a spare bedroom.

'I was thrilled to death with the job – I loved it! Mind you, we were always busy. My duties included cleaning the platform and waiting rooms, although I did not have to polish the windows because they had been painted blue, due to the blackout. I helped look after the goods yard and to load the goods each night – there were lots of factories around Rothley and Mountsorrel at that time. The draymen used to bring in huge crates of boots, mainly for the Army I suppose, and great hampers from the hosiery factories. I had to do the billsticking – pasting up the timetables, seaside posters and that sort of thing. There was one massive board at the top of the bank by the bridge; I used to have to carry a big, heavy step-ladder up there and get it over the fence before I could start my slap-dabbing. And then the damn wind would come and wrap the poster around my head! The only job I did not have to do was to climb the signal posts to bring the oil lamps down for trimming and cleaning – that had to be done every day you know.

'All the villages were about a mile from the station; there was Rothley, Thurcaston, Cropston, Swithland and Mountsorrel. We used to have passengers from them all – they came in shoals and a lot of them used bicycles. There was a bike rack all along one wall of the porters' room and they were allowed to use the estates office as well. We literally had hundreds of passengers every morning, mainly going to Leicester. There were all sorts of people, not just those going to work in factories but the owners of big shops, solicitors, architects and suchlike.

'We had fifteen trains each way and I used to have to get there in time to unlock the station for the first one – at 5.56. The clerk, who had to be there at the same time, lived about two doors away in the cottages and we used to run down the cutting side together. It was quicker going that way and across the track rather than round the lanes to the front entrance. If I got over the fence first I'd call out "Are you there?" and a voice in the darkness would answer "Right behind you", and then we'd go slithering down the bank together.

'We had a nice do one morning in that blizzard in 1916. The snowdrifts were hedge-high all up the road. There were three steps down from the cottage door – but not that morning. I even walked over the top of the gate without seeing it! Then we had to knock up the Station Master to get some shovels to dig out the station gateway. Eventually we got it clear and went down onto the platform; all the telegraph wires were down across the line and we could hardly see where the posts were. Soon the Leicester bigwigs, who lived along Rothley Lane and The Ridgeway, and the boys on their way to school in Leicester arrived, and we set them on helping to shovel and sweep.

Above Newstead Colliery was the second coal mine to be passed in the first two miles of the walk. Closed in 1987, it is seen here awaiting demolition. *Author's collection*

Right Newstead Colliery village in happier days: retired pitmen relax and exchange a joke with the photographer. *Bill Vincent*

Above The Rolls-Royce Flight Testing Establishment at Hucknall put some strange craft into the air, and in their day the two seen here probably caused more comment than most. The Wellington bomber has had its rear gun turret replaced by an early Rover jet engine. When jets were in their infancy and most people knew nothing of them, locals were surprised to see this aircraft flying with stationary propellers, while emitting a deafening roar from its rear end! *Rolls-Royce Heritage Trust*

Below But the strangest aircraft of all had to be the 'Flying Bedstead', a vertical-take-off pioneer of the early 1950s. *Rolls-Royce Heritage Trust*

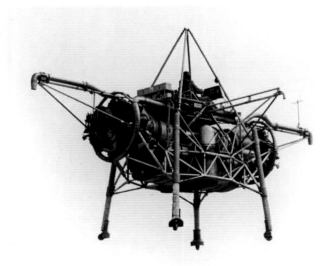

The disappearing railway: Bulwell Common Station, in a northern suburb of
Nottingham, is seen in 1956 and (*below*) twenty-five years later. Only the skyline
and the industrial building, visible through the signal gantry, remain unchanged.

The workmen's train in the upper picture, hauled by an ex-Great Northern
Railway 'C12' Class of 1898, was known locally as the 'Dido'; for almost sixty
years it meandered up and down the Leen Valley for the convenience of railwaymen
who lived in Nottingham and worked at Annesley. There are at least three theories
of how the name originated. Some say it was because the service ran Day In Day
Out; others thought the train a bit of a joke (a 'dido' is an antic, caper or prank,
according to the *Concise Oxford Dictionary*). On the other hand, the origin might
reflect the humour of a classically educated railwayman, for Dido was the

mythological first Queen
of Carthage, whose name
derived from the
Phoenician for wanderer,
and the train certainly
wandered – up one side
of the valley by the
GNR line and back
down the other by the
Great Central route.
Both Bill Reed

Above The handsome frontage of Nottingham's Victoria Station in 1901. The platforms were behind the building and fifty feet below street level. *Courtesy of Nottingham City Council and www.picturethepast.org.uk*

Below Following redevelopment the old station clock tower pokes skyward among the concrete slabs to form a singular, decorative feature in the harsh townscape. *Author*

The palatial interior of Nottingham Victoria when new. *Courtesy of Nottingham City Council and www.picturethepast.org.uk*

Above **A quiet day and faded grandeur in the 1950s.** *Courtesy of Nottingham Historical Film Unit and www.picturethepast.org.uk*

Below **The same scene today.** *Author*

Above A handsome engine in a fine station: Great Central 'Atlantic' No 1085 stands at the south end of Victoria Station in this pre-1923 shot by Nottingham photographer Gordon Hepburn. Designed for the fastest expresses and resplendent in Brunswick green and crimson lake livery, with polished brass beading over the wheel splashers, she was, on this occasion, waiting to take a slow train to Leicester. Note the distant clock tower, situated midway along the length of this immense station. *T. G. Hepburn, Rail Archive Stephenson*

Below An early-1930s scene of the southern end of the station, then only a little over thirty years old. Aficionados will be pleased to note all trains are still in the hands of former Great Central and Great Northern engines. *J. R. Hollick, author's collection*

Two men with memories of Nottingham Victoria Station: George Fox (*right*), born in 1889 and evicted from his childhood home to make way for its building, is seen here in his nineties, having just performed in a concert with the Carlton Male Voice Choir.

George Chambers (*below*) was the driver of the last passenger train to leave the station. He is seen here driving a St Pancras-Nottingham express in the 1960s, photographed by his friend and colleague, **Bill Reed.** *Bill Vincent/ Bill Reed*

Percy Ablitt, the author's late father, recalling memories of Nottingham Goods Yard when he was a boy during the First World War. *Bill Vincent*

Nottingham can still deliver a few surprises, such as this view of a working windmill standing on a green hilltop and framed by tower blocks, typical of the many that scar the city. *Author*

Above Inside the bell foundry at Loughborough. *Taylors, Eayre & Smith Ltd*

Below 'Great Paul', Britain's largest bell and Taylor's most famous product, on its journey from Loughborough to St Paul's Cathedral. Three steam traction engines were employed for the eleven-day haul in May 1881. *Taylors, Eayre & Smith Ltd*

Above 'Recreating the Experience': former Southern Railway 4-6-0 *Lord Nelson* lives up to the motto of the preserved Great Central Railway as it leaves Loughborough with a train for Leicester North in July 2008. *Author*

Below Loughborough Central Station, terminus of the preserved section of the Great Central Railway. *Author*

Left   A sunny morning inside Loughborough signal box on the preserved Great Central Railway. *Bill Vincent*

Below left   A giant at rest: inside Loughborough engine shed. *Author*

Below   Madge Sleath, who worked as a porter on Rothley Station during the First World War and returned to run the refreshment room of the preserved railway in 1975, celebrates her 89th birthday on Loughborough Central Station. Forming a backdrop to the family group is the only surviving Great Central Railway passenger engine, 'Director' Class *Butler-Henderson*. *Author's collection*

Above Leicester Central Station has suffered partial demolition, neglect and ruination, but occasional relics of better days survive. *Author*

Left A wrought-iron gate incorporating the GCR monogram. *Author*

Above Other than the station, the only remaining Great Central building of significance in Leicester is the former power station, which stood in the goods yard and generated electric and hydraulic power. It is now a student bar. *Author*

Left The ruin of a Roman Bath House, adjacent to the Jewry Wall Museum. One the largest Roman ruins standing in Britain, the archways formed the main entrance. *Author*

Right The Blackfriars Roman mosaic pavement is seen here in its original position in the special room that the Great Central Railway built for it inside the structure of the viaduct. *Courtesy of Leicester City Museums*

Left Leicester's Town Hall Square is a peaceful oasis in a bustling (and sometimes tawdry) city. *Author*

Below Leicester's colourful daily market offers bargains by the score and a remarkable cacophony of traders' calls. *Author*

First they cleared the platform edge and we put some sand and salt down. Of course, we all had a good snowball fight while we were about it and I'll always remember the fun we had that morning. But it was nearly dinner time before the snowplough broke through and the first train arrived.

'I remember some other funny incidents too. There used to be two local coal merchants who used the yard, Joseph Ellis & Sons and Freddy Ross. Well, I'd just weighed out Joseph Ellis's cart when Freddy Ross poked his head round the corner and asked me to wait a minute until he was ready. So I picked up a bit of rope and started skipping to pass the time. When I arrived back on the platform Mr Hodgkinson, the Station Master, greeted me with the words: "Madge, in my office – you're on the carpet !" When he sat down, he showed me this telegraph message that read "FEMALE PORTER SEEN SKIPPING IN GOODS YARD STOP HAD SHE NOTHING BETTER TO DO STOP". I suppose someone important must have seen me from a passing express, so I told him what had happened and added that a bit of exercise never did anyone any harm. I never found out what his reply to the message was, but he just told me to keep out of sight of expresses next time I'd got nothing useful to do!'

Rothley station occupied an isolated site and there were a couple of occasions when Madge felt unnerved. As my father, in his infancy, had feared the suffragettes, Madge feared the German prisoners who visited the goods yard to load potatoes they had picked while working on nearby farms.

'One of them used to watch me around the place. I don't know what made him, but every time I looked across to where they were loading sacks of potatoes into wagons, he would always be watching. As I walked home last thing at night, after the 10.50 had gone, I imagined his face peeping round every gateway I came to, ready to leap out at me.

'Apart from the German lad I only had one other fright. It was getting on for midnight, with an air-raid warning in force, and we were waiting for the last train, which had been delayed because they were ordered to stay where they were when the sirens went. I was in the porters' room, under the steps which lead down from the street entrance. Except for a small hole, so that I could see the signal, all the windows were painted blue for the blackout – and I was alone. There was a girl clerk on duty too, but she was locked in the office. I tried to read, then wrote some letters; when it was quiet I often passed the time writing letters to friends. Then, over the bridge came the sound of dragging footsteps. At first I thought it was some drunken bloke going home and that he wouldn't bother me, but then they came slowly down the stairs. I sat listening as they shuffled down, just above my head, onto the platform and round towards my door. I wanted to lock myself in, but I had left the key on the outside. I was breathless with fear when the door opened and a bull's-eye lantern shone on me. I can't tell you how relieved I was to see it was the fat old policeman from Leicester. He had walked all round Thurcaston and Cropston, looking for chinks in the blackout, and was hoping to get a train back to Birstall.'

Madge talked on, about how, in the evenings, she would rush back to her lodgings for some supper between trains, about the pay, nineteen shillings for a seventy-two-hour week, and how she paid eight shillings for board and lodging. 'Mind you, I helped my landlady a lot when I was off duty' – which could not have been very often with six twelve-hour shifts and alternate Sundays to be worked!

'When it was my weekend off I would finish at 5.30 on the Saturday and return to duty for the 10.26 on Monday morning. So I'd go rushing off home to Ibstock, travelling to Loughborough and then changing onto the old London & North Western's Charnwood Forest line. Then I would have to leave about eight o'clock on Monday morning to start the journey back, dashing across the town to catch the 10.15 train from Loughborough Central. And then I had to start shutting carriage doors as I got off! When I told my lads about it they could never understand how I managed, but it was my job. And you have got to do your job, haven't you?'

It was hard work for poor pay, but Madge found most people to be friendly and kind. Although if she had been as sociable and helpful with the passengers as she was with me, they would have found difficulty in being otherwise. But the real proof of their respect for her still stood in a corner of her room, a treadle-operated Singer sewing-machine that the regular passengers had given her as a wedding present. She still used it to make her own clothes and confessed that she knew that it had cost £27 – about half a year's pay. Carefully preserved in one of her numerous scrapbooks was the letter she had received with the machine. In faded blue ink, on paper disintegrating along the folds where it had lain for nearly sixty years in the machine table drawer, it spoke of her 'constant good nature and readiness to help'. It had probably helped with lady porters being a bit of a novelty and many folk around Rothley being pretty well-heeled, but it was a generous and thoughtful gift by any standard.

And some of the passengers really were well-heeled. She remembered the not infrequent occasions when a telegraph message would be received to say that an express would be making an unscheduled stop.

'That usually meant that the Earl of Lanesborough would be spending a few days at Swithland Hall. He was an Army officer, living in London, and sometimes would bring a few friends to visit – people like Lord Stuart of Wortley [a director of the railway]. We knew we had to work fast to cause the least possible delay to the express, so the Station Master, Alf, the porter, and I would wait where we knew the guard's van would stop. As soon as the train came in, the guard would start pushing stuff out – great hampers full of rations, bottles of plonk and suchlike. There was all their kit as well. I would often help Lord Lanesborough carry his bags up the steps and, usually, he gave me sixpence as a tip.'

After leaving the job in 1919, Madge became fully occupied with her family and, although she never lived more than a few miles away, had no cause to make a return visit. It was fifty-six years later that she read of the plan to re-open Rothley Station, which had closed in 1963, and asked one of her sons to take her there. Word eventually reached the railway's publicity officer, who sent an invitation to the opening ceremony and arranged for her to meet the directors. She thoroughly enjoyed the occasion, made another visit, made new friends, and soon took on a job in the refreshment room. Had she any previous experience in catering?

'I'd been baking cakes for the British Legion for forty-four years and the Evergreen Club for eighteen, so I managed. Whenever I was rostered to work they would always send a car to collect me. I used to be due to start work at 10.00am, but usually got up about six o'clock to bake cakes, pastries, mince-pies and that sort of thing. Then I'd make a loaf up into sandwiches and make sure that I'd got a pint of milk as well, because the milk used to be delivered on the first train and I'd usually have a crowd waiting for tea before it arrived.'

Madge worked in the refreshment room every weekend until 1980, when her doctor opined that 'no sensible woman of eighty-four would be going out to work' – so she retired.

'I had to do it if I was to prove I was sensible, but I wished I could have kept on – I fretted ever so about it.'

She shuffled through the Christmas and birthday cards, sent regularly by the present station staff, and turned the pages of photographs of the special events she had attended. On one occasion she is with a television personality, another with the now elderly daughter of her old Station Master.

'And this one is of me with the present Lord Lanesborough, President of the preserved railway. I once asked him at one of these dos why he never gave me sixpence like his uncle, the last Earl-but-one, used to do. He looked at me for a minute and said, "You don't have to answer if you don't want to, Madge, but why did uncle used to give you a tanner?"

12
WALKING INTO LEICESTER

I walked down the ramp at the end of Rothley Station platform, past the buffer-stops that marked the end of the line in those days, over a masonry bridge that spanned a quietly flowing brook, and rejoined the trackbed. Trees grew tall on either side, oak, ash and hawthorn, while ballast crunched rhythmically underfoot – the only human sound to be heard in the summer air. From the embankment there was a fine view of green rolling countryside and a golf course, glimpsed through gaps in the undergrowth. This is a scene that can now be viewed from the carriage window of a steam train, for this section of line has since been re-opened and trains now run to a new terminus on the site of the former Belgrave & Birstall Station, on the northern outskirts of Leicester.

The way became progressively more tranquil, with no sound other than the buzzing of insects, the rasping, warbling, noise of crickets and quiet birdsong. Large brown dragonflies darted and soared over the wild flowers, like miniaturised versions of ancient biplanes. The line, now in a shallow cutting, had less of the look of a railway than a country lane

of centuries gone by. Vegetation reduced the track width to three or four feet and, rarely trodden, it was a type of walk long since disappeared into history. Modern intrusion was entirely absent and almost all trace of the railway itself had disappeared. The thought of 'The South Yorkshireman' and 'The Master Cutler' speeding along this route seemed pure fantasy. Powerful freight locomotives hauling long trains of iron ore and coal, or fast mixed-traffic engines hurrying Grimsby fish to London and the South West, might as well have not passed for a thousand years, such scenes seemed so distant.

A long, largely overgrown cutting led to Belgrave & Birstall Station, later to become the southern terminus of the resurrected railway. It had been identical to Rothley, but now presented a scene of dereliction. The steps down from the road bridge were intact, but the sturdy timbers of their canopy were splintered and charred. Of the platform building, only a gable end and a short length of wall remained. This ruin had once been the waiting room and there, exposed to the elements and surrounded by rubble, was a corner fireplace identical to the one so lovingly cared for at Rothley. As I photographed the scene, a figure appeared in the viewfinder. Initially tiny, it grew rapidly, proportionate to its hurried approach, and I lowered the camera more intrigued that annoyed by the intruder. A man of about thirty years, naked to the waist, muscular torso carpeted in black hair, pushed a double pushchair on a rapid, twisting course between the heaps of rubble.

'Why's this station all broken, Daddy?' the slow-speaking voice of a young child reached me clearly.

'Because some people who live in Birstall prefer a rubbish dump to a railway,' came the prompt and bitter reply. Then man, children and pushchair came to an abrupt halt and he greeted me, warmed by my interest in the ruin.

The vandalisation of the station was particularly saddening to him, with his childhood memories of having boarded a train there to visit an air display at Hucknall Aerodrome, which I had passed shortly after setting out from Annesley. Later, in the early days of the preservation scheme, he had helped repair the station.

'We re-covered the roof over the stairway – where the yobs have sprayed "Leicester City FC" – but we had to abandon the work because the Loughborough to Rothley stretch of line was all that the Steam Trust could manage at that time.'

We discussed the conditions I could expect to encounter as my walk took me further south and he told how, when walking near Rugby, he had been challenged as a trespasser and threatened with a shotgun. Behind a fixed smile, I nurtured the hope that he was prone to exaggeration. After he set off again, pushing the children on their hair-raisingly rapid journey through weeds and debris, I found a comfortable spot in the shade of a horse-chestnut tree, sat with my back to yet another golfcourse and surveyed the scene. Just to the south of the derelict station, a blue-brick retaining wall in the side of a low cutting indicated the position of a demolished signal box.

As I walked on, the cutting soon gave way to an embankment and I found myself at the site of the first of many demolished bridges to be encountered while passing through Leicester. Standing there, looking down on a busy roundabout and listening to the continuous roar of traffic, I realised how deceptive had been the rural feel of the last couple of miles; the old railway, deep in its cutting, had formed a long finger of countryside to penetrate the city's sprawl.

Leicester spread into the distance, wide and flat, its skyline punctuated by tower blocks. These buildings of the 1960s never reach skyward with the elegance of the church spires and factory chimneys that they overshadow, but use their bulk in a bellicose challenge to good taste – like aggressively clenched fists raised above the crowd on a football terrace.

The course of the railway was more intact than it had been in Nottingham, easily followed by scrambling up and down embankments where bridges had been demolished. Gradually its nature changed with the appearance of a few more items of litter, followed by polythene sacks that overflowed with household refuse, progressing to burnt-out cars and industrial waste. Then the path opened out into a wide expanse of broken land where weeds and thistles grew waist-high among mounds of brick rubble. In the middle of this wasteland stood a goods shed, built in the style of a Dutch barn. Abbey Lane Sidings had been here, laid to handle the Great Central's coal traffic to this prosperous city in the days when every home was heated by coal fires and every factory powered by steam.

Leaving the site of the sidings, downed bridges, chain-link fences and barbed wire made progress on the embankment impossible, but its course, like that of the following viaduct that carried the line for more than a mile across the city, could be followed along adjoining streets. On one section, isolated by demolished bridges, a signal gantry stood gaunt against the sky, leaning slightly from the perpendicular. It would be easy to say that it leaned drunkenly, but this was not the comic drunkenness of a fool; this relic had more dignity, like a tired old man who might have had just one drink too many.

The streets in this part of Leicester were not intended for pedestrians, 1960s planners having added footways as an afterthought. There was no shelter from the afternoon sun, beating down mercilessly, or the noise of traffic roaring round the loops and curves of these urban speedways. A bridge, which shuddered and vibrated under the weight of speeding vehicles, crossed the River Soar, whose lily-covered waters were below street level and strangely isolated from the surrounding hurly-burly.

The remains of the Great Central Hotel still stood on Northgate Street – a large chalet-style building, with glazed brick on the ground floor and stucco to the first, under wide Tyrolean-style eaves. The roof bore the faded legend 'Great Central Hotel', while a sign on the wall proclaimed it to be 'The Van Dam Bar' – clearly a recent owner's attempt to rid the building of its railway image – but the boarded-up doors and windows advertised failure. A massive iron-plate bridge was still in position over Soar Lane, the only intact bridge I had come across in this part of the city. Forming the northern approach to Leicester Central Station, it had a triangular plan to accommodate the tracks as they fanned out to the platforms. Now, ironically, heavy lorries were parked on top. The station, in Great Central Street, was a handsome structure, though modest in comparison with Nottingham Victoria. The long front wall, separating the covered approach from the street, was of pressed red brick with decoration in cream terracotta, while the entrances were guarded by ornate iron gates. This part of the building was in use as a warehouse, with packing cases and drums stacked high behind unsightly wire-mesh fencing.

Inside the main entrance, two feet protruding from beneath a partly dismantled van turned out to belong to a middle-aged man with an oil-smudged face who readily gave permission for me to look around. A place so misused and neglected should have had a forlorn air, but that was not possible with the sun shining so brightly through the roof lights. The booking offices were still there and, by the passageway that had once led up to the platforms, a peeling notice warned passengers of the impending closure of the station and withdrawal of the Nottingham (Arkwright Street) to Rugby service on 3 May 1969.

From Great Central Street a ramp led up to the platform area, which had been built partly on a viaduct and partly on a vast embankment. Of the massive island platform, which once had double bays at each end, little remained, although the ornate upper storeys of the booking hall were visible from this point. Terracotta urns on Flemish gables contrasted strongly with the utilitarian lines of the two industrial units that had been imposed on the remainder of the site. At the southern end, in the midst of a car park of rolled hardcore, part of a platform remained, its asphalt surface cracked and crazed by advancing vegetation.

13
LEICESTER

For a half mile to the south of Central Station the viaduct and several heavy bridges had been demolished, giving free reign to the urban speedway constructors. Yet among the whirling roundabouts and concrete underpasses Leicester still managed to preserve some of its treasures. On the corner of a massive road junction, next to a side street named Holy Bones, stands the city's ancient parish church, dedicated to St Nicholas. The Saxon church on this site was built of Roman stones, some of which are said to be incorporated in the present building, and among the gravestones were a number of Roman columns, but the immediate area contains even richer relics. Hard up against the western boundary of the graveyard stands part of the massive sidewall of a Roman bath house.

Immediately behind the wall, the concrete and glass of the long, low, Jewry Wall Museum lay partly concealed in its sunken sanctuary. It had an interesting layout, with the museum building forming one boundary and the old bath house wall the other. In this surprisingly peaceful setting, below the level of present-day streets, lay the bath house foundations. And, from this side, the sidewall was even more impressive, rising to a height of about forty feet. The ruins date from about 130AD, but for many centuries only the wall had been visible until the remainder of the site was excavated in the late 1930s. Viewed across the museum lawn, it was a curious scene with ancient foundations visible in the grass, backed by the massive Roman wall and the old churchyard beyond, while a few yards to the right modern traffic sped by in the shadow of a multi-storey Holiday Inn.

The Jewry Wall Museum deals with the archaeology of Leicestershire up to the year 1540. Exhibits range from Roman shoes, buckles, brooches, cinerary urns of human remains and skeletons recumbent in their coffins, to fine mosaic pavements and wall paintings. The Blackfriars Roman Pavement, the largest in the museum, has an interesting history interwoven in recent times with that of the Central

Station. First discovered in 1830, it remained in a basement despite an 1852 proposal to move it to the Crystal Palace and a later one to transfer it to Leicester Museum. When the Great Central Railway was being built through the city, the house above was demolished to make way for the station, but the conflicting needs of preservation and progress were met when the railway company built a special chamber beneath the viaduct to house the mosaic. It remained there, strikingly colourful against the lavatorial glazed brickwork of the room, even after the closure of the railway. However, by 1977 water leaking through the neglected viaduct had begun to damage the pavement and an ingenious rescue operation was necessary to save it.

First, the surface of the mosaic was cleaned, then animal glue was used to fix a layer of muslin and scrim to the surface. Next, the rescuers drove long blades under the pavement to separate it from the floor, before carefully cutting it into sections, which were lifted out and laid face-down. The original mortar was then removed from the underside, to be replaced by a stronger combination of modern mortar and glassfibre. The sections were then turned the right way up and the muslin and glue washed off before transportation to the new museum, where the parts were bolted together and relaid, just a few yards from the original site. Following removal of the mosaic, the earth below was excavated to reveal one of the city's best finds of pre Roman pottery, including examples originating from such diverse locations as Italy and Colchester, which suggested the existence of a fairly important settlement even before the arrival of the Romans.

Leicester is a busy, modern city that remains proud of its past and maintains an interesting network of museums. I made a point of visiting the Museum of Technology, housed in a redundant sewage pumping station about a mile north of the city centre. A pleasant stroll through the beautiful Abbey Park, part of the thousand acres of open space of which, even back in the 1930s, the city could be justifiably proud, and a path along the bank of the Soar brought me to the museum. Here, set in well-kept gardens, was a fine example of Victorian municipal architecture and engineering. The distinctive engine house, with its tall brick chimney and clerestory roof, was originally built to house four giant beam engines and their eight Lancashire boilers.

Today, the engines remain in all their glory, and masses of oil-smeared machinery and ornate iron columns fill the palatial hall, but seven of the eight huge boilers have been removed from the adjoining boiler house to make way for other exhibits. These beautiful engines, last used in 1964 and each capable of pumping 108,000 gallons of water per hour through a height of 165 feet, were cold and dead on the day of my visit. But I was pleased to hear that they are steamed occasionally and that, as the venerable old beasts stir into gentle movement, the engine house is again filled with the once familiar odour of steam and hot oil, while a new generation attunes its ears to the subdued sounds of machinery able to combine power with a leisurely pace.

Although the character of the boiler house museum has changed significantly since my visit, as a consequence of the creation of a new 'Discovery Park' near Coalville I was able to view a diverse collection of exhibits ranging from horse-buses to motorcycles, from horse-drawn fire pumps to one of Sir Frank Whittle's jet engines. To my enduring disbelief, a light aircraft engine of the 1950s, weighing only 300lb, exhibited a claim to be as powerful, at 170 horsepower, as each of the two-hundred-ton beam engines in the next room – further strengthening my suspicion of facts, figures, statistics and, in particular, horsepower ratings. Another section was devoted to the development of knitting machinery, illustrating the phenomenal pace of 19th-century innovation. Side by side, and merely fifty years apart, stood an 1820s hand frame and an 1870 Cotton's Patent machine. At the beginning of a period spanning only two-thirds of a modern lifetime stood a crude wooden contraption and, at the end, a sophisticated piece of modern-looking machinery.

One of the most impressive exhibits stood in the grounds, a steam-powered excavator directly descended from those that had helped to build the Great Central. Like most of its forefathers that laboured on the construction of the railway, this machine was built by Ruston-Bucyrus of Lincoln but, when completed in 1935, the end of the species was in sight. Even the maker's descriptive pamphlet was prefaced with the admission that 'Although steam has been supplanted largely by diesel, petrol and electric motive powers for excavators, there are still instances where steam is preferred, especially in quarries and opencast mines where electric current is not available or where the cost of electricity is prohibitive for shovel work.'

This shovel may not have been the largest built, but with a weight of eighty tons and a bucket capable of holding 2.5 cubic yards of earth, it presented an impressive sight and gave some idea of the awe that must have been inspired when these monsters first appeared on the Victorian scene. Like the pumping engines, the steam-shovel remains in full working order and periodically demonstrates its abilities to visitors.

There was much more to be seen here: a garage containing a carefully restored Leicester Corporation double-deck bus and, among other treasures, an old fire-engine with a long turntable ladder. But it was perhaps the workshops that intrigued me the most, forbidden territory to the public but readily peepable-into by the curious.

After leaving the museum, Leicester's city centre was a pleasant place in which to roam that day, from the vast and busy market, with its cacophony of traders' calls, to the peaceful gardens in front of the Municipal Offices, where trees offered welcome shade and cool water tumbled from a handsome fountain. The Council Offices were housed in a building less grand than that in Nottingham – its mellow brickwork and stone dignified yet familiar, homely. Tastefully decorative, an ornate clock tower rose from one corner to overlook gardens possessing a formality so friendly that the sound of birdsong seemed entirely natural in the centre of this bustling city.

Leicester has prospered for centuries and, even in the depressed times of the 1980s, exhibited an uncontrived air of affluence. Because of good fortune in trade and the diverse range of its industries the city has frequently renewed itself, usually tastefully. Even the Haymarket Shopping Centre seemed less bombastic than its equivalent in Nottingham – and here the promise to include a theatre had been honoured. Whole areas of fine Victorian and Edwardian buildings stood proudly intact, often modest in size, but almost always visually pleasing. In Gallowtree Gate, Thomas Cook's offices of 1891 caught my eye. It was in Leicester in 1840 that the travel agency business was born when Cook organised a railway trip to Loughborough. Fifty years on, the firm had these offices built and when I passed they rose elegantly above the plasticised frontage of a shoe shop to exhibit to the passer-by a frieze depicting the company's growth. An ancient-looking train depicted the inaugural 1840 railway excursion, a slightly more modern one took visitors to the Great Exhibition of 1851, in 1884 Cook's customers viewed the pyramids from a Nile steamer while, in 1891, an even more modern train traversed a backdrop that included a more contemporary wonder of the world – the Forth railway bridge.

Recession had begun to hit this city in the mid-1970s, with a disastrous impact on the previously prosperous footwear and hosiery industries. Soon smaller firms, subcontractors dependant on the large manufacturers, and other industries fell victim. But the city authorities fought back with a variety of tactics; a promotion campaign was launched in co-operation with private business interests, job creation schemes were undertaken and vigorous efforts made to attract new industry. On paper these schemes appeared similar to those now common in other areas, but here they gave the impression of having worked better, perhaps due to that confidence born of previous prosperity. Or, possibly Leicester, with its clean image and frequent train service, fast enough to whisk its citizens to London in an hour and a quarter, was close enough to the favoured South East to stave off the worst of the devastation afflicting communities further north.

My return route to the Central Station area wound through narrow backstreets where tall, elderly buildings cast refreshingly cool shadows and the city's bustle was muted. But the peace was soon destroyed by the broad expanse of an urban speedway, which pedestrians were forced to cross via a dank and vomit-stained subway. This dreary grey world was the chosen environment of a small group of youths with partially shaven heads, whose scalp-veins pulsated as they guzzled cider from large plastic bottles. Sounds were of speeding traffic above, discarded drink cans rolling underfoot and, during a brief lull, a leather-jacketed girl cackling appreciation of her companion's fart, almost before it had finished echoing raucously along the tunnel. A plaque proclaimed that the subway had been opened in 1969 by the Lord Mayor – later to become Chairman of the English Tourist Board.

Back on the surface, a street called The Newarke led past mellowed buildings and a gate in the old town wall, which beckoned from an even narrower side street. The handsome frontage of The Newarke Houses, home of the city's social history museum, concealed a fine period garden while, a little further on, a pleasant park on the site of the castle brought me back to the River Soar and the vicinity of the Great Central. From West Bridge the view was of shabby, modern industrial buildings, covering the site where the Leicester & Swannington Railway had once terminated at West Bridge Station, alongside the River Soar. It seemed shameful that such a historic place should play host to that mundane sprawl, but the City Council did have plans to lay out the site of the station as open space adjoining a riverside walk and providing a modest reminder of its former importance.

It was in 1829 that the businessmen of Leicester met George Stephenson to discuss the feasibility of a railway to bring Charnwood Forest coal to the town, and promptly raised £90,000 to get the project under way. Completed five years later under the direction of Stephenson's son, Robert, the railway was an awkward combination of cable-hauled inclines with locomotives working the more gently graded sections. But it did boast the 1,796-yard Glenfield Tunnel, at that time the world's longest, and brought cheap coal and building materials into the expanding city.

In 1846 the Midland Counties railway took over and converted the line into a through route by extending westward to Burton-on-Trent and building a link from Desford to its own main line south of Leicester. The Leicester to Swannington line survived largely in this form, Stephenson's famous tunnel being worked by locomotives with specially reduced cabs and chimneys, until that section of the route and West Bridge Station closed in the 1960s. At the time of my visit, the Leicester to Burton line carried no passengers and had reverted to its original function of transporting coal and stone.

A few hundred yards south of Central Station, near the end of a truncated section of viaduct, stood a massive lattice-girder bridge that had carried the Great Central tracks over Braunston Gate, at a point where the road was itself bridging a branch of the river. The railway bridge was attractively restored and painted green and cream, with details picked out in red, colours once favoured by its original owner. This spot marked the city end of Leicester City Council's Great Central Way, a through route for walkers and cyclists that linked the heart of the city with open country. When I passed by, this part of the route was unfinished, but I was able to join the pathway about a mile further south, after exploring the remains of the Great Central Goods Yard.

14
SOUTH LEICESTER

The Great Central's Leicester goods offices still stood, rather proudly, on the Western Boulevard. Three storeys high, they were very similar to the Nottingham offices but, at sixty-six acres, the yard they served was twice the size. I found the noise of traffic on the Western Boulevard intolerable and walked for a while beside the Soar, which flows at a lower level and parallel, only returning to view a decrepit red-brick building with a tower, which once housed machinery for generating electric and hydraulic power for use in the yard. Most of the land near the road had been taken over by a scrap merchant, and huge mounds of cars, fridges, washing machines and other consumer 'durables' awaited their fate at the hands of a shredder. Cast-offs of consumerism were fed into one end of this machine to be spat out at the other as a constant stream of hand-sized pieces of metal. Amidst the bedlam of screeching, tearing and clanking noises in this mechanical charnel-house was a small compound where a monumental mason attended to his work. The cold marble and polished granite headstones, silently awaiting names and epitaphs, adding an air of unreality in the incessant din.

Later, from the bridge that had once carried Upperton Road across the south end of the goods yard, it was possible to survey the untidy mess that this well-laid-out railway had become. The main running lines, their course now weed-covered, had cut through the yard from north to south; to the west was the great hulk of the goods warehouse with the power station nearby. Beyond, the Holiday Inn pointed skyward, offering what must have been a fascinating view of industrial dereliction to the occupants of its bedrooms. Surprisingly, the scrapyard retained a railway connection, a single track from the Leicester to Burton line, along which a few elderly coaches had made their last journey to await the scrapman's torch. South of the road bridge, the building that had once housed the Great Central's wagon repair shops still stood, its clerestory roof adding a touch of distinction amidst the surrounding drabness and dereliction.

Adjacent to a bridge carrying the Leicester to Burton railway line across the course of the Great Central, it was possible to rejoin the track. Leicester engine shed had once stood close by, but no trace remained. Until closure in 1964, the shed played an important role on the Great Central system, due to the practice of changing the engines of express passenger trains at Leicester Station. Normally accommodating a score of locomotives, Leicester Great Central engine shed had housed some fine machines over the years, from John Robinson's beautiful Great Central 'Atlantics' to Sir Nigel Gresley's massive 'A3s' and 'V2s'; even the legendary *Flying Scotsman* had been resident for a number of years in the early 'fifties.

From the direction of the Midland main line a train came into view and approached rapidly along the Leicester to Burton line, swaying on the neglected and uneven track as it climbed the long gradient, its driver staring impassively ahead, solitary and remote behind the high windows of his cab. The powerful diesel growled past, trailing a long line of stone-hoppers, each successive pair of wheels springing the track up and down in the oily ballast.

After walking over the next section of cutting, newly filled and being prepared for industry, I arrived at the start of the Great Central Way. The path was not inspiring at this point, falling as it did between two stools – neither railway nor country walk. The cutting, which would have offered a degree of seclusion and formed a haven for wildlife, had been infilled and an asphalt path meandered over it, through coarse grass and saplings, in a contrived attempt at informality.

A small knot of people, mainly children, standing where a road crossed the path parted slightly as I approached to reveal a policewoman holding a clipboard. She was young, plumpish and probably pleasant, but barred my way firmly. Solemnly and importantly, she asked whether I had already made a statement. In the moments of silence before answering, I became embarrassingly aware of my unconventional appearance: forty-something, bearded, dressed in shorts and frequenting the sort of place where children like to play.

'Statement?'

'Haven't you heard?'

'Heard what?'

My ignorance of events seemed to sound incriminating in itself. As the children and a man on a stationary bicycle looked on curiously, she held up a card of double-spaced typing, which, in that pedantic style peculiar to the police, told of the discovery of the body of a murdered woman. I raised my eyes slightly, only to meet hers over the top of the card, staring, inquiring and accusing. Lowering my gaze, the words became a blur as I tried to think where I had been on 30 July, and progressively the feeling of unease grew in me. In lame tones I told my inquisitor and the gaping-mouthed audience of my interest in the Great Central Railway, its London Extension and my intention to walk its course. She interrupted to ask if I had been in the area on the 30th and suddenly became bright and friendly when I said not. Pointing down the path, she told me I was free to walk ahead but not to the left, where a search was being made for clues. Our parting was almost congenial as we wished each other success and I walked on, leaving her to await the next suspect.

On wasteland near the Grand Union Canal, to the east of the railway, more police searched a roped-off area for clues to the murder. And ahead, alongside the path, a figure lounged in a picnic chair. Gradually it took the shape of a youngish constable, who wished me a good afternoon and quite clearly lacked the discomforting intensity of his colleague. He carefully placed his science-fiction paperback down on the grass, open pages downwards, alongside a carrier-bag containing sandwiches, Thermos flask and yet more books, and remarked that he was only there to keep people out of the search area.

'It's a twelve-hour shift so I thought I'd make myself comfortable and soak up a bit of sun. What are you doing here anyway?'

For the second time in fifteen minutes I explained about the railway and my walk, but, inevitably in the circumstances, the conversation drifted back to murder.

'You get used to them, you know. Although there aren't as many as people think, we probably get four or five a year in Leicester and they are usually sorted out pretty quickly. The vast majority of murderers know their victim and most of them are related. Sometimes, someone will just walk into the station and tell us what they've done. You get hardened to it eventually – view it as a chance for a useful bit of overtime. And, as I've got to be here, I thought I might as well make the best of it.'

Soon, the track re-crossed the River Soar on a handsome bridge with decorative cogwheel corbel work around both of its arches. On this stretch, dead straight and mostly raised on a long embankment, the local authority's methods were seen at their dreariest. The track was wide, asphalted for half its width to form a cycleway, the remaining strip of ballast supporting a few plants. Black tarmac stretched away into the distance, shimmering in the hot sun, like some pedestrian version of a motor road. A distant blob, distorted by heat-haze, turned out to be a bicycle, with a policeman's coat draped over the handlebar, leaning against the centre girder of a steel-plate bridge. Its owner was nearby and I explained again about my journey and my earlier meetings with his colleagues, as he sat uncomfortably on the side plates of the bridge.

Visibly overheated in his dark uniform, this man had no books, no chair, sandwiches or any other creature comforts and I succumbed to the temptation to tell of the luxury enjoyed by his comrade.

'Bloody deck-chair?' He shuffled around. 'I've been sat on these sodding rivets for the past six hours!'

No industrial archaeologist could have failed to have been impressed by those perfectly formed domed rivet heads, evenly spaced at three-inch intervals along the edges of the steel plates, thus making it impossible not to sit on at least two at any one time. And that group of robust men who laboured so diligently to build the bridge would undoubtedly have enjoyed a smile had they known how much discomfort they would cause a bony-arsed copper almost ninety years on! It was then that I realised there was something about this Great Central Way that actually pleased me – all of the steel bridges were resplendent in a new coat of green paint and kept in good repair.

The walk was getting a feel of rurality again, but despite the view across a field to a canal lock, with brightly painted narrow boats and a whitewashed cottage, it was illusory. For Aylestone and Braunstone were pressing hard on either side and ahead a road was being built across the track. But it was pleasing to see how it was to be carried over on a bridge and I began to feel a little guilty for having griped about the unimaginative landscaping of the path. At least Leicester had the initiative to preserve part of the route as an amenity, an attitude far more enlightened than that of many local authorities.

At Glen Parva the scene changed, where a deep cutting terminated in a near vertical wall of refuse. A climb over the rubbish and past the ruins of a brickworks, where youths raced motorbikes around a home-made scramble course, brought me to the River Sence. An insignificant tributary of the Soar, sharing its valley with the Grand Union Canal, its presence obliged the railway to build a thirteen-arch viaduct to cross the valley and a plate-bridge to cross the canal. Viewed from the meadows below, it was a clean, good-looking viaduct of the standard Great Central pattern, with Roman-style arches of blue brick. Again, I repeated the mistake, first made at Wilford, and found the succulent-looking fruit of a lineside pear tree to have the taste and texture of a wooden chair leg.

A further quarter of a mile brought me to the bridge over the London & North Western Railway's Leicester to Nuneaton line, where an impenetrable barrier of corrugated iron and barbed wire forced a diversion along the Grand Union towpath. After idly watching a narrow boat pass through a lock, the Leicester to Lutterworth Road brought a harsh return to the modern world; the traffic noise was deafening and yet I was the sole pedestrian. By this route, both hectic and lonely, I entered the village of Whetstone.

15
WHETSTONE TO
LUTTERWORTH

The Great Central's embankment skirted the western edge of
Whetstone for a few hundred yards until coming to an abrupt end
at the site of the station, with a view typifying the fate of so many
English villages. To the east, the church spire rose timelessly from the
treetops, to the west stood a farmhouse, substantial with courtyard and
outbuildings, while ahead an estate of private houses, another
dormitory for the city's overspill, was being built. Station Road offered
a quiet route into the village, past the much-altered Station Master's
house and some pleasant Edwardian villas. In the garden of the Bull's
Head I sat for a while with a glass of Everard's mild ale, beneath the
majestic canopy of a great beech tree. And that heinously noisy road
that had brought me to the village seemed a thousand miles distant.

At the entrance to the half-built housing estate that had usurped the
station, a sign bore the legend 'Spinney Halt – Value for Money
Homes'. Dust clouds swirled over the unmade road as I headed for the
trackway beyond. Like a mirage in this arid scene, a show house stood
resplendent with lace curtains, lawn and flowers. An immaculately
coiffured young woman of synthetic appearance and a salesman in an
equally synthetic suit leaned idly against the front fence, watching a
half-stripped labourer sweating as he hewed at the rock-hard earth,
with that aloofness so carefully cultivated by first-generation upstarts.
The houses were of that standard 1980s design for 'sensitive areas',
equally likely to be found filling a gap in a city conservation area or
standing on the pinch-penny fringe of a dormitory village. There must
be scores of thousands like them around the country; squarish, terraced,
with stainless-steel gas flues poking through their pantiled roofs –
symptomatic of an age of coal-effect gas fires and geranium-filled
chimney pots.

The walk soon became pleasant again, with a good cross-country view from the forty-foot-high embankment that carried the track for the next three miles. But traffic noise grew as the M1, an unwelcome neighbour from here to Lutterworth, closed rapidly from the west, and it was a relief to find the overbridge intact where the motorway passed beneath the railway. This section of motorway opened in 1965, in the dying days of the Great Central route, and many a railwayman must have looked down from this bridge with feelings of injustice and despair, comparing the systematic run-down of the railway with the limitless funds poured into motorway construction. Over the years it has been asserted that the Great Central failed because it followed a route through lightly populated areas, yet it was a route largely duplicated by and considered perfectly suitable for Britain's first motorway. The bridge provided a grandstand view of the M1 at its worst as speeding vehicles, many carrying loads more suited to rail, thundered beneath. A liquid oxygen tanker approached much faster than the others, weaving through the traffic with surprising and frightening agility. It flashed by, giving a fleeting glimpse of a tank emblazoned with warnings of its explosive contents, a blonde woman in the passenger seat and a little girl asleep on the engine-cover.

As the noise of the motorway faded, birdsong became the dominant sound, a young rabbit hopped nonchalantly across the path and butterflies basked on wildflowers. Again, all seemed set for an idyllic stroll – until progress was barred by a fence near the village of Cosby. And beyond the first fence were dozens more; the land having been sold as garden extensions to adjacent houses. I regained the embankment after diverting through a sports field, only to find the problem repeated a few yards further on. While walking a narrow strip of pasture between the privatised embankment and the M1, under the inquisitive gaze of a herd of Friesians, the absurdity of a policy that allowed an 850,000-cubic-yard embankment to become garden plots was blatantly apparent.

The trackway became accessible again where it crossed a road linking the villages of Cosby and Countesthorpe, although an uneasy feeling persisted that this section too might be privately owned. Again, the motorway was close by yet, despite the perpetual noise, the walking was pleasant. Soon a steel-plate bridge carried the path across a deep and overgrown cutting, marking the course of the Leicester to Rugby line of the Midland Railway, closed in 1961.

Further on the Great Central also entered a long cutting, with the motorway running parallel, hidden but not silenced, and soon the Leicester to Lutterworth road crossed overhead on a high three-arched bridge. This was a pleasant place and, I now realised, private in all senses of the word. A crudely painted notice nailed to the bough of a

tree, in the way they used to be pictured in children's comics, bore the solitary words 'KEEP OUT!'. The warnings became frequent, and their message insistent, but, with barbed wire on one side and the motorway on the other, the only options were to advance or retreat. And if this happened to be the territory of the gun-toting landowner I had been warned of back at Belgrave & Birstall, retreat would have been no less hazardous than advance – so I pressed on. As the way became more secluded and overgrown the feeling of being isolated in hostile territory grew, until progress was halted completely by a fence more suited to protecting a nuclear installation than the trackbed of an abandoned railway. Exchanging shorts for jeans, I forced a way through the undergrowth that grew up the cutting side, briars tearing mercilessly at any exposed skin, and after squeezing through yet more barbed wire found myself in a forest of saplings at the edge of the motorway. And there I sat to eat a sandwich, plagued by flies, acutely aware of the illegality of being on the motorway and wondering quite what to do next.

The Ordnance Survey map showed a public footpath leading to the village of Ashby Magna and the bridge carrying it over the motorway was just a couple of hundred yards distant. But although the plantations alongside motorways may look like easy territory for a stroll, this one proved to be one of the most impenetrable thickets I have ever had the misfortune to struggle through. Thistles and nettles grew waist-high. Ankle-ripping brambles concealed dead branches that snapped underfoot to emphasise, with spine-jarring suddenness, that terra-firma was eighteen inches lower than it appeared. Eventually I reached the footbridge and climbed over the railing. Public right of way or not, the end nearest the railway was barricaded by a mound of earth topped with barbed-wire in the manner of a First World War trench parapet, presumably built by he who had fenced off the trackbed. And, for good measure, a generous quantity of manure had been added as a further deterrent to those naive enough to believe they had a right to walk the designated footpaths of England.

Just what motivated this unseen adversary? What self-righteousness led him to demand that I should obey his diktat, while he defied the nation's laws? But, as I was heading away from his land, there was no need for confrontation. The bridge, a long span of concrete, led via a broken stile into a meadow, where sheep ran bleating before me as I followed the course of the long neglected and almost invisible footpath. Following the uncertainty and trepidation of the previous couple of miles this cowardly flock imparted a sense of confidence as they fled before me and, again, I felt master of the land I surveyed – at least until entering the next field. The sheep were still fleeing, but with a more obvious purpose as they ran to and behind a gigantic brown bull, then stood to stare at me from the safety of his rear. He stood four-square and magnificent at the head of a woolly phalanx, wearing an expression both inquisitive and defiant. My retreat, as dignified as I could make it, was watched by bull and sheep, motionless, silent and superior.

A factor overlooked by my land-owning adversary, in his obsessive drive for privacy, was that people who cannot pass by one route will do so by another, sometimes more destructively. And I strode through his

wheat field, relieved to be leaving this unfriendly place, feeling justified in adopting the philosophy of 'sod the man and sod his wheat'.

A short walk through lanes led to the site of Ashby Magna Station where the overbridge, now packed solid with earth beneath, provided a good vantage point. A few yards to the north someone had created additional landscaped space in his garden by scooping an amphitheatre from the embankment and adding conifers, running water and a rockery. South lay a wide cutting that had once accommodated the station. All railway structures had been cleared and the land occupied by the makeshift buildings of a sawmill. But here the owners were friendly, having made the acquaintance of other railway walkers who had passed this way, and readily agreed to my crossing their land. The sides of the cutting, which led the short distance to Dunton Bassett Tunnel, were honeycombed with rabbit burrows, whose residents seemed unconcerned by my presence and hopped about with a touching, if misplaced, trust in humankind. After making the acquaintance of a pair of fine chestnut mares and their foals, I passed through the ninety-nine-yard-long tunnel. Very similar to the one at East Leake, the bore was in excellent condition and used for storing a surprising array of junk that ranged from a two-man crosscut saw to an aged petrol pump.

Five miles remained of the walk to Lutterworth and they passed uneventfully. The motorway, never more than a few yards distant, was not particularly obtrusive, hidden by trees and banks of earth that deflected most of the noise skyward. There were more fences and warnings to trespassers but I ignored them, taking the view that, if I did no damage, no one would have cause for complaint. On one occasion it was necessary to leave the track, where mud had been dumped on it, resulting in a crop of chest-high thistles. More 'Keep Out' signs, with their implied threat, detracted from the pleasure of this stretch; and the realisation that a lifetime spent working for the country would never earn one the freedom to walk its soil unhindered was a bitter one.

The approach to Lutterworth, along a grubby corridor of track hemmed in by the M1 and the back of an industrial estate, was unimpressive. But here was one of the few railway buildings to be seen for miles – a platelayers' hut, of brick and concrete. And I felt privileged to see the back of a biscuit factory that proclaimed itself to be 'The Home of Wagon Wheels', bringing back memories of one of the many sweet and sickly indulgences of a distant childhood. Eventually, industry colonised the trackbed and I found myself climbing over mounds of rusting iron castings at the back of a foundry. A dark satanic place, with a yard ankle-deep in moulding sand, it looked derelict. But through the open doorway men could be seen working in the gloomy interior. Working conditions in foundries – dirty, dangerous, noisy and hot – are far from the air-conditioned offices in which modern mythology tells us England earns its living. Yet a sign at the main entrance read 'WELCOME', in English and Arabic – so perhaps this dirty corner of this pleasant town did still rank as one of the workshops of the world.

The small town of Lutterworth has links with two men whose work, in very different ways and separated by almost six centuries, affected the lives of millions. It was here that John Wycliffe made the first translation of the Bible into English. And it was here, as well as nearby Rugby, that Sir Frank Whittle carried out much of his work on the development of the jet engine during the Second World War.

Whittle's work in the town is now commemorated by a public house bearing his name, standing opposite the site of the factory where some of the early tests took place. For a modern pub its appearance was surprisingly pleasant with a well-kept lawn, picnic tables, rockery and a beautiful mature fuchsia, all open to the road and undamaged by vandals. As I stood in the lounge, sipping a glass of disappointingly fizzy beer, the pub was quiet and I learned a little of the birth-pangs of the jet engine. A model of Britain's first jet aircraft, the Gloster E28, dangled on a thread from the ceiling, a plaque recalled the day in 1969 when one of the co-directors of Whittle's firm, Powerjets Ltd, gave the pub its official opening, and a framed magazine article told the story of his invention. It was a fascinating story from the first patent, in 1930, through the first near-disastrous test at Rugby in 1937, to the first flight in 1941.

Two local men, the only other customers, leaned against the bar and told the landlord their opinion of those responsible for closing the town's railway station. I eavesdropped for a few minutes, thinking how many times I had heard similar conversations and how, as government policies continued to make the railway's future even more precarious, it seemed the people wanted their railways even more.

Lutterworth was a town of contrasts, from its ancient church, set among fine trees and approached along a street flanked by timber-framed houses, to the busy main street, marred by the constant din of heavy traffic. Even when used as a car park, the Market Place was pleasant, although architectural styles ranged from thatched cottages on one side to a brash supermarket on the other. The side streets contained surprises too, with a haphazard mix of ancient and modern, but the overall impression was of a pleasant little place, sometimes sleepy, sometimes bustling as its people went about their business.

As is now common, the church was locked, but it was pleasant to sit in the shade of a yew to absorb the atmosphere and think of the town's history. John Wycliffe came here as rector in 1374 and stayed until his death ten years later, publishing his translation of the Bible in 1382. His doctrine of demystification would have been as welcome to the Pope as the free and universal distribution of antibiotics would have been to a medieval pox-doctor, and it was, perhaps, fortunate that Wycliffe's great work appeared when his life was almost at its end. Nevertheless, the strength of his following and the threat it posed led the Vatican to decree that his remains be removed from consecrated ground, an act said to have been carried out during a raid on his grave organised by the Bishop of Lincoln.

St Mary's Church is largely 13th century, with later medieval additions, although the greatest change to its appearance came with the building of the present tower, following the destruction of the old, taller spire by a gale in 1703. The interior is said to be very fine, with beautiful stained glass and two frescoes, one featuring John of Gaunt – Wycliffe's patron. Until recent years, various items in the church, including the pulpit, were claimed to have been used by Wycliffe, but all are now thought to be of insufficient age for that to be true. More information about the town and its church would have been welcome, but it was Saturday and the Tourist Information Office was closed.

Judging by the coaching inns that lined one side, the main street must always have been busy, but it was never intended to accommodate the thundering and rattling procession of heavy lorries that marred my visit. A tea room above a dress shop offered refuge and a chance to observe local life, although it seemed much the same as teashop life anywhere. At first sight it was a place of plump matrons, feasting on cake and saccharin-laced tea, but there was a sprinkling of younger folk, including a strikingly beautiful teenage girl with long blond hair. Wearing a tabard-style blouse with admirable nonchalance, the side-openings revealing all but the nipple of her breast, she engaged in hushed and urgent conversation with a youth of similar years. They postured, the need to save face overruling true feelings. Her attentiveness embarrassed him, the subtle pouting lips and repeated touching of his thigh, observed by me from my corner and his friends from across the room. His manner was as clumsy as hers was sophisticated, yet her hands, which gestured so eloquently and brushed him so lightly, were disfigured by cruelly bitten nails.

When the moment came she rose and left, gliding past the seated matrons with carefully studied grace. For a moment they neither spoke, chewed nor drank, but stared in envy, jealous and silent. The boy regained his composure and, as his friends crowded round, dismissed from his features that fleeting sadness to assert that she was a slut, who he had rightly sent on her way.

16
RAMBLING INTO RUGBY

S tation Road, leading off the Market Place, was soon crossed by a steel-plate bridge with tell-tale lattice fencing. Lutterworth's station house was occupied and well cared for, but the remainder of the station site was filled with houses indistinguishable from those at Bulwell Common and Whetstone. On top of the embankment a long mound of overgrown rubble marked the southern end of the platform. The trackbed, still almost cheek-by-jowl with the motorway, headed relentlessly on its straight, southerly course towards the metropolis. A little further on an embankment crossed the valley of the Swift and gave a fine view of the town with roofs stepping up the sunny hillside to the four-pinnacled church tower.

After dodging the traffic on a motorway approach road, which cut through the embankment, I continued for about a mile along a pleasant tree-lined section of the route, passing yet another golf-course. Since leaving Leicester the track seemed to have been bordered on one side by golf links and on the other by the M1, which had probably attracted the golfing fraternity to settle in the area in ever-increasing numbers, taking over farmland in the process. Abruptly, in a shallow cutting, the track ended at the edge of a cornfield. So I took to a nearby lane that led into a motorway maintenance depot, where I skirted mountains of salt and sand before crashing through otherwise quiet woodland on an overgrown footpath. Here the railway was being used as a linear muck-heap and the smooth surface of a lane, running parallel near the village of Cotesbach, brought welcome relief. This really was part of England's green and pleasant land. In a field of ripe, golden corn a combine harvester worked in a cloud of dust, framed by the gnarled trunks and dark green leaves of old oak trees. All around were views of a type usually seen in the glossy pages of brochures produced by the English Tourist Board. Waving corn, fields of sheep, meandering lanes, ancient trees, old red-brick cottages and traditional fields with hedges combined to form an almost timeless scene – apart from the harvester and distant smoke billowing from burning fields of stubble.

North of Shawell a path led up a hillside towards the railway, but wire mesh fencing barred the path into an unusually barren-looking cutting where grass and wild flowers had given way to rough, naked clay and only bramble and hawthorn survived. A slight movement among the bushes was followed by a sudden grunt, like the primeval snort of a fairy-tale ogre. Gradually the outline of a well-fattened pig took shape, then, through the briars, a whole colony became visible. An undignified end for a proud railway, but infinitely better for the pigs than another farm I was to see later.

The lane continued down into Shawell, where an old man stood in his doorway to greet me with a slow "ow do?". His cottage was one of a row with timber framing, mellow brickwork, thatched roofs and unusual semi-circular thatched porches. In the gardens were hollyhocks, sweet peas and other flowers that had long passed out of fashion, sharing the land with wholesome-looking vegetables. Except for the white haired old man, tall, sinewy and dignified in his ancient waistcoat with silver watch chain, the village was deserted. But it was to last only moments before the swish of tyres on tarmac intruded and three cars braked to a halt by the green. The new red Volvo, the new blue BMW and the new red Ford disgorged their drivers – well-built, well-heeled and searching for the cricket club. Unable to help, I left them standing in a small knot, looking intently around as if expecting the club house to materialise amongst the cottages.

Alongside a bridge, a gap in the fence led down to the railway trackbed again and I headed south, acutely aware of the pigs upwind. Inevitably, barbed wire was not far distant, protecting from intruders a vast sward of nettles that covered the track ahead. Fortunately, a little-used footpath ran parallel, eventually leading to a field below the embankment, where the canopy of an ash tree provided shade beside a brook, and solitude for reflection.

The approach to the A5 road was across a wide field, a temporary home for hundreds of sheep, which bleated imbecilically as they fled. Originally, provision had been made for a station to be built where the line crossed over the road, but even the bridge abutments had been removed in a road-widening scheme. After crossing the road and entering Warwickshire, the track was again cut, this time by the M6, forcing a detour along the A5 and a minor road. That half-mile walk along the A5 was miserable, with verges too rough to walk in comfort and too narrow for safety.

A little north-west of Newton I slithered down loose infill, recently tipped into a deep cutting beneath a tall five-arched viaduct, soon to hide it forever. But it was good to be on a clear track again and heartening to see the way clear of fences. Despite the closeness of Newton, there was solitude here; bulrushes grew by a blocked drain, the rhythmic tapping of a thrush breaking snail shells was the only sound to compete with my footfalls, and the feel of the Great Central Railway was with me again. Looking back, three elegant bridges spanned the straight and purposeful track, their arches rising successively higher into the distance and the deepening cutting. Within a mile, on its final approach to Rugby, the trackway emerged onto an embankment and an estate of modern houses appeared close by the west side. But the walk remained pleasant and, for a little longer, unabused by litter-dumpers. There were a few people: a young girl on a bicycle and a family picking wild blackberries. The crickets were noisy, butterflies profuse and, over to the east, cattle grazed in lush meadows, softening the skeletal appearance of the masts of a radio station.

After crossing high over the infant River Avon, the track ended abruptly on what had once been the northern abutment of a viaduct. Climbing round the corrugated-iron fence, covered in tasteless graffiti, opened up a view of the landscape that had faced the railway builders before they crossed this wide valley. Now the railway had disappeared, only a scar on the earth remained to mark the line of two viaducts and an embankment, although visible in the distance a little to the south of Rugby's surviving station, a girder bridge still spanned the West Coast Main Line and its mass of overhead electric wires. A few hundred yards to the west, the Oxford Canal crossed the Avon on a stone aqueduct, almost hidden among trees, before passing immediately below my vantage point, from which I could look down on a traditionally decorated narrow-boat as it cruised by with its cargo of holidaymakers. Leaving the railway, I followed a path that crossed a field before tunnelling under the canal embankment and joining a road that led through an estate of warehouses and into the town.

17
RUGBY:
AN INDUSTRIOUS TOWN

The road into Rugby passed through a narrow tunnel under the vast embankment on which the town's surviving railway station stood. The station was an impressive structure with a massive island platform and tall buildings – reminiscent of Nottingham Victoria though lacking its opulence – that sheltered beneath an overall roof of gargantuan, if inelegant, proportions. There was an air of neglect; trains frequently sped through, and others stopped and passengers alighted or embarked in reasonable numbers, but the station had been built for better days and absorbed the travellers without bustle or fuss. Somehow it seemed half-forgotten, its buildings dead, most of their doors permanently locked. High on the side walls that supported that great roof, by then devoid of glass, vegetation was growing. Through this giant Dutch barn of a place passed a tangle of overhead wires, adding further untidiness to the combination of solid Victorian architecture and 1960s bodge-ups. Unusually, despite its size and importance, the station was not graced by a proper booking hall or imposing façade and was approached instead through a dismal subway from a shabby side street. But it was four-square and substantial, in keeping with the industry that had brought wealth to the town.

This northern side of Rugby was where its people earned their keep, largely from industry originally attracted by the London & Birmingham Railway, later absorbed into the London & North Western. That track skirted the built-up areas, without troubling to leave the valley, and industry took root alongside while working-class housing grew up between the new factories and old market town. And there, apart from a few recently built estates, is where local industry had tended to remain.

When the railway arrived in 1838, Rugby possessed a fledgling cement industry and two small factories, one making hats, the other chairs. But that was soon to change as the web of steel rails spread across the nation and the town came to occupy an important position in the network. Trains brought coal from Leicestershire and gypsum from the mines near Nottingham, to be used with local clay and blue limestone by the Portland cement industry. And trains were readily available to carry the finished product wherever it was needed to satisfy the voracious needs of the 19th-century construction boom.

The railway itself generated employment and industrial skills; locomotive repair shops, wagon works and engine sheds all depended on the new breed of industrial worker, and by 1900 one-fifth of the town's workforce was employed by the railway. Soon the presence of large numbers of skilled workers in such a favourable location was to prove an attraction to other industries.

In 1897 Willans & Robinson moved here to make their famous three-cylinder steam engines, which were to find their way into every sizeable power-station in Britain and the engine rooms of the warships of countries as diverse as Portugal and Japan. But Willans & Robinson contributed to industry something far more important than an efficient steam engine, which in any case was to be superseded all too soon by the newly developed turbine. Their gift was the introduction to the engineering industry of the tolerance system of manufacture. Under this system the firm produced all its components within predetermined, permissible, margins of error, making it possible for any spare part to be purchased off the shelf, and laying one of the foundation stones of mass-production.

Five years later, in 1902, the British Thomson Houston Company began production of heavy electrical goods in a new factory that faced Willans & Robinson across the tracks of the London & North Western Railway. British Thomson Houston, which owed its origins to the American inventors Elih Thompson and Edwin Houston, established itself in Rugby at a time of massive expansion of the electrical industry. Electric tramways were becoming common, electric railways had made their debut, electric lighting was taking over from gas, factories were beginning to exploit this new source of power and, to meet the need, generating stations were being built in all major towns. So British Thomson Houston prospered, its original 25-acre site growing to 165 five acres and, in its prime, employing a workforce of ten thousand.

But perhaps the most significant work undertaken at Rugby was the development of the jet engine, and it was the skill and expertise of the local workforce that attracted its inventor to the town. Sir Frank Whittle fought two important battles here; one was an inspired campaign to push back the frontiers of technology, the other was a long-running and debilitating struggle against vested interest and bureaucracy.

Whittle was born in 1907 to working-class parents in nearby Coventry and, as a boy, helped his father, who had once worked as a mechanic in the Lancashire cotton mills, with his small and struggling engineering business in Leamington Spa. He was a bright child, stimulated by this background of practicality, and, at the age of eleven, won a scholarship to Leamington College. In 1922 he applied for an RAF apprenticeship, but was rejected as being too small. However, after forcing himself through a programme of physical training to increase his height, he was accepted the following year. It was as a cadet, in 1928, that Whittle conceived the idea of using a gas turbine to drive an aeroplane propeller and, the following year, went on to evolve a concept that would dispense with the propeller and used the turbine to produce a jet-thrust sufficiently powerful to push an aircraft through the atmosphere.

The Air Ministry rejected Whittle's proposal as impractical, citing the lack of suitable materials to withstand the high temperatures encountered in a turbine while being light enough for aircraft use. Undaunted, he patented his idea in 1930 but allowed the patent to lapse five years later, allegedly due to lack of the £5 re-registration fee. Through the early 'thirties he searched for an industrial backer, invariably being rejected due to the problem of materials or development costs. But success eventually came into sight in 1936 when, having set up Powerjets Ltd with the help of a fellow former cadet, he persuaded British Thomson Houston to become a shareholder in the company and to co-operate on development work. BTH, which had recently built an extra-high-pressure turbine that had withstood temperatures of 1,000 degrees Fahrenheit, allowed Whittle to conduct his experiments at its Rugby works and the world's first jet engine was constructed there in 1937.

The experience gained during those early tests in the factory yard provided convincing evidence that, if nothing else, a safer site was necessary, and Powerjets rented a disused foundry from BTH. It stood alongside the Great Central Railway line at Lutterworth and, years later, Whittle was to reminisce how locomotives seemed to habitually stop and blow-off an ear-splitting jet of steam directly outside his office window, which must have been very close to the spot occupied by the manufacturer of chocolate Wagon Wheels I had noticed on my journey through that town.

As the pace of development increased the Government began to take an interest, giving financial help in 1938; the following year, as war loomed with Hitler's Germany, it underwrote the project. With the programme becoming increasingly urgent, the Gloster Aircraft Company was given the job of producing suitable test aircraft, and in 1941 the E28 made its historic seventeen-minute flight with one of Whittle's engines. It may not have been the world's first-ever jet-powered flight – the Germans had achieved that a few months previously – but it was the first to be rated a success. Within three months BTH had completed a second engine, to be exported to America for copying.

Development of jet-powered flight might have been a British success story, but the tale of its gestation was an unhappy one. Following the success of Whittle's struggle to gain backing for his idea, he was soon to suffer intense disillusionment with the companies with which he worked, and many hours were lost wrangling over problems that should never have arisen in a country threatened by war and destruction. Not only was British Thompson Houston uncooperative when it came to implementing some of his solutions to mechanical problems, but it also had designs on some of Powerjets patents – despite having already benefited from Whittle's inventiveness through its shareholding in that company. Relations were to reach such a low that the Government encouraged Powerjets to co-operate with other manufacturers, including the Rover Car Company, which built the first engine supplied to Rolls-Royce and was flown from Hucknall in that peculiar adaptation of a Wellington bomber, mentioned in Chapter 2.

By 1943 Whittle was so concerned by the behaviour of the private firms that he asked for Powerjets, which he envisaged as the future manufacturer of his engines, to be nationalised. Stating that the Government had provided 99% of the development funds and that all of the leading figures in jet-engine development had been in Government employ, he argued for public ownership on the grounds that 'a few private firms should not be allowed to grasp the benefits for their shareholders which should properly be the property of the state'.

His Majesty's Government did buy out Powerjets the following year, but on the worst terms Whittle could have feared, and a promise was given to the private manufacturers that they would not face competition from the state-owned company. Instead, the firm, which had struggled to develop the new engine, was to become, at the very dawn of the new era of aviation that it had created, a mere research organisation to service the needs of those who had contributed less.

While Frank Whittle had been busy with his pioneering work, earning himself a deservedly important place in history, Rugby's industries continued to prosper, although a considerable amount of regrouping took place. In 1919 Willans & Robinson became part of the newly constituted English Electric Company, forming a group capable of manufacturing all the machinery necessary to equip a complete power station; in 1928 British Thomson Houston joined Associated Electrical Industries. Eventually, in 1968, these conglomerates combined under the name of the General Electric Company and the factories, which had for so long faced each other across the railway tracks, came under the same ownership.

The merger led to rationalisation and redundancy on a scale then unfamiliar in Britain, but the Rugby plants survived. Even in the 1980s, after the loss of half the town's engineering jobs in the decade to 1972, one-third of local workers continued to be engaged in electrical engineering. Fifty per cent of all male employment remained with four manufacturing firms, while only five per cent earned their living in service industries. The company continued to supply heavy electrical products around the world, from turbine generators for the Siberian gas pipeline to power station equipment for South Africa. And that fledgling Portland cement industry was to become a major manufacturer with interests as far afield as Australia and the USA.

Despite its proud past, the irony is that Rugby is not best known as a centre of industry and innovation, or even as the town where the jet engine was born, but as the place where a Victorian schoolboy picked up a football and ran with it. Instead of receiving the good hiding that would probably have befallen a working-class lad, he entered history as the inventor of Rugby football, and can be credited with the high incidence of broken noses to be found where the game is prevalent.

The Market Place was a good spot from which to begin exploring the town. Occupying the middle ground between the gentility of the public school to the south, and industry to the north, it was an interesting place where evidence of the developer's onslaught and attempts to resist it stood side by side. Here the architecture and commercial vitality contrasted strongly with the devastation and squalor on the route from the station, where Victorian pubs stood isolated on wasteland and brash façades of motor-tyre shops clashed with the remaining red-brick terraces. The town gave the appearance of having tried hard, if a little late, to preserve its character. Modern bus shelters were embellished with Victorian frills, and pedestrianised streets planted with young trees, ornate lamp standards and seats. But many of the fine buildings were interspersed with gaudy shop-fronts and concrete monstrosities. The Bull, with its barley-twist pilasters, and the fine old Three Horseshoes Inn, stood in a scene dominated by concrete and brick hulks bequeathed to the local heritage by F. W. Woolworth and The Boots Company.

In common with most other towns and cities in the land, there was an undercover shopping centre. Mercifully, the townsfolk had been spared some of the vulgarity visited upon other communities by Mammon's architectural minions, and the Rugby Centre was cleverly concealed from the Market Place behind a handsome façade that had once fronted The Bear & Ragged Staff Inn. Opened in 1980, the centre's frontage was a response to the public outrage caused a decade earlier when the full extent of the damage these centres were causing to our urban environment became so tragically apparent. But their promoters made only a nominal concession. The Bear & Ragged Staff merely provided the beast with an acceptable mask, behind which the centre's interior displayed no more elegance than an industrial shed, while the view from the rear was as bad an example of mid-Atlantic design as may be seen anywhere. How much better it would have been if the façade had opened onto a hinterland of human-scale streets and arcades, where the town's shoppers could have strolled in fresh air.

Rugby Borough Council had published a town trail leaflet, prepared in association with the local Civic Society. Although muted in its criticism of the town planning policies of the previous generation of officials, the leaflet was an invaluable guide to visitors wishing to appreciate the varied styles and fine buildings to be seen within a short walk of the town centre. It led me to such places as The Shambles, diminutive buildings thought to have descended from lock-up booths that had once stood in the ancient market place, and on down the pedestrianised Sheep Street, which became increasingly well preserved in the vicinity of that well-heeled school.

Lawrence Sheriff Street, with the school's fine architecture on one side and carefully maintained shops on the other, had a rare and timeless atmosphere, while round the corner in Barby Road, expansive playing fields gave that feel of affluent tranquillity reminiscent of parts of Oxford and Cambridge. Near here, just inside the school gates, a plaque commemorated William Webb Ellis, the boy who got away with picking up the football, and further on a statue of Thomas Hughes MP, who used his experience as a Rugby pupil as the basis for *Tom Brown's Schooldays*. The trail continued through tree-lined streets of well-to-do houses and passed by the birthplace of Rupert Brooke, best known for romanticising the First World War with fine poetry, which probably resulted in a few more young men rotting beneath the corner of a foreign field than otherwise might have been the case.

Quiet footpaths and a pleasant park led to St Andrew's Church, an unusual concoction incorporating a 19th-century spire at one end and a Saxon tower at the other – and each with its own set of bells! Returning to the bustling streets, the trail continued by a roundabout route back to the Market Place, having provided a valuable insight into this industrious town.

18
THE LINE THROUGH RUGBY

In comparison with the arrival of the London & Birmingham Railway, the Great Central Railway's passing of Rugby, on its eastern edge, had little effect on the town's development and, at the point where I rejoined the track, it could never have looked anything other than a poor relation. Some half-mile distant to the north, beyond the multiple tracks of the West Coast Main Line, was the abutment where I had stood to look down on a passing canal boat. The area between was a wasteland where once had been a succession of lineside features, any one of which could have been the subject of a story to entertain passengers on the Great Central for the remainder of their journey to Marylebone.

From the north, the line first bridged the Oxford Canal on a viaduct of fish-bellied girders, the building of which was quite remarkable. Iron caissons had to be sunk through the waterproof clay lining of the canal, itself on an embankment, to provide a firm foundation, and under the terms of an agreement with the canal company this had to be done without spilling water or obstructing navigation. The problem was solved by constructing a steel trough, eighty feet long and eight feet wide, with removable ends. The trough was floated into position on the canal and sunk hard up against one bank. Temporary dams were then built from the outer corners of the trough to the opposite bank of the waterway, permitting the isolated half-width of canal to be drained and the caissons sunk into the embankment, while boats were able to pass through the steel trough. When the caissons were in position the waterproof clay puddle was repaired, the dams removed and the trough refloated, before being moved to the opposite bank for the process to be repeated.

Leaving the steel viaduct, Great Central trains then travelled along a very substantial embankment before another viaduct, this time fourteen arches of blue brick and stonework, carried the line over the London & North Western Railway's sidings and branch line to Peterborough. In the years following the Second World War British Railways' Locomotive Testing Station stood alongside this viaduct. Heralded as the most advanced in the world at the time of its completion, its opening marked the culmination of twenty-one years of work on the part of its advocates. Test plants of this type were a Russian invention of the 1870s and for many years one built by the Great Western Railway, at Swindon in 1903, was the only example in Britain. However, with the increase in size and power of locomotives, the Swindon plant became inadequate and was eventually relegated to running in new and overhauled engines.

The story of the Rugby installation began in 1927 when Sir Nigel Gresley, of the LNER, one of the giants of locomotive engineering, spoke of the need for a testing plant to be built as a joint project shared by all of the British railway companies. Previously, locomotives, other than those belonging to the Great Western Railway, had been tested on the track, with results seriously affected by gradients, curves, headwinds, the need to slow for signals and a host of other variable factors. Clearly, the system invented by the Russians so many years before, where the locomotive remained stationary while its wheels revolved on rollers, possessed an inherent superiority, and Gresley's proposal was taken up by the four major companies. Unfortunately, economic depression led to the Southern Railway and the GWR withdrawing their support, and it was not until 1936 that the LMS and the LNER decided to continue the project alone.

Rugby was chosen as a site convenient to both companies and a start was made on construction, only to be halted for four years by the Second World War. Eventually the testing station opened under British Railways ownership towards the close of 1948, and served the industry well until alternative methods of assessing the performance of the new generation of diesel and electric locomotives brought its work to an end in 1959.

Under test, an engine would be mounted with each wheel on a pair of rollers, up to five pairs being driven by the locomotive's driving wheels. At the rear, the drawbar of the engine was attached to the piston of a hydraulic cylinder, in turn anchored to a framework of girders. This framework, weighing sixty tons, was set in the foundation of the testing equipment – a massive concrete block that measured one hundred and three feet in length, varied from six to seventeen feet in depth and weighed three hundred tons. Despite the massiveness of this structure, it still had to be physically separated from the walls of the building and their foundations to avoid damage by vibration. The building that housed this equipment was designed by the LMS and was one hundred and seventy feet long, sixty-five feet wide and fifty-five feet in height.

As the locomotive's wheels revolved, the resistance of the rollers could be controlled by a hydraulic brake, so measuring the horsepower and torque at each set of driving wheels, while the pull on the hydraulic cylinder at the rear measured the drawbar horsepower. The equipment was capable of handling locomotives running at simulated speeds of up to 130mph and generating 4,500 horsepower. Because the locomotive was stationary, coal and water consumption could be measured accurately for a given power output, while the behaviour and temperature of steam, flue and smokebox gasses was monitored, together with a host of other data essential to the understanding of steam engine performance.

Rugby Testing Station served British Railways admirably for eleven years and a wide variety of locomotives was studied there including, in 1957, an English-Electric experimental gas-turbine-powered design. But the plant had been primarily designed for steam engines and, sadly, steam traction was dying. Results of the test programme now reside in the library of the National Railway Museum, but until perhaps a change in the availability of oil forces a change in policy, they are of little use outside the hypothetical debates of steam enthusiasts.

Leaving the testing station behind, the Great Central line crossed onto the girder bridge spanning the West Coast Main Line, which once offered a view of another wonder of the railway world, the 'Rugby Bedstead'. So-named by the Great Central's signal engineer, for reasons obvious to all who saw it, this was commonly, though mistakenly, thought to be the largest signal gantry in Britain and stood a few yards to the east of the bridge. Built for the London & North Western by the Great Central, which was held responsible for the cost of signalling alterations necessitated by the building of the new line, it carried no fewer than forty-four signal arms. Arranged in two tiers, the lower semaphores repeated the positions of those above. This arrangement ensured that the upper signals, positioned seventy-four feet above track level, could be seen at a distance, even from the curved cutting by which northbound trains approached, while at close quarters the lower ones were more easily observed.

Most of this was a memory when I passed by; the viaduct over the canal had disappeared and a great brown scar of bare subsoil marked the position of the embankment. The massive empty hulk of the testing station had survived a little longer, its title and the 1950s logo of British Railways fixed high on the wall; 1930s utilitarian in style and built of that yellowish brick so popular in those days, it stood disused until

1984, its broken windows looking forlornly over wasteland where sidings and a locomotive depot had once stood. The brick viaduct had gone too, together with the branch line it had once crossed, while the 'Bedstead' had been replaced by colour light signals as long ago as 1939. All that remained of the Great Central's presence here was the heavy lattice-girder bridge that spanned the main line, its battleship grey paint darkened by age, rust and neglect – and even that has been removed since.

19
ON TO DAVENTRY

Turning from the view of the West Coast Main Line, I followed the Great Central track into a long cutting. At this point the course of the line was owned by Rugby District Council and seemed little changed since the lifting of the rails. Passing through a thickly populated area, it provided some welcome open space, and nature added its own scheme of colours. In the mortar courses of a road bridge abutment wallflowers had taken root and flourished high above ground level. A little further on yellow-flowered ragwort grew in broad swathes on either side of the trackbed, while a vast array of willow herb gave a misty purple hue to the cutting sides, their colours contrasting with a beauty that seemed too orderly to have resulted from the fickle chance of nature.

The site of Rugby Central Station was a few minutes walk from the West Coast Main Line and a flight of recently dug steps led up to Hillmorton Road, where the bridge provided an excellent vantage point. To the west was a good area of the town, where no out-of-character development had marred the appearance of the well-to-do residences. Perhaps the most interesting was a house with bow windows and an ornately curved iron gallery surrounding a tower that emerged from the centre of the roof. But, as is so often the case, the railway had formed a borderline and untidy industry had taken root on the other side of the track. Below the bridge the single island platform sprouted vegetation while the trackbed on one side was marshy, with reeds and bulrushes growing to a height of five or six feet. On the sides of the shallow cutting rhododendrons and other shrubs from the station garden formed a colourful wilderness and campion flowered in huge clumps. A youth threw a stick for his Jack Russell terrier, an agile creature despite an absent rear leg, which demonstrated its adaptability by invariably cocking its stump rather than its remaining back leg whenever the need arose. Down at the south end of the platform, an iron ring, bolted to the ground, marked

the position of a water column for replenishing the tenders of southbound trains.

The goods yard was host to a timber company, which had been there when the railway was operating, and the old goods shed still stood, though surrounded by newer buildings. High on the wall, the legend 'Great Central Railway Goods Warehouse', painted in white on a black ground, survived. It was a plain though not unattractive red-brick building with the top of its square chimney stack corbelled out to provide some modest ornamentation, although the loading bay had been bricked up and the roof slates replaced by asbestos sheets.

A little further on, the cattle and goods platforms could be seen among the tangle of undergrowth and, walking on, the sound of crickets became more noticeable than the distant whine of sawmill machinery. It was a pleasant place, with silver birch trees rising from the trackbed and tall hawthorns foresting the sides of the rapidly deepening cutting. A few local people walked their dogs: young children, with mothers who should have known better, attempted to catch butterflies with fishing nets, while more adventurous youngsters practised a high-level balancing act on the parapet of an overbridge that still bore the marks of locomotive smoke. Someone's raspberry canes had gone wild, producing an almost impenetrable tangle around trees that bore bitter-tasting apples. A young rabbit hopped from beneath the bushes to crouch motionless in the long grass, confident in his ability to flee if I should move closer – and I hoped he would never meet a man with a gun.

The cutting became deeper and more enclosed. A fine three-arched bridge carried a road high overhead and the rapidly growing woodland crowded in – sycamore, oak, hawthorn, apple and birch. It seemed a fine facility, which the town ought to keep for its people. There were no crowds, but someone was usually in sight and those who came here appeared to respect their environment. People walked alone, or with their dogs, sat on the grass or played with their children and generally behaved well.

Soon the path emerged onto an embankment with views across fields of ripe corn dotted about with trees, although to the east the scene was dominated by the masts of a radio station. A bridge over the lane to Barby had been removed and beyond was an almost impenetrable barrier of barbed-wire. The owner was probably to be found at a nearby farm, which emitted more machinery noise than an urban factory owner would dare to contemplate, but there was no need to plead for his permission to pass because a lane ran parallel. From a bridge over the M45, deserted and closed as repair gangs laboured in the shimmering heat, there was a good view back towards Rugby. In the distance a massive concrete water tower overlooked the area, like some contraption from an alien planet, while over to the west stood the rather elegant pile, complete with tower and dome, of a private school at Dunchurch. Special forms of education seemed to thrive around Rugby – and the map also indicated the near presence of one of Her Majesty's Borstal Institutions.

Soon the lane bridged the Oxford Canal and the towpath offered a route back towards the railway. It was easy walking near the road, where fishermen had kept down the undergrowth and some of their number had left behind evidence of their occupation – lunch wrappers and odd pages of a pornographic magazine. But soon, though pleasanter and litter-free, the way became difficult. On one side the towpath subsided into the water, on the other a rough hawthorn hedge pushed its thorn-laden branches across the way. In some places the bank had been reinforced with steel piles and mud from the canal dumped onto the

path to dry rutted and uneven, providing the ideal conditions for a notably pernicious species of thistle to thrive. I went blundering through this miniature nature reserve, disturbing copulating butterflies and hard-working bees, giving what I hoped was a cheery-sounding greeting to the relaxed folk who cruised by in their boats.

Near a hump-backed bridge I parted company with the canal and set off across fields to rejoin the railway. Centrally positioned in this green and pleasant scene was Her Majesty's Prison Onley. Constructed in the style of an estate of 1960s council flats surrounded by a concentration-camp-type fence, it presented a hideous and incongruous sight. Alongside the prison the trackbed had been obliterated but soon reappeared and seemed largely untouched in its rural setting. A permanent way men's concrete hut, standing half wrecked in the midst of a herd of cattle, was only one of a number of railway relics along this section. For a couple of miles the canal ran parallel, though usually invisible from the railway, until it swung away eastwards to join the Grand Union at Braunston. During the construction of the railway, materials were delivered by canal boat and transhipped at this point.

In this area the railway took a solitary course with no human presence evident for several miles. A lightly wooded cutting gave way to a much shallower one, where grass on the trackbed had been scorched brown by the sun, and I strolled with only crickets and butterflies for company. With the ballast removed, concrete channels at the side of the trackway protruded above ground level, resembling kerbstones as they stretched away into the distance towards a forlorn-looking signal gantry that had somehow survived the attentions of salvage men and vandals – even after almost twenty years of disuse. Intermittently the peace was shattered by jet aircraft screeching low over the fields while, high above, a sailplane soared in silent elegance against the distant blue sky.

From an embankment, where a bridge had been removed, a steep and slippery slope led down to a farm track and onto the main Coventry to Daventry road by the village of Willoughby. The map indicated a public house on the main street, which led through what seemed a hotchpotch of a village with styles ranging from old ironstone cottages to modern pinch-penny semis and 1930s pebbledash. But sure enough, round a bend in the road, was the sign of The Rose. My step quickened across the asphalted frontage, aware of the pool of sweat in the hollow of my back and moistening my parched mouth in anticipation of a thirst-quenching drink, but it was not to be. At exactly two o'clock the door was locked as tightly as if it had been screwed to its frame! After peering through a window at a view of a towel-draped beer pump, I retreated to a bench by the road and contemplated Willoughby darkly. The image of the traditional English public house was there all right, complete with thatched roof and painted sign, but mine welcoming host was not. A tall woman, wearing culottes that resembled an outsize and flowing adaptation of Second World War British Army shorts, replied with some aloofness that she was not aware of whether or not

The Rose normally opened at lunchtime, and for good measure added that the village shop was closed too. I sat on that bench, so thoughtfully provided for travellers barred from the inn, picking grass seeds from my socks and chewing a dried-up sandwich. A police panda car drove by, then returned and slowed to a crawl as I returned the driver's curious, unfriendly, stare. He knew I did not belong there, and I could well imagine the sort who did.

On rising to leave, I noticed the pub garden was now being tended by a middle-aged man in bathing trunks. Publicans in my part of the world tended to be slicker-looking than this man and I wrongly assumed him to be the gardener. But he happily owned up to being the landlord, explaining that the premature closure of the pub was due to the lack of lunchtime trade, Willoughby being a dormitory village with its menfolk working in the town. Soon I was seated in a corner of the garden, enjoying a drink and taking a kinder view of the village from the shade of an ancient tree. The Rose was built of ironstone and thatch, with a red-brick and slate extension stuck onto one side. The lawn was well kept, bordered with marigolds, moon daisies and a profusion of other flowers, while a fat tortoiseshell cat surveyed her territory from between the front wheels of a car as she sought out the engine-warmth even on that hot day. Across the lane was the old school, now a dwelling, bearing a plaque dated 1816 that pronounced it to have been built by the trustees of a local charity. The village seemed different now, and not only did I owe a debt to that unlikely looking figure in bathing trunks but, in my opinion, so did the people of this otherwise unwelcoming place.

Back on the main road I braved The Sleepy Sausage Cafeteria to order an egg and tomato roll, the reason for the lengthy preparation time only becoming apparent when the fried and grease-laden concoction was served. Naively, I had expected a sandwich of mashed hard-boiled egg with slices of fresh tomato, but I was a stranger to transport cafés and their practices. This world of solitary folk, smoking cigarettes and reading tabloid newspapers over greasy plates on Formica tables, accompanied by the incessant noise of a radio somewhere in the kitchen, was alien to me. So was the special offer of 'cab-in with facilities' at £1.75 – sleep in the lorry you've driven all day, wake up to take a wash in the back of a transport café and face another day behind the wheel on yet another breakfast rich in artery-clogging, gut-griping fat.

A few yards away the road had once passed under the railway's high embankment, but the bridge was long gone and bullocks grazed on the station site. Across the fields to the east was Braunston, prominent on a ridge, with its tall church spire and windmill tower reaching skyward.

Braunston was really two communities, the original village and a later canal-side settlement. Situated at the junction of the Grand Union and Oxford Canals, it had lived by water traffic for a couple of centuries and continued to do so. By the time commercial carrying had ceased in the 1960s, pleasure boating had already become sufficiently well established to offer the village a new purpose, its position at such an important junction, with a picturesque flight of locks and a two-thousand-yard tunnel close at hand, being ideal for the leisure trade. Old reservoirs became new marinas, shops and restaurants appeared, and a couple of the old pubs were adapted to serve the new breed of visitor. But it remained an interesting place where traditional-style narrow-boats were still built, although of fabricated steel instead of timber.

Strolling along the high, wide embankment of the railway, now divided by a fence running longitudinally, I was preceded by a vast herd of sheep whose massed bleating was suddenly drowned by the screech of warplanes. First appearing in pairs over Braunston, they dropped down from the ridge to skim low over the fields, and even lower over the embankment, to make practice bombing runs at a village a couple of miles westward before veering away to stand on their tails and blast themselves high into the clear sky.

About a mile south of Willoughby, the embankment ended where the map showed that a viaduct had once stood. Thirteen arches that had spanned a 186-yard-gap across a valley had disappeared completely, leaving only a few blue bricks laying as stepping stones on the bed of a stream. This part of the walk was very pleasant: good views of rolling country with plenty of trees, hedgerows and small fields of grazing cattle. For some reason the occupation bridges had been different for much of the way from Rugby, the building contractor having a preference for the steel-plate type, but ahead on the outskirts of Wolfhamcote, a traditional and elegant Great Central-style arch came into view.

Here the Grand Union Canal passed beneath the railway in a shallow cutting, but the bridge had been removed, forcing a short diversion along the towpath to where a cart track crossed the cut. In an idyllic setting under the shade of gnarled old trees a boy fished from a narrow-boat with two men, who I assumed to be his father and grandfather. The *Honeypot* was an unusual craft, a handsome cross between a working boat and an Edwardian pleasure cruiser, with an awning extending forward from her rear cabin over an open section to her prow. The oldest of her occupants, big, white-haired, stubbly bearded and stripped to the waist with that confidence that comes to a man when he no longer cares what others think of his body, welcomed me with a leisurely greeting. For a few minutes we talked of fishing, the canal, the railway and, finally, his boat, which owed her unusual shape to having spent her early years as an engineer's inspection craft. We wished one another well as I left them to their fishing, the older men looking content, the boy excited and enthused by beginner's luck and enjoying success for its own sake.

After crossing the trackbed of the Daventry to Leamington branch of the London & North Western Railway, the path entered a long cutting near the village of Flecknoe. This would have been pleasant, too, and it probably was for the reeds and marsh grasses that flourished so successfully in the soggy wetness of the undrained trackbed. Concrete signal-wire channels formed a pathway of sorts, but so uneven and perilous that progress was painfully slow. And, as the sun beat down mercilessly, the still air hummed to the tune of a multitude of carnivorous insects that forsook even the beasts of neighbouring fields to feast on me. Suddenly the track was again on an embankment, which would have provided a pleasant walk, with teasels growing tall and straight for hundreds of yards on either side, but the heat of the day had taken its toll and exhaustion was setting in. This was pretty countryside, but on that day it would have looked much prettier from the window of a speeding train.

From a grassy resting place, above the Daventry to Leamington Spa road, Shuckburgh Park and Beacon Hill were visible. In the other direction, eastward, fields of ripe corn led up to a distant ridge dominated by a vast, modern warehouse on the outskirts of Daventry, while ahead the trackbed headed towards Catesby Tunnel, but it was time to leave the track and take to the road. I was thankful to get a lift to Daventry, where an indifferent bed, followed the next morning by a mediocre breakfast, was provided by a boarding-house landlady, who welcomed me with a demand for payment even before I stepped over her threshold. But not all of the town's facilities were poor; the well-grilled steak at The Wheatsheaf more than compensated for the lacklustre welcome and persistently cold shower at the guest house.

Next morning the air was damp and the ground wet after a night of heavy rain. The moulded plastic seats of the chairs in The Wheatsheaf garden each held a pool of water, while the masts of the radio station that dominated the town from a neighbouring hill were lost in grey cloud. Daventry seemed to be a town of the present, yet undecided whether to break completely with its past, giving it all the maturity of style of an adolescent first venturing into the world of adult fashion. Perhaps the town had grown up too quickly, transformed to accommodate the overspill population of Birmingham in the 'sixties and 'seventies – when all that was new was thought to be good. But, in fairness, it had faced the problems of rapid development rather more suddenly than most, and more recently had striven to preserve some of what remained. The pedestrianised Sheaf Street, with its harmonious frontage of modest small-town architecture, and Main Street, leading into the triangular market place below the classical Georgian ironstone church, were pleasant and worthy of the protection given them. But it was a sham, like a town of film-set façades. There were no mysterious lanes or alleyways to be explored. Those that survived merely led behind the street frontage to open onto wide roads or car parks surrounded by modern shops. Behind the plate glass window of one, a deserted supermarket, a rotund shopgirl stood by her till, yawning repeatedly as she gazed onto the unlovely quadrangle of wet tarmac and dreamed of better things, trapped in the drudgery of her work and imprisoned like a fish in an aquarium.

20
CATESBY TUNNEL

A tunnel the length of the one at Catesby was no place to venture alone, with the ever-present risk of injury and the awesome possibility of lying helpless in the dark with little chance of discovery, so its exploration was omitted from the main part of the walk and I returned later with a companion. When exploring the tunnel north of Nottingham Victoria Station I had been accompanied by Stephen Best, a friend and local historian, and my father – almost eighty years of age and treading in the footsteps of is own father, who had been forced to walk through when there had been no trains available in the general strike of 1926. At Catesby, I had the company of Ian Lambert, another friend and rail enthusiast from Nottingham.

As we joined the trackbed where it crossed the Daventry-Leamington Spa road, the view was deceptive. True, there was a substantial cutting visible less than half a mile ahead, but the deep cleft that preceded it was a surprise. This had once been spanned by the nine-arch, 357-foot-long Staverton Viaduct, but now only a few scattered blue-brick copings remained as witness in the poor grey soil at the end of the embankment. After crossing the stream, which gurgled through concrete pipes at the bottom of the cleft, the following embankment offered fine views of rolling countryside, until the path entered a half-mile-long cutting. Immediately after came Catesby Viaduct, crossing the deep valley of the River Leam. High, graceful and imposing, it presented a fine sight from the east side, but a sad spectacle from the west. From the corners of its tall piers, which supported twelve fine arches, great chunks of blue facing brickwork had broken away to expose patches of underlying red brick, resembling the livid ulceration symptomatic of some awful disease. Walking across, alongside the vandalised parapet, the reason for such a rapid decline became apparent; large areas of bituminised hessian, which had provided a waterproof membrane, had been torn up by the bulldozers as they scraped away the ballast, allowing water to penetrate the structure.

A low embankment followed for half a mile or so, until giving away to a short cutting on the final approach to Catesby Tunnel, whose portal was partially concealed behind an occupation bridge. On the hillside west of the tunnel stood Catesby House, whose owners had caused more than a few problems for the engineers by refusing permission for working shafts to be sunk within the grounds. Close to the tunnel mouth the gloom was brightened by a few flowers, survivors from the abandoned garden of a linesmen's hut, now a skeletonised ruin of stark grey concrete. Casting its sombre shadow over this silent scene was the blue-brick and smoke-blackened masonry of the portal, an elliptical void flanked by curved buttresses and surmounted by a rectangular tablet bearing the completion date of 1897. Like the tunnels at Nottingham, the sheer size was impressive; rising twenty feet above rail level and with a width of twenty-seven feet, its darkness beckoned. Once inside, it became possible to discern the faint speck of greenish light marking the other end, 2,997 yards distant along the dead straight bore.

The northern part was the deepest and most difficult for the men to dig. Burrowing through limestone, while being drenched in water as the massive timber roof supports creaked and groaned around them under the strain, they must have cursed the landowner who forbade the use of working shafts. According to L. T. C. Rolt, in *The Making of a Railway*, the initial bore had been about nine feet square, sufficient to allow a small locomotive to enter with trucks to haul out the spoil; this had later been widened out to its final size. In this way they toiled through the first five hundred yards; the remainder of the tunnel, cut through clay with the benefit of working shafts, was built full size at what was then a record speed of 110 yards per month.

Within a few yards of the entrance, water covered the floor to a depth of an inch or two, but it was soon to deepen. All track ballast had been scraped out, except for a ridge that adhered to the tunnel wall like concrete and provided a useful, if precarious, path above the flood. Jets of water poured through cracks in the mortar courses of the wall, deposits of lime forming around them to create deathly white gargoyle faces, uncannily bearded with red clay that oozed through from the depths and clung to the tunnel side beneath each fountain. Water was everywhere, dripping, pouring, even gurgling below in long-neglected culverts. Looking back, a 300-yard-long lake mirrored the silver light that streamed through the tunnel mouth. Forward was darkness devoid of life – only stalactite-gargoyles and more gurgling awaited us. Conditions in here must have been abysmal for the builders.

Eventually the first air shaft came into view, a distant patch of pale amber light reflecting on the floor. Reference books gave its distance from the entrance as five hundred yards, but it seemed nearer to a thousand. Water came down like a heavy rainstorm, penetrating the walls of the vertical shaft to fall on one of the few unflooded sections of the floor. The air shaft, rising high above track level, had begun life as one of the nine working shafts and had been made fifteen feet in diameter, fifty per cent larger than its four companions, in an attempt to ventilate the long northern section of the tunnel. The engineers had attempted to solve the problem of water penetration by incorporating a ring of specially shaped brickwork to form a circular gutter around the vertical shaft a few feet above its juncture with the tunnel roof. From two opposing points on this ring drainpipes, recessed into the tunnel lining, descended to floor level. Between the tracks a culvert ran the length of the bore to carry the water down the gradient to the northern portal, along the cutting and onto the embankment before depositing it into the River Leam. Even then it was not wasted, but put to use on its way to the river by powering a ram pump that supplied water to the village of Catesby. The ruin of the pump-house still stood, alongside the embankment a few hundred yards north of the tunnel mouth, although no longer functioning and probably unnoticed by most who passed by.

The drainage system, which barely coped during the tunnel's working life, had since been overwhelmed by two decades of neglect. Careless scraping away of the ballast had caused obstructions in the culvert, brackets supporting the drainpipes had corroded through, and water gushed through the loosened mortar of the shaft wall with such pressure that it sprayed too far out to be caught in the gutters anyway.

There were no limestone sculptures in the southern section, just mounds of bright red clay below the more forceful leaks, while regularly spaced air shafts lifted the spirit as their passing indicated our progress towards the outside world. Adjacent to one ventilator, a rectangular chamber, similar to those in Nottingham's Mansfield Road Tunnel, had been formed and lined with the same blue brick as the walls of the bore. Unlike the underground room in Nottingham, this one contained no racks, cupboards or other relics – nor a bed, for this peaceful countryside would not drive a man to seek refuge underground. But it was impossible not to think of those who had spent their days here, whose daily work had brought them into this black world. They would have taken their meal breaks in this sooty room while water dripped about them, with massive freight engines belching steam and sulphurous smoke as they struggled to haul their heavy trains up the gradient within the tunnel, or express passenger trains roared by at frightening speeds merely feet away from these unsung heroes. And the advent of diesel traction would have brought little relief, only the replacement of soot and smoke by foul-stinking fumes.

Many tasks had to be performed in that murky world and platelaying gangs were based at each end, each with half of their 'length' in fresh air and the other half in the tunnel. The structure itself was maintained by men of the Civil Engineer's Department at Woodford, who worked from a wagon equipped with a gantry to give access to the roof and walls. In the biting cold of winter, when the dripping water formed icicles so long and heavy that they threatened the safety of passing trains, these men worked from the same wagon to smash a way through the ice barrier; unknown and unthought-of by passengers as they grumbled about the delay to their schedule.

Ahead lay another underground lake, knee-deep and with no ledges at the tunnel sides, which made wading the only way forward. We strange-looking creatures were glad this underworld was private, with trousers rolled up above our knees and pale, thin-looking legs terminating in bulbous hiking boots, bodies clad in waterproofs against the perpetual dripping from above, and hung about with lamps, cameras and other impedimenta peculiar to the eccentric explorers of disused holes. It was a farcical scene, icy water filling our boots, caustic comments combining with the sound of splashing water to echo along the otherwise silent tunnel.

Approaching the south portal the floor became dry, although the water in our boots remained and gradually warmed to body temperature, providing a new and squelchy walking experience. The south end of Catesby Tunnel, at 503 feet above sea level, was the highest point of the route and a watershed, drainage water from the tunnel flowing north into the Leam and, eventually, the Bristol Channel, while a few yards distant the Cherwell began its journey south to join the Thames and the North Sea.

Emerging into the open, the sun was warm as we rested on the side of the cutting to dry ourselves and survey the scene. The grass was a lush shade of green and wild flowers grew unmolested, while trees had set themselves near the tunnel mouth and grown to near maturity since the day the last train had passed this way.

21
JIM ANSCOMB:
WOODFORD'S HISTORIAN

A local bus provided transport from Daventry back to the route on the day I by-passed the tunnel, and the countryside was still damp from the heavy overnight rain when I alighted in the village of Charwelton. Of the station, only the overgrown platform remained with one of the trees, which grew from the asphalt, already taller than the overbridge. Along the goods yard drive the wet grass was long and rarely trodden, although the former Station Master's house looked well-kept and homely. But this was a situation too good to last and, a short time after my visit, the road was diverted from the bridge, across the station and along the line of that secluded drive, encouraging traffic to speed through the village unhindered by those undulations and bends that once typified the English country road. By the goods yard gate the infant River Cherwell gurgled into pipes that carried it under the main road, before flowing lazily beneath a 13th-century packhorse bridge. It was near here that the river rose, reputedly from an unlikely source in the cellar of a house, before meandering through the countryside to join the Thames at Oxford, where its muddy bottom is disturbed by the poles of punters and its waters reputedly cavorted in by naked dons at a place known as Parson's Pleasure.

The village was quiet, with most occupants of its ironstone cottages away at work elsewhere. But there was once work and industry here – a brickworks, ironstone quarries and the railway – before the village returned to slumber and most of the populace became commuters. One of the steam shunting engines survived to decorate a park in Daventry where for many years it stood as a source of fascination to children and nostalgia for the elderly.

On the bridge over the station I waited for Jim Anscomb, a retired foreman of the goods yard at Woodford, who had offered to act as my guide. The bridge was a good vantage point from which to see the spire of the village church, rising above the treetops almost a mile from the community it served, and the railway, as it headed south through the trees towards Woodford and north to Catesby Tunnel, the latter marked by its row of chimney-like ventilators rising out of the hill. With no sign of Jim, I set off walking. Again the trackway was reminiscent of a green lane, with trees rising high on either side and long grass underfoot. Eventually a distant figure, standing in the centre of the track, became discernible as a man dressed in a summer jacket and lightweight cap. When we met, Jim was collecting flowering grasses – not pulling them out by the root but, in that methodical way common with the elderly, carefully cutting their stems with a small penknife – 'for a friend who appreciates them'. Jim had chosen to wait for me on the parish boundary of Woodford-cum-Membris, observing territorial formality in a manner befitting a local historian. And, as we walked, this remarkable man, who had reached retirement age when the railway had closed two decades earlier, pointed out features of interest with the authority of one who had always taken an interest in his surroundings and remained blessed with powers of accurate recall. But for him, I would have overlooked the overgrown mound of rubble that marked the site of the pump house for Charwelton water troughs.

Water troughs, invented by John Ramsbottom, the engineer of the London & North Western Railway, were a common feature on British and American railways, until they became redundant with the demise of steam. They consisted of a water-filled metal trough laid between the rails, which allowed an engine's water tank to be replenished by a scoop lowered from the tender as the train passed over. Ramsbottom's invention was especially ingenious because, even though the fireman lowered and raised the scoop to control the amount of water collected, it could not strike the end of the trough if lowered too soon or raised too late. This was achieved simply by arranging for the rails at each end to be sufficiently high to prevent contact while for the length of the pick-up section they were a few inches lower, allowing the scoop to dip below water level.

The troughs at Charwelton were brought into use in the summer of 1903, making it possible for express trains to run non-stop between Marylebone and Sheffield in three hours and ten minutes. Built at a total cost of six thousand pounds, each trough was 874 yards long, sixteen inches wide, and heated in winter by a steam pipe to prevent freezing. All this could be deduced from reference books, but it took Jim Anscomb to locate the ruin and explain how water was pumped up the embankment from the small reservoir, known as the Hollowell Pool, that had previously supplied drinking water to the ancient village of Charwelton.

Soon the trackbed fanned out as we came to the site of Woodford 'New Yard' sidings, built in 1941 when the yard's capacity was greatly increased to meet the needs of the war effort. It was difficult to imagine now the rows of tracks, the thousands of wagons, the incessant clanking of couplings and thumping of buffers as men and machines went relentlessly about their business through day and night. Heavy coal trains arrived here from Annesley to be split into sections for London or the South West. Long rakes of empties arrived to continue their northward trek for replenishment in the nation's coalfields; Grimsby fish sped south and bananas from Avonmouth hurried north. In the distance, to the east of the yard, had stood wagon repair shops next to the locomotive shed that had exuded a sulphurous haze over the green rolling landscape. Now it was wasteland. On the left, a brick-built water tower, to the right a few half-wrecked concrete huts, ahead an immense expanse of emptiness. But the desert was gradually being reclaimed; a poor-looking crop of cabbages struggled to raise their heads from the cinder-strewn earth and, beyond, sheep grazed on mean grass.

G C R^Y

W METER

5 FT

Jim new the place intimately, the purpose of every relic: a heap of cast-iron pipes, now mostly broken, had once carried water to the loco shed, and rows of stubby brick piers had been lamp post foundations, now exposed to view by the removal of ballast. Other similar-looking structures were manhole covers over a culverted stream that passed beneath the vast embankment on which the yard had been built. We surveyed the bleak scene from the high ground where his office had been during the days when he was foreman, and images of a lost time filled my mind.

As we turned away, Jim retrieved his ancient bicycle from a hedge bottom and wheeled it, creaking and squeaking, down a cinder path to a tarmac lane and, ultimately, to his home on a nearby council estate. He was quartered in a modest first-floor flat, one of four in a pair of semi-detached houses. It was a surprising place, not for the manner of its decor or furnishings, for old men tend to have simple needs, but for the equipment he had accumulated in the pursuit of his hobbies. A good-quality camera lay on a bureau, a slide projector stood amidst paperwork on the dining table, and among other homely clutter was a cassette recorder and typewriter.

Before going to the kitchen to prepare lunch, Jim handed me his railway scrapbook – a massive volume of photographs, documents, maps and written observations about Woodford's railway. It must have been a gargantuan task for Jim and his two companions when they had produced it, back in 1956, for there were no photocopiers available to ordinary folk in those days and each item had to be cut out and pasted in, or laboriously copied. So well-thumbed was this tome that its original covers had long since disintegrated and been replaced with vinyl floor covering, which gave a superficial impression of amateurism; but the book was an invaluable record of the village and its people. Here was Woodford before, during and after the building of the Great Central Railway. Long-dead people were summoned to life in its pages: hard-working navvies, visiting journalists, railway people at work and leisure, instructions and letters from the General Strike of 1926, railwaymen in trade union and public life.

Long before I had explored more than a fraction of this Aladdin's Cave of local history, he was clearing a space on the table for two plates of lamb chops and potatoes, a simple well-cooked meal made all the more enjoyable by the morning's walk and given as if we had been lifelong friends. And then back to the scrapbook, with the fascination increasing as we turned the pages. The parish of Woodford-cum-Membris includes the twin villages of Hinton and Woodford, both possessing a manor but only the latter a church, separated by a few fields that the railway covered with its vast embankment. There was a railway here before the Great Central, but its owners considered the villages unworthy of a station and the single track of the East & West Junction Railway, later renamed the Stratford-upon-Avon & Midland Junction, was content to meander through the southernmost fields of the parish.

Ironically, the E&WJR benefited considerably from the building of the Great Central, carrying almost all of the materials to the site of the new line; bricks for the bridges and the lining of Catesby Tunnel, timber for fencing, even the contractors' locomotives were transported to the vicinity of Woodford over its metals. Permanent connections were made later, curves joining the two lines to allow both northbound and southbound Great Central trains to turn westward along the other company's line, and although the southern connection was soon taken out, through carriages from Marylebone to Stratford-upon-Avon used the north curve until 1936.

The building of the Great Central was a time of considerable upheaval for Woodford, but despite the Parish Council's complaint in 1895 about the nuisance caused by the advance guard of navvies dossing down in outbuildings, the villagers seemed, in the main, to welcome the prospect of steady work and good transport. By 1898, with the line well on its way to completion and most of the five hundred navvies properly housed in a hutted encampment, the council was in an altogether more enthusiastic mood. Realising that the inhabitants of their soon-to-boom town would need addresses, they entered into the spirit of things by naming the streets. But here a touch of farce entered the tale in the person of the District Auditor, who ruled that it was not within the power of a Parish Council to erect street nameplates – and promptly surcharged the members for their trouble. Good sense did, however, eventually prevail and the penalties were cancelled.

In Jim Anscomb's scrapbook the human aspect of history was well to the fore, not only the familiar, humorous tales of the navvies and their escapades – in one case they buried their illicit beer stock in the side of a cutting to conceal it from an inquisitive excise officer – but also more moving stories. Perhaps the most touching was that of Adeline Pym, who gave so much to help the hardworking builders of the line. Nowadays, the common image of the railway navvy is of a course, aggressive, hard-drinking, insensitive figure and few bother to think of the man beneath the exterior shell, but Adeline Pym new better. In 1895 she opened a free reading room for them and the *Northampton Mercury* reported how men crowded in night after night. She provided games, periodicals, newspapers, writing materials and, taking the view that it was their room, raised no objection to the men wearing their working clothes. The reporter also wrote of the many hours she spent getting to know the men, listening to their problems and, when asked, giving help and advice. Later in the same year she bought a house, strategically placed opposite the Hare and Hounds, which she converted into lodgings. A caretaker was employed and contemporary reports spoke highly of the home's comforts and cleanliness, uncommon luxury for men sometimes forced to sleep in earth shelters.

Jim had been unable to discover much more about this little known Victorian heroine.

'I know she was a maiden lady, but I don't know where she came from. We do know that she left here in 1898, though, when the navvies' work was finished locally, to go to Staines and set up a similar home there. We know that because we have a newspaper report of bankruptcy proceedings taken against her in London. She worked alone, without an organisation, and ended up with no assets and debts of more than £2,000.'

It was a bleak end to what should have been a happy tale and, for a few moments, Jim was silent.

Completion of the Great Central transformed the village. Between Woodford and Hinton was now a great embankment topped by a station, marshalling yard, engine shed, wagon works, a power station supplying electricity for the lamps that illuminated the sidings, and a gas works that provided fuel for a gas-engine that powered the generators. By 1901 the population had more than doubled to 1,220 people and, although the navvies had vacated their lodgings and huts, 136 company houses introduced the alien architecture of an industrial town. But the advantages of urban life were not always quick to follow and although the locals, looking forward to seeing their village grow into a full-blown city, tolerated the inconveniences familiar to country folk, newcomers from the towns of the Great Central's northern heartland cursed the muddy, unpaved streets.

When Jim Anscomb arrived in the locality, in October 1939, those pioneering days were over; the population was almost 1,800, the Second World War had just started and the village had given up trying to grow into a town. For Jim, Woodford was the last stop after two decades of railway wandering that had begun seventy years before I met him, and yet he related his story in that clear manner I found typical of old railwaymen. Just like Bob Sharp, back in Nottingham, he was able to give the dates of events that had occurred more than half a century previously.

'I was born in 1900 in New Southgate, although before the First World War my parents moved first to Enfield and then New Barnet. In September 1914 my father joined the Army and my mother, finding she could not manage on the separation allowance, decided to move to her old village in Norfolk. That was early in 1915 and, two years later, I joined the railway to work as a porter. At that time, newly joined staff were described as "extra labour" and I was sent to work at various stations as a relief man – that was my status until they made me a full-blown porter, late in 1917. But the nomadic life continued until the start of the eight-hour day, and then I was needed at my home station of Flordon, about seven miles south of Norwich.

'When I first started, the twelve-hour day was normal. True, we were allowed two hours for meals but, if you were needed during those two hours, you did not get paid for it. For instance, during the 1918 influenza epidemic, I was sent to Aldeby, a little town near Yarmouth, and all except the Station Master were off sick. So I was working from six in the morning to nine-thirty at night. Mind you, when I say working I really mean that I was on duty all that time; sometimes there was nothing much to do, but the point is that I did not get paid for the extra time.

'I stopped at Flordon until February 1928, when I moved to Mansfield and got a Class 4 shunter's job, which turned out to be helping a guard get traffic out of Rufford and Clipstone Collieries. We'd take a load of empties up to, say, Rufford in the morning, dispose of them, move the loaded wagons out and the guard would work them back to Mansfield concentration sidings. Early in the afternoon he would be back with more empties, I'd be waiting for him, and then we would make up another train of coal for him to work back to Mansfield.

'At Clipstone we did the same sort of thing, but it was worked rather differently. We would take in a load of empties, dispose of them, and then the engine would go round to the loaded sidings to pull out about twenty wagons. We'd go with them to Rufford Junction, where we would put them into the loop, which was usually filled right down to the concentration sidings. There would be a string of perhaps eighty or ninety wagons there and they would keep drawing them down, a few at a time, into the sidings, while my guard kept adding his ten or twenty to the rear of the line. About dinner time we would go back for another load of empties, dispose of them and start fetching the afternoon wagons out. And that was how we went on for most of the day.

'I left in May 1929 to go to Immingham as a Class 3 shunter working on the coal hoists, which were used to load ships. The system there was that a pilot engine would put wagons into a siding that led down to the hoists and the brakes would be pinned down. I would go up and unhook six of them, lift the brakes and allow them to run down the incline to the hoist, where I braked them again. The capstan man would uncouple a wagon and release the brake. If the wagon needed turning, he would put it on a turntable and spin it round so that the end door was ready to tip the contents into the boat. When the hoist came down, he would run the wagon on to it and up it would go, be tipped into the ship, then be lowered halfway down to a platform where another shunter was waiting to run it down the incline to the sidings. He would begin by pinning down the brakes of two wagons at the bottom of the gradient, to form a stop block, then he would let perhaps a dozen others run down into them. Again, he would pin down the brakes of the last two, to act as a stop block for the following ones, and then take the first twelve down to the sidings and brake them, ready for the empties pilot to take them away. That was how we worked all day long except, occasionally, when there wasn't a boat to load – and then we would just sit around.

'That was when I learned to play pontoon. For the tippers it was different; one of their gangs always played bridge, although the favourite among them was solo-whist, while we shunters always played solo or pontoon. Sometimes we'd have a drink as well, bottles of what we knew as aniseed gin, which we got from some of the Dutchmen; I don't know what it was, but it wasn't a bad drink. We used to get tobacco off them, too, awful stuff that we called Rotterdam hay – but some managed to smoke it.

'My next move was to Boston, where I planned to work a summer before settling down in Lincoln, but hard times were affecting the railways, like everything else. And it so happened that, soon after I arrived in Boston, a Class 3 shunter broke his leg and was unable to restart work; that made an opening for me and I stayed there – simply because I couldn't get a job anywhere else. I worked there for ten years and was in the same position when I left as when I started – bottom of the list! So, for promotion, I applied for a job at Woodford. In those days a man would move home for five shillings a week. The pay for the lowest-grade shunter (Class 4) was fifty shillings a week and each grade received an extra five shillings, giving a Class 1 man sixty-five shillings a week.

'So I arrived here as a Class 1 shunter, just as the Second World War was starting. I thought I was in clover – working every third Sunday for one thing. So, not only was I getting sixty-five shillings instead of the fifty-five I'd received at Boston, but was also picking up a Sunday at time and a half. But that meant working two weeks without a break, which didn't leave time for much else; by the time you had dug the garden, or been shopping with the missus, that was it! Of course it was extra traffic created by the war that made Sunday working necessary.

'I don't remember ever working a Sunday at Boston; there was some overtime, but not very often. And, if we thought someone deserved to be brought out of the goods shed to become a shunter, we would refuse to work overtime until management was forced to promote him. So I have little sympathy with the way some trade unionists behave today – going out on strike if their overtime is stopped.'

In those early days of the Second World War, when Jim first arrived in the village, there were fears that the Woodford marshalling yards, especially being situated so close to an important junction, would be a prime target for enemy bombers. But even if the fear was a real one for the authorities, it did not seem to have percolated down to Jim and his mates.

'There was supposed to be a blackout, and for the first few months we had a fire-watching scheme going in the village. People did turn out and supposedly watched for fires, but it was a bit of a rum do. Anyway, all lights on the railway were supposed to be concealed and the big lamp posts in the yards had tarpaulin skirts fitted around the top, like giant lampshades, to direct the light downwards. But as time went by they all got blown off and nobody bothered to replace them. Of course, if ever there was a night-time air raid alert, they were all put out immediately.

Also there was a man watching for aeroplanes, twenty-four hours a day, from a dugout up near where the yardmaster's office was later built, and he would give a warning if he spotted anything – but that was very rare. Mind you, there were a few bombs dropped around here, although none did any damage. I remember one of those candelabra bombs coming down near Charwelton, lighting the whole place up, and a couple of bombs were dropped behind the loco shed one night, but no damage was done. I never even heard the damn things, we were so busy in the yard, with all the clanking and thumping and noise going on. And some others dropped at the side of the village, but they exploded harmlessly as well.'

The war was to have a great impact on the railways; at Woodford it led to a massive increase in the size of the yards and ended the extravagance of allowing privately owned wagons to be used solely for the carriage of one company's products. During Jim Anscomb's early months in the village considerable time and effort was wasted shunting wagons around so that they could be returned empty to one particular colliery or factory. The introduction of the 'common user' system ended that wastefulness and contributed greatly to efficiency.

At the time of their building the Woodford yards had been extensive and a further six sidings had been added in 1934, but it was in 1941 that the new yards were built to increase capacity so dramatically. Originally an 'up yard', for traffic heading south, had been built east of the running lines between the station in the south and the engine shed in the north, while the 'down yard', for northbound traffic, had occupied a corresponding position to the west. The new yards were built north of the engine shed, stretching into the parish of Charwelton, and had storage capacity for 1,991 wagons, bringing the total for the whole complex to 3,255, although this number could be increased to 3,638 when necessary by storing wagons in the four running loops. Another improvement made at this time was the replacement of the locomotive turntable by a triangle of track behind the engine shed, permitting larger engines to be turned at the depot. The new yards, linked to the old by tracks independent of the running lines, were built over the site of the derelict Charwelton brickworks and on the west side covered the site of a flooded clay pit, earning them the nickname of 'Duckpool Sidings'.

To the men working in the yards, the first indication of the approach of a train would come when the control office telephoned the appropriate Woodford signal box. If the train was approaching from the north, the call would come from Rugby Control to the signalman at the north end of the yard, who would relay the message to the foreman shunter, who would decide where the train should be positioned on arrival. Before moving from the reception sidings it would be checked by the wagon examiner and his 'fat lad', the examiner checking for faulty wheels by tapping them with a hammer – a dull sound meant a cracked wheel – and the 'fat lad' topping up the axle boxes with grease. Then the process of sorting wagons and attaching them to trains heading towards their final destination could begin.

WOODFORD № 3

Throughput at Woodford was impressive and the figures Jim obtained from the yardmaster for his 1956 study show that between 1932 and 1941 more than eight million wagons were sorted, while during the ten years to 1951 the number reached 9,938,000. All of this was handled by a staff of two inspectors, three foremen, three Class 1 and five Class 3 shunters – all under the authority of the yardmaster.

Jim Anscomb had not been resident in the village very long before taking his first steps into public life.

'Like most railwaymen, I was a trades unionist and I'd already joined the Labour Party at Boston, so I very soon got roped in as secretary of the local party. A case of make the newcomer work, if you will!'

It had been the arrival of the railway workers, unaccustomed to doffing their caps to squire or parson, that had brought both Nonconformism and working class politics to Woodford. Trade union branches were formed even as the line opened: the Amalgamated Society of Locomotive Engineers & Firemen was the first, followed by the Amalgamated Society of Railway Servants, forerunner of the National Union of Railwaymen, and the National Union of Vehicle Builders, although their local branch later transferred en bloc to the Engineering Union.

Railway people also brought their traditions of self-help, particularly, in those days prior to the National Health Service, in the form of organisations providing funds for hospital or medical treatment. Jim, who became secretary of one such organisation, takes up the story.

'In those days pay was poor and the work dangerous, yet anyone needing treatment was expected to pay for it. The system was that members of the local gentry would make an annual donation to the hospital and would reserve a number of "letters of introduction". If you were ill, you would ask one of them for a letter – in Woodford it was usually the parson. Well, local railwaymen soon got fed up with having to go cap-in-hand to him, especially the radicals and the Nonconformists, whose lives could be made quite difficult, so they started their own scheme to buy letters. Initially they relied on fund-raising events, collections, fetes and band concerts. The men of the locomotive depot went further and formed the "Blue Hungry Band". This was a comic band with a variety of instruments, though mainly kazoos – they were attired in blue tunics, yellow trousers and strange hats. Every summer they played a game of comic cricket against a team from the London & North Western Railway's Rugby depot for a cup, specially made in the workshops. But occasional events were insufficient to maintain the necessary income and, in 1927, the men voted to set up the Woodford Workers' Hospital Fund, financed by a payment of one old penny deducted from each pound of their earnings.'

Jim was secretary of the fund from the early war years until it was wound up with the birth of the National Health Service in 1948. It had certainly been a proud achievement for Woodford's workers, but self-help schemes were never a proper substitute for a real health service. As Jim pointed out, 'Not only were the funds often inadequate, but the hospitals were never able to plan forward and develop as they later did under the NHS.'

As a result of his early success with the hospital scheme, doubling its annual income to £600, he was offered the position of treasurer of the chapel accounts and, later, the branch of the National Union of Railwaymen. Soon he was noticed in other quarters and, when a vacancy arose on the Parish Council in 1943, he became a co-opted member – the normal procedure while elections were suspended during the war years. In 1944 he joined the Rural District Council, a position he held through all subsequent elections until 1971, serving as its Chairman for eight of those years. In 1946 elections were restored and Jim became the first railwayman to represent the Byfield Division on Northamptonshire County Council and, with one three-year break, he served on it until local government reorganisation in 1973. When I met him, in his mid-eighties, he remained a parish councillor, with over forty years of continuous service.

At work, his promotion continued to be gradual and, after becoming a guard, he thought he had no further ambition in that field.

'I was a goods guard, and hated passenger work, mainly because I knew little about passenger train working. Sometimes I would be on a station, perhaps on my way home, and people would ply me with questions I just could not answer, so I sometimes used to feel a bit of a silly bugger. And then, on top of that, I started to get so bored with the work that, at night, I found myself dropping off to sleep half the time –

and that can be flippin' dangerous. So I became a yard foreman to escape.'

The 1950s were not good years for railway workers; money could be earned more easily elsewhere and the consequent low morale was reflected in the attitude of some of the men.

'One problem I used to come up against as foreman was that some guards would work a train into Woodford with a Great Western guard's van, but then refuse to work it out again. You see, the Great Western guard's van had an open platform at one end only, unlike the normal double-ended type. So, if they arrived with the platform end of the van trailing they would be expected to leave with it facing forward and some of them objected to having to go out into a facing wind to operate the brake. Of course, the Western men had always worked that way and accepted it, but it caused problems for us at Woodford.'

The attitude of higher management was ambivalent, probably due to the difficulty of keeping men when pay and conditions were so poor, and this made life even more difficult for those in Jim's position.

'One day a guard refused to take out a Western brake van with the platform facing forward; we had no means of turning it, so I cancelled the train. Afterwards the yardmaster told me that I had acted correctly – but never to do it again! On another occasion, when I was being interviewed for an inspector's job, they asked what I would do if a shunter refused to uncouple a train. I said that I would uncouple it myself and sort things out later. They told me that I should not go doing things like that – so God knows what they expected me to do!'

As time passed, the Beeching Plan to rationalise the railway began to bite hard into the system and the threat of closure loomed over Woodford, but many railwaymen viewed this threat with disbelief.

'Right up to the last few months some were saying we were too busy for them to close us down, but how wrong they were. The run-down was very rapid when it came; I know from the figures found in the yardmaster's office after closure that, for example, four thousand wagons passed through on 21 January 1964. Yet on 25 February all except mineral traffic was diverted via Birmingham and the only mineral loads continuing to use the line were those between Great Central stations, along with a small number of empty mineral wagons heading for Scunthorpe.'

On 5 April 1965 the yard closed completely and Jim spent a year on the dole before drawing his pension. Most of the younger men found work in Daventry – and Woodford became a dormitory.

22
WOODFORD AFTER
THE RAILWAY

Woodford village in the 1980s was a strange place. Never having grown into a town, as some had envisaged it would, the rural and former industrial parts stood either side of Church Street like separate communities. On Percy Road, Sidney Road, Cherwell Terrace and Castle Road the feel of the solid red-brick terraces was of an industrial town or colliery village, even to the scabrous patches of recently applied stone cladding that scarred a few of the walls. Turn the other way, walk along School Street and enter a village of ironstone cottages, with its manor house fronting directly on to the street near the premises where Miss Pym had run her home for railway navvies. Continue along High Street, high because it's on a hilltop, where flowering sweet peas may be glimpsed in gardens, and pass the Edwardian-style school to The Fleur-de-Lys. This was a rare find in the 1980s, an ungentrified country pub where ruddy-faced men drank pints of froth-free Bass, which flowed from a hand pump and harked back to the past – a past when other men had sat in that same room in their railway uniforms to play cards or dominoes and talk of the day's happenings.

The Fleur-de-Lys had played a full role in the life of the village. A brick extension at the rear housed the first-floor clubroom, where the Woodford branch of the Amalgamated Society of Railway Servants had been formed and continued to meet, latterly as the National Union of Railwaymen, until the railway was closed. Across the yard was the hut where the Woodford and Hinton Band had practised for many years and added its brand of culture to the village.

Woodford had supported two bands, excluding the comic 'Blue Hungry Band'. The grandly named Woodford and Hinton Silver Band was known locally as 'the beer and bacca band', which clearly differentiated it from the Methodist Brass Band. Local folk were in the habit of dubbing grand organisations with less than grand titles, so the

Methodist band became known as 'the bun and monster band', the monster in question being a popular fruit drink of the time, sold in unusually large bottles and said to be the favourite tipple of chapel folk. But history favoured the beer drinkers; the bun and monster brigade folded in 1922, while the beer and bacca men lasted into the early years of Hitler's war.

St Mary's Church seemed a logical place to visit after the pub. Approached along a narrow road, where the severe, fortress-like Moravian Church added yet more incongruity, St Mary's stands appropriately adjacent to both the rural and former railway communities, on a hillside overlooking fields and the site of the locomotive shed. Jim Anscomb was an invaluable guide around the graveyard, despite expressing such a low opinion of headstones that he had already made arrangements to be cremated rather than rot beneath one.

Under one patch of neatly mown grass lay the remains of a one-time vicar of the parish, Richard Walter, who had fought and been wounded at Trafalgar, then served at Woodford for twenty-three years as curate before becoming vicar for his last five. But the graves of two working men stimulated more curiosity: William Davis, a twenty-one-year-old railway fireman, was laid to rest in 1864 after being killed by the exploding boiler of his locomotive at Camden, on the North London Railway, while William Marriott had earned his reputation as a singer, poet and thatcher before being interred in 1871.

The interior of the church impressed me with its richness – a richness of craftsmanship and architectural line rather than an extravagant display of monetary wealth. Parts of the building are 12th century, but it has been added to and rebuilt over the years – certainly with good taste on the last occasion in 1878. There was an overall feeling of airiness and there was some fine woodwork to be seen, especially on the ends of the benches and high in the barrel-vaulted roof. On a wall near the tower was a wooden plaque, splendidly painted with the coat of arms of the Great Central Railway by a serving railwayman who had once worked at Woodford as a fireman. It had been placed in the church by the Great Central Railway Enthusiasts Association, which still thrived in the village, to honour the railway's contribution to village life. And standing in a corner was the parish chest, an impressive box, its ancient timbers bound with broad bands of iron. Jim told me that it contained cleaning materials!

The streets of railway houses would provide little interest to the average passer-by, but not so Jim Anscomb. He showed me where the butcher's shop had been, with its slaughterhouse at the end of the yard, and the off-licence that never was, because it never succeeded in acquiring a licence. And he told me a sociological anecdote too, about Percy Road being known as 'Liver and Bacon Street', or 'Piano Row', because the better-off railway families tended to live there.

On Sidney Road, with the house gardens stretching down to the Cherwell and overlooked by the vast embankment, we paused near a gap in the terrace of houses. Long overgrown and neglected, this patch of land must have occupied an unenviable place in the memories of many Great Central railwaymen. On this spot stood the enginemen's hostel, unofficially known as 'the barracks', where, for fifty years, accommodation of an indifferent quality had been provided for visiting train crews. The hostel began its loveless existence in 1907, when four adjoining houses where converted to accommodate men sleeping between shifts, prior to working their trains home. Originally the sixteen bedrooms were converted into thirty cubicles, while a rest room and dining room were provided on the ground floor, kitchens were situated in the basement and, somehow, space was found to accommodate the caretaker and his family. As the depot and the yards became busier the hostel was extended by building a canteen in the garden and converting the ground floor rooms into a further six cubicles. According to Jim Anscomb's research, production-line techniques made it possible to accommodate up to three hundred men a week in the barracks, with each guest at least having the privacy of his own cubicle, if not the sole use of two sheets – normal practice was to replace the bottom sheet with the top one and to provide a clean upper sheet as each new man arrived!

During the early years of the Second World War the unpopular practice of sending crews on lodging turns ceased at Woodford and the hostel was used instead to house men drafted to the depot from other parts of the country. Later, it gained further notoriety when used as accommodation for young firemen who were unable to find lodgings in the village, and was still being used for this purpose when gutted by fire and subsequently demolished in 1957. Thirty years on the site remained empty, derelict land overlooked by a derelict embankment.

Near the station approach, the down-at-heel Sir Winston public house, The White Hart Hotel of better days, clung perilously to existence. Precious little remained of the station itself, just a pair of blue-brick arches spanning the road, parallel with each other, which had once supported the north end of the main platform and provided public access by a stairway between them. On the embankment, where the busy station had once been a stopping place for expresses travelling between London and the North, and others heading for the South and South West coasts, nothing remained. Neither was there any trace of the side platform, where the Stratford-upon-Avon train used to wait for the arrival of its main-line connection. Now the ground was occupied by a campsite, where travelling showmen weathered the winter months, and along the scrub-covered fringe of the station yard were a few untidy garages and huts.

Down the road to the west was Hinton Manor, a modest house of mellow stone, facing an extravagant-looking mock-Tudor building, which had begun its existence as the Hinton Gorse Hotel. Built with the intention of serving the needs of visiting hunting folk, who arrived with their mounts by train, the hotel had fallen on hard times with the ascendancy of the motor horsebox and, after a brief period as a grain store, was eventually purchased in the 1950s for use as the British Railways Staff Association Club. When I visited the village, the building housed the Woodford and Hinton Social Club and, among other functions, served as the meeting place of The Great Central Railway Enthusiasts Association.

The Association was formed in the mid-1970s, following a visit to the National Railway Museum by a party of local ex-railwaymen and, over the years, helped to keep alive an interest in Woodford's railway history. In the early days former railwaymen predominated among the membership, but time slowly took its toll until they became a minority and the task of keeping the organisation alive fell to other enthusiasts. For a group based in such a small community, they were very successful and published a monthly magazine, 'The Windcutter'. A modest publication, but well produced and full of interest, it was named after the fast coal trains that once plied the line between Annesley and Woodford. These were reputed to provide the best service of non-vacuum-braked trains in Britain but, somehow, the name seemed wrong and more appropriate to a patent remedy for the guts-ache than a heavy freight train. But it was fitting that those enthusiasts named their publication not after one of the glamorous expresses, but in honour of the heavy coal trains that were once the lifeblood of the line. For a number of years the president of the Association was Richard Hardy, who had been the locomotive shedmaster at Woodford for a short period at the end of the 1940s. A distinguished railwayman and author of a number of railway books, Richard Hardy had a special affection for the Great Central and I was to meet him some time later at his home, near the line, in Amersham. Sadly, in the late 1980s, as older railwaymen died or left the village and interest in Woodford's railway past began to wane, the Association was wound up.

As we stood on the site of the station, Jim mentioned that Woodford had been the scene of an accident in December 1935, which, though relatively minor in terms of damage and injury, made a permanent impact on the way the railway was worked. Since the summer of 1906 it had been the practice for the 18.20 Marylebone-Manchester express to carry a through coach for Stratford-upon-Avon. As the express did not stop at Woodford, the coach was 'slipped' from the rear of the train by the guard, who would then bring it to rest in the station, ready to be attached to a local train for Stratford, while the forward part of the express continued its journey. On this occasion the brakes of the main section of the train failed, bringing it to a rapid halt, and the slip coach ran into the back of it. Although only a few passengers were slightly injured, the accident resulted in the end of slip coaches on the Great Central, after more than thirty years of extensive use.

Walking on, past the spur that had led up to the Stratford-upon-Avon & Midland Junction Railway, and passing beneath the bridge that carried its trackbed over the Great Central, we left behind Woodford and Hinton, sleepy villages separated by the vast embankment that had once united them with a common purpose. The railway had brought noise, grime, alien architecture and an influx of industrial working-class folk to the Northamptonshire countryside. It had also brought a lively injection of new culture and talent from distant parts of the country: diverse qualities, combining traditions of the countryside and the town in a community given cohesion by membership of what Jim Anscomb called the railway family.

In those sixty-odd years that the railway gave life to the village, the people here had not only shifted tens of millions of wagon loads of the nation's food, its raw materials and the products of its industry, and maintained the locomotives, rolling stock, tunnels, bridges and track of their railway; they had also settled into their new community and given it guts. They developed political skills, took over the council and ran their village. Not only railway apprenticeships were served here – the Adams family alone sent two sons up the line to become Lord Mayors, Thomas in Manchester and Samuel in Leicester. From the 'Blue Hungry Band', acting the fool and raising money for good causes, to the dignified Woodford and Hinton Silver Band, the horticultural and athletic societies, chapels and trade union branches, it was a proud and remarkable record for a small place.

Jim left me on the southern boundary of the parish, just as he had met me on the northern one, and I continued the journey south while he returned to his village. After a few moments, I turned to watch the receding figure of the man to whom I owed most of my knowledge of Woodford. In his mid-eighties, long after most of his contemporaries had died or given up, the old railwayman continued his work as parish councillor, local history scholar and writer, and still found time to be hospitable to visitors.

23
SULGRAVE

At first the going was easy, through a cutting that was home to a group of chestnut hunters, who had grazed part of the following embankment to the appearance of a closely cropped suburban lawn. The embankment was a gigantic earthwork, extending the mile or more to Culworth Junction and providing an unsurpassable vantage point from which to view the lush green landscape. On high ground to the west lay the village of Eydon and, in the foreground, a combine harvester went about its noisy and necessary business.

At Culworth Junction another immense embankment, which had once carried a nine-mile-long spur, diverged in a south-westerly direction to join the Great Western Railway at Banbury, while the Great Central main line continued towards the metropolis. Little else remained at this once important place – the fire-gutted remnants of a platelayers' hut, built of old sleepers, the foundations of the signal box and, in the vee of the junction itself, the empty shell of a small concrete building. Later the embankment gave way to a marshy floored cutting, where nettles and thistles grew densely and the dank stink of decay pervaded the still air. At the site of Culworth Station the way was blocked by agricultural buildings, but an occupation bridge offered a route to the Moreton Pinkney road.

The bridge offered a view of an ugly and depressing place, with only the bridge and station house remaining as reminders of the railway. A tall silo towered over huts like the watchtower of a prison camp, and from the gloomy interiors of those vast corrugated-iron sheds came the unmistakable noise and odour of closely confined pigs. Agricultural machinery, much of it rusting and abandoned, littered the track as it led towards the next cutting, which had been partially filled beneath a tall triple-arched bridge that carried a lane over the line. But soon all ways were barred. A sign ahead claimed the land was private, and one on either side warned that there was no public footpath, yet the map showed otherwise, and a recently fixed local authority sign proclaimed a public right of way to both left and right! Clearly, it would have been impossible to please the landowner so, rather than trespass on a stony trackbed, I followed the designated path, through a field where hay was growing, until it joined a winding and undulating lane, with views across wheat fields to a massive embankment, before entering the village of Sulgrave. Along the main street rain began to fall softly, airborne droplets shimmered in the bright sunlight and the wet leaves of two great copper beech trees glistened like jewels. In the shelter of their canopy were the village stocks, a picturesque scene to those whose nostalgia is blind.

There was a warm welcome from Mr and Mrs Cherry, their two sons, two dogs and fat cat at the farmhouse where I was to spend the night. I was given a large cup of tea in the kitchen, where a kettle simmered perpetually on a Rayburn stove, before being shown to my room. It was large and comfortable, bright, clean and fresh, with stone mullioned windows – one looking out beneath thatched eaves to the green, the other across open country, for this was the last house of the village.

A hot bath, so effective for soothing aching limbs and insect bites, was the first priority, and the next was a search for food. My first stop was at The Star, where I savoured my first ever drink of 'Old Hookey' – a fine traditional old ale brewed by, and at that time rarely available outside the vicinity of, the very traditional Hook Norton Brewery. But The Star was an ale house that served no food, and 'pricey' was the landlord's view of Sulgrave's only restaurant. Instead, he suggested a dinner at a pub some two miles distant, and I set off to add yet more miles to the day's total.

It was a good dinner of gammon, new potatoes and salad in a pub that had developed along lines very different from The Star, being close to a main road. The place had become more of a restaurant than a pub, but a bar survived to serve the locals. The company was fascinating: a local lad impressing his girlfriend, a quiet American with his wife, and two less than quiet couples who hailed from the vicinity of Birmingham. The Americans, having been persuaded to change their order from baked potato to salmon trout, murmured the words 'veery nice, veery nice' almost continuously throughout their meal. The Brummies, meanwhile, resplendent in polyester and crimplene, the women's hair lacquered to the texture of steel wool and their menfolk's blazers adorned with regimental badges, made a great fuss. Every drink in stock was discussed with the landlord before the men eschewed hand-pumped ale for keg bitter and each of the women settled for a yellow-coloured concoction they called a 'snowball'. Chef was brought from the kitchen to explain each item on the menu before the men chose steak and the women scampi, as we all knew they would. But the food was good, strengthening me for the walk back to Sulgrave and an evening in its wonderful pub.

Sulgrave was fortunate to have such a gem as The Star, with its flagstone floor, overlaid with carpet at the posh end. The single room was graded without any physical dividing line and the same bar served all customers, irrespective of whether they came from the end with the bare stone floor and simple furnishings or the carpeted area with ex-chapel pews fitted around the walls – a use unlikely to meet with the approval of their previous owner. It was the sort of pub that had almost died out thirty years before, to be imitated later by the very same pub companies that had destroyed them in the first place. One customer who described it as a typical English country pub was corrected by another, who remarked it was now anything but typical. The Star seemed to be one hundred per cent genuine, and so did Jack, the landlord, a one-time railway platelayer who shared my enthusiasm for 'Old Hookey'.

Jack and his regulars soon knew my purpose in the village and welcomed me into the group. We talked of my walk, Jack's days on the railway, their memories of express trains speeding along the top of Sulgrave embankment, and trips up the line to Nottingham Goose Fair followed by yet more visits to that city, then so well provided with young women and lively public houses. It was a good night, our conversation unimpeded by the flashing lights of gambling machines or piped music. And, as more ale was poured, directly from a barrel in the little half-sunken cellar at the back of the bar, people, words and memories merged into a pleasurable blur.

Next morning I arose feeling remarkably fresh to face the sort of breakfast I had previously thought was a myth perpetuated by country cookbooks and tourist board brochures. There, among the fine old furniture of Mrs Cherry's dining room, I sat in splendid isolation at a great table to eat a breakfast of fruit juice, muesli, bacon, egg, tomatoes and fried new potatoes, followed by thickly sliced toast and a large pot of tea. Sitting back afterwards, as sunlight streamed through the window, thinking of the previous evening and marvelling at the lack of a well-deserved hangover, it all seemed unreal – far distant from the crumbling inner-city, murderous traffic, aggression and mind-bursting noise that constitutes the environment in which too many of us live.

Sulgrave, a pretty village of mellow limestone, wisteria-clad walls and neat thatches, is probably better known in the United States than in Britain, due to its association with the Washington family. The manor house, where they lived for a hundred and twenty years in the 16th and 17th centuries, stands at the eastern end of the village and attracts sufficient visitors to justify an expensive hotel as a neighbour.

The house was the birthplace of Lawrence Washington, whose son John emigrated to Virginia in 1656 and took with him the family coat of arms of three stars and two stripes, said to have inspired the design of the American flag. The original emblem may still be seen at Sulgrave Manor, carved above a doorway.

The village church had connections with the family too – their pew, memorial brasses and the south porch, which was built on the instructions of Lawrence Washington. St James's was a pleasant mixture of a building, part Saxon with a 13th-century tower, and a delightful avenue of Irish yew trees leading to the north porch. Nearby were Saxon earthworks and, across the fields, an oddly restored windmill; converted into a private house, its newly castellated rim and flagpole provoked one villager to draw comparisons with a sandcastle. But it had at least been saved from dereliction and it seemed likely that the proud owner would lavish care and affection on it for many years to come.

Before leaving the village I stood in a meadow to look again at the house that had been home to the forefathers of the first President of the United States – a peaceful scene on a sunny morning, yew hedges, rose, rock and kitchen gardens, the United States flag hanging limply in the still air and a herd of immaculately clean Friesian bullocks watching me through their soft brown eyes. All would have been calm were it not for the great man's descendants. But even they quietened the engines of their warplanes when flying low over those fields. Darkly sinister against the bright summer sky, these thermonuclear demons possessed an evil, awe-inspiring beauty. Yet local people hardly seemed to notice, having accepted them as an everyday part of the Cold War scene. And the bullocks, doomed like all of their kind, grazed unperturbed.

24
SULGRAVE TO BRACKLEY

The walk along the bridleway back to the GCR trackbed was enlivened by the company of an elderly woman, whose equally elderly spaniel had befriended me within minutes of leaving the village. Tall and stately, she picked her way over the uneven ground with the caution of one aware that old bones break easily and heal slowly. And as her gaze roved over the countryside, her eyes protected from the sun's glare by one of those green celluloid shades favoured by telegraph operators in films of the Old West, she reminisced. Her memories were of a time when the patchwork pattern of fields and the area's mixed farming, which I valued for the variety it brought to the scene, did not exist and this was a land of rich grazing with not a cereal crop to be seen. She envied me the walk along the embankment, now too steep for her to climb, where the flowers and butterflies of her youth flourished unmolested by chemical farming. We parted company in the cool mouth of the tunnel that carried the path through the embankment and which was now showing signs of decay. Climbing the steep bankside, I caught sight of her again, vainly calling after the spaniel, which had suddenly rediscovered some of its youthful vigour and disappeared into a cornfield.

For the two miles to Helmdon high embankments, giving wide views of fine countryside, alternated with soggy bottomed cuttings in a continuous succession of heavy earthworks as the line traversed a rolling landscape. This was a scene of constantly changing interest, from the playful antics of young rabbits to the beauty of a tree; from the surprising majesty of a bridge to the unexpected discovery of a piece of limestone ballast, broken to reveal the perfect fossil of a shellfish.

A little to the north of Helmdon village the line crossed a valley and the disused trackbed of the former Northampton & Banbury Junction Railway on a fine nine-arched viaduct. But signs of neglect were evident; the scraping away of the ballast having destroyed the waterproof covering at the ends of the structure, allowing erosion to occur and, near the middle, a parapet wall bulged perceptibly outwards. As I walked across, between parapets smeared all over with cow dung, a figure came into view and gradually took the shape of an elderly man. Fit, with features almost unlined, he was clad in a flat cap, green knitted cardigan, corduroys, open-necked shirt and heavy wellington boots. His sun-tanned face creased into a grin as he asked if I was walking to London, before adding that I would not be the first. And was I planning to write a book, because I wouldn't be the first to try that either!

From then on he asked no questions but talked at length about his long life in Helmdon. It was a story that he wanted to tell, and I was happy to listen. Prompting was unnecessary – he had such a lot to say and said it so well that it would have been impertinent to interrupt, even to ask his name, so I never learned it. We stood for an hour as he faced me squarely and fixed me with an intense eye from which mine deviated rarely, and then only slightly. In a field far below, in direct line with a point about an inch from his right ear, an amorous cow was showing commendable persistence, initiative and perhaps a little progress in her efforts to arouse a bull whose paddock she shared. In the time we spent together, nothing else distracted me from the man's interesting tale.

After seventy-five years in Helmdon this man still loved the place, walking along the old railway every day 'except when the snow's too deep'.

'Can you tell me anywhere in England with finer views than this? I often tell them in the village to get up on the bank and really see the countryside, but not many do – in too much of a hurry to rush off somewhere foreign, just to show they can afford it!'

Looking down from the viaduct onto the trackbed of the Northampton & Banbury Junction line reminded him of his childhood, as the son of a platelaying ganger who had worked on that railway. His father had not enjoyed the length of retirement common today, but died, worn out by hard labour and poverty, within months of leaving his job. And now, as he looked down that trackway, he remembered the old man's backbreaking toil. Even the sun's pleasant heat brought forth memories of how, during dry weather, the wooden 'keys' that secured the rails into the cast-iron chairs mounted on the sleepers, would dry out, shrink and be shaken free by passing trains. He had seven miles of track to care for and a daily inspection was necessary in dry weather conditions. The memory was vivid of his father walking the line with a long-handled key-hammer – specially shaped with a narrow head for driving the wedge-shaped keys between the chair and rail – carried over one shoulder and a basket of spare keys slung over the other. But in that cursed dry weather he could rarely carry sufficient keys to replace all

those that had split, or been lost, and frequently had to trudge back to the store for a fresh supply.

It was a life of long working hours rewarded by poor pay, and made even harder by the necessity to grow much of the family's food. To families such as his an allotment garden was a necessity rather than the basis of a satisfying hobby. He held the memory of his father in deep respect, feeling gratitude for all he had provided, but remembered bitterly the tearful evenings spent working in the garden from schooltime until dark, while his better-off friends played.

'My father's aim was to produce a ton of potatoes each year. That sounds a lot, and it is when you are growing them, but it is not too many when you have got to feed eleven people for three hundred and sixty four days.'

The family also kept pigs and, as George Chambers had done, he told of the slaughtering, butchery, salting and drying of ham in the alcove of the cottage fireplace. He came from a background where nothing was wasted; even potato plant tops were dried out, some to form a bed on which the potato sacks would be placed to prevent the damp earth rotting them, while others were thatched to provide a roof for the potato store.

Much of his own life had been hard too.

'I left school one Friday afternoon in 1924 and started work for a gentleman farmer at seven o'clock the next morning – and I stuck that life for the next twenty-six years. Most of the time I was working with cattle, seven days a week, fifty-two weeks a year for a pittance. Gradually, after the war, I began to realise how badly off I was in relation to other people, and when my brother got me a job with a maintenance gang on a local RAF base, paying more for five days than I had been getting for seven, I jumped at the chance.

'As soon as the boss heard I was leaving he came to see me, walked into the cowshed in a suit that would have cost what he paid me for six months' work, and told me I couldn't go – because I was one of the family. One of the family! In twenty-six years the only room of the house I ever saw was the kitchen. But I used to get on well with his little daughter, teaching her about the animals and showing her the newborn ones. He made a lot of that, saying how much she would miss me and there could be no question of me leaving. Eventually, he offered more money, but not much more. When he saw how determined I was, he wished me success in the future and asked who my new employer would be and what work I would be doing. But I never told him because, as an ex-Army officer from a wealthy farming background, he could have easily got me the sack, even before I started my new job. Then I would have had to have gone back on his terms – and then we really would have found out how much a member of the family I was. I made the break in 1951 – never regretted it and worked on the airfield until I retired.'

He was clearly enjoying that retirement, especially the walks on the bank that he almost seemed to regard as his own property, even insisting on acting as a guide to show me the way down. Perhaps it was really an excuse to point out the tunnel that took a bridleway through the embankment, and to enthuse about the quality of the brickwork. His father, who had watched the line being built, had pointed out that very same brickwork to him when he was a boy. And like so many others with an appreciation of craftsmanship, he regretted that the like would not be built again.

His father would also have remembered the contractor's depot, situated next to the line on the valley floor, and the temporary railway linking it to the Great Central line high above. The scene would have been incredible to the inhabitants of this peaceful landscape – steam-navvies relentlessly going about their work and portable steam engines powering machinery for mortar-making, stone-dressing, joinery, blacksmithing and pumping water, while steam-driven cranes raised heavy loads of building materials high on to the piers of the unfinished viaduct. But one of the most impressive sights would have been the contractor's temporary railway. To avoid the expense of heavy infrastructure work, the line climbed steeply to the level of the new railway, presenting a formidable challenge to the drivers of the diminutive locomotives. In his book *The Making of a Railway*, L. T. C. Rolt wrote about the work of the contractor's locomotives at this site and how, given favourable conditions, those tiny engines were able to haul seventy-five-ton loads up a 1 in 9 gradient on the sharply curving track, presumably accompanied by a spectacular display of belching smoke, sparks rocketing high into the air, thunderous exhaust beats and the squealing of steel-flanges against steel rails.

Helmdon Station was decaying gracefully, its platform well grassed and roses from the garden flowering in a tangle on the bank. There was still some atmosphere too; the Station Master's house looked unaltered and a small office remained by the yard entrance. A modestly proportioned goods shed stood in the yard, now used as a coal merchant's depot and dotted about with heaps of shiny black anthracite. Nearby, three teenaged boys entertained themselves on bicycles; determined to fly, they had built a ramp that catapulted them and their bikes through a trajectory of six or seven feet when approached at breakneck speed. The porters' room, in the central pier of the overbridge, still had its iron window frames. They gave a strange view into the cutting beyond, the wide floor carpeted with grass, close-cropped by grazing sheep, while trees grew either side to give the illusion of a well-maintained avenue.

Next came an embankment, a mile or more in length, bordered by trees to give a secluded atmosphere to the path, which really belonged to rabbits, birds, insects and other small creatures who watched from the undergrowth. The line seemed to have been forgotten here, its intact, if unspectacular, bridges offering good vantage points from which to view the surrounding country. Near Radstone, the side of a cutting, otherwise made drab by its use as a linear manure-store, suddenly exhibited a blaze of colour where sweet peas flowered, as if in defiance of an adjacent dump of empty polythene sacks and chemical drums. This was the start of two cuttings, one quickly following the other, totalling one and a quarter miles in length and forming the approach to Brackley.

Passage was difficult here, the trackbed marshy and the cutting sides thickly overgrown with hawthorn and briars. This was a place where humans rarely trod, leaving other creatures in relative peace. Eventually, after negotiating briars, bogs and barbed-wire, the way was blocked by a twenty-five-foot-high pile of earth and rubbish. Ahead was a timber yard and, having no other choice, I headed for a road via the edge of a cornfield. That field of golden corn was less pleasant than I had expected, the crop growing waist-high from dry, dusty-looking soil. Cornflowers and poppies, which had flourished on the railway, were withered and black here, like burned corpses; only a few straggly nettles and a host of pernicious blood-sucking flies survived in that sea of golden yellow. But the field gave access to the road that led into the town.

The Great Central Railway origins of Brackley Station were easy to recognise, although it had not been one of the company's finest. Down in a cutting, the platform was no longer to be seen and the bridge had gone in a road improvement project. But the booking hall, partly screened by Scots pines and set back from the road instead of occupying the usual position on an overbridge, survived as a tyre sales depot.

There had once been a fair-sized goods yard here, and a warehouse still stood alongside the track, but all around the characterless structures of a modern industrial estate were rising.

25
BRACKLEY AND FINMERE

The road into Brackley was heavily trafficked and dusty pavements, fronted by mundane buildings, smothered the memory of the nearby countryside beneath a depressing and familiar cloak. It seemed typical of so many old towns whose ancient hearts still beat proudly while the gangrene of mediocrity attacks their extremities. But the drab scene gave way to better things: a smallish, well-kept park owned by the National Trust; fine old buildings of local stone; and surprising spaciousness as the road widened into the High Street and acquired small greens and trees on either side, while dropping downhill to the Market Place. A wide range of architecture fronted this open space at the town's centre, and all were compatible. Local stone predominated, from the ancient Magdalen College School and the handsome Town Hall of 1707 to the imposing Tudor-style Bell Tower Hotel and the small, quaint and Victorian Fire Engine House, while thatched roofs and ornate ironwork added richness to the mixture.

Brackley has a long and chequered history and, in its time, has been influential and famous. It was at the castle here in 1215 that the barons opposed to King John met and presented their claims, which later found expression in the Magna Carta. At that time the town was prospering on the wool trade, but decline was to follow, so much so that comment was made during the early 16th century that such a poor place still had a mayor. Yet it still had importance in other ways for, in 1447, Magdalen College School was founded there to give refuge to Oxford scholars fleeing the plague. And it still survived in the 20th century – as a mixed comprehensive.

Local dislike of the monarchy continued long after King John's day and manifested itself again in 1642, when the town's people attacked Royalist troops who were travelling through the town to do battle with Cromwell's men at Oxford. Brackley's irregulars used a motley collection of weapons with devastating effect against Charles's army and the town benefited considerably from the spoils of the ambush, numerous folk celebrating the occasion with the acquisition of their first horse! Such stirring acts of rebellion seem to have ended with the Civil War, the town thereafter settling down to a humdrum existence. And it was the 1832 Reform Bill, rather than the townsfolk, that ended the corrupt arrangement allowing thirty-three privileged and wealthy residents to be represented by two members in Parliament.

Today Brackley is probably best known for its proximity to the motor racing circuit at Silverstone and, on the evening of my arrival, the motor vehicle appeared to be master of the place. It seemed unjust for such a fine town centre to be rudely assaulted by traffic, that a juggernaut lorry should be allowed to manoeuvre back and forth in the historic Market Place as, like some great beast, it prepared to bed down for the night.

The town was quieter the following morning and its charm more readily appreciated, although an attractive-looking public house proved disappointing. The modernised interior had been allowed to keep some of its earlier character – but not much! Although the floor was still made of worn flagstones, the ceiling suffered from a surfeit of newly manufactured beams and the rough-plastered walls supported a brash collection of lamps, with aluminium shades anodised to imitate copper. A microwave oven had pride of place on the bar, dominant among cluttered accoutrements of the fast-food business. Recent successes of the Campaign for Real Ale ensured that hand-pumped beer of a reasonable quality was available, but the food was another matter. My Cornish pasty arrived garnished with a paper napkin, cut in half in an extraordinary exercise in parsimony. Plastic cutlery completed the sad display, although the knife easily cut through the anaemic snack and, unintentionally, the plate of soggy cardboard on which it lay.

Until the late 1950s Brackley had been well served by railways, the seven thousand residents benefiting from the services of two lines. First came the London & North Western Railway's branch from Bletchley to Banbury, opened in 1849, some fourteen years after the people here first petitioned for a railway. A modestly engineered route, following the Ouse Valley, the line made little impact on the landscape. But, typically, when the Great Central came along, half a century later, it marched by in a much grander style, crossing the Ouse Valley on an embankment and an adjacent one on a great viaduct just to the east of the town. This graceful structure, more than one hundred and fifty yards long and carrying the tracks some sixty-two feet above the valley floor, must have offered passengers a fine view of the town, a pretty sight in those days before the raw carcasses of modern warehouses had begun to sprawl over the surrounding fields.

The viaduct was to dominate the valley for more that three-quarters of the 20th century but, a decade after closure of the line, neglect was bringing its problems and the threat of demolition loomed. Local people wanted to keep it and public meetings were held in the Town Hall. The Council did its best to help the campaign, but funds could not be found and the viaduct met its end. The town guide for 1980 carried two photographs of the valley, one taken in 1978, before demolition, and the other the following year. In the intervening months the structure had been blown up and its entire fabric ground down to form hardcore. No trace of it remained.

The ends of the embankments, which had once led to the viaduct, still protruded from either side of the valley. The southernmost one led into a cutting, with a waterlogged floor of heavy red clay. Untidily strewn about with rubbish, its only virtue was to support trees bearing the only edible apples to be found since leaving Annesley. Near here the course of the Great Ouse made a U-turn and a little over a mile from the viaduct the line was again crossing its valley, this time on a high embankment. Brackley remained visible for a time, the Town Hall tower protruding from the skyline and overlooking a patchwork of fields in the undulating countryside. To the west cattle grazed, while to the east were fields of corn, their borders marked by hedgerows and gnarled old trees that almost concealed the roofs of the village of Westbury.

Some of the smaller bridges had been removed along this section, but not the rather plain structure that crossed the river at the spot where Northamptonshire, Oxfordshire and Buckinghamshire all met together, such that a three-legged man could have stood with one foot in each county. Also surviving was the steel-plate bridge over the Banbury branch of the London & North Western Railway, itself on an embankment at that point even though its builders had chosen to follow the river's meandering course. Having parted company with the Ouse for the last time, the Great Central again plunged into a cutting where mare's tail, clover and cornflowers were gradually creeping over the trackbed, and I enjoyed the colourful company of butterflies. For more than a mile the trackbed was host to a line of electricity pylons. But the cutting was remarkable for more than that: in one place sweet peas thrived profusely, completely covering the hawthorns that grew on the bankside. It was here that a variant of the normal brick-arched occupation bridge made its appearance, the vertical abutment walls being taller and the arch much flatter, resulting in a slimmer and more elegant shape that those further north, although most of these had lost their parapet walls.

There was a short break in the cutting near the pretty village of Mixbury and an embankment gave a good view of its 14th-century church tower. Back in the cutting, a few hundred yards on, the line of pylons veered off eastward and a kestrel circled above a rubbish dump where a lane had once bridged the railway. Perhaps the power lines were a fortuitous obstacle to further infill and habitat destruction, not that the rubbish dump was without life – as the kestrel well knew. But death was here too, and its presence came as a shock. Some innate streak of curiosity compelled me to lift the lid of a discarded washing machine; its drum contained four dead rats, the biggest I had ever seen! Somehow comical, they reclined on their backs, mouths partly open in toothy grins. But this was death, the grins were grotesque and blowflies crawled on the bodies, filling the drum of the washing machine with incessant buzzing.

Across the lane the cutting was unspoilt, with tiny flowers dotted about the well-drained track and apple trees that bore fruit. Someone had been planting here too; among the self-set hawthorns were young oaks and sycamores supported by stakes. A mile or so north of Finmere Station the cutting became overgrown as broad-leaved woodland crowded down to the narrow path and even formed an arch over it. From a neglected footbridge made of ancient bull-head rails and rotting sleepers, it was possible to look along the line, but quite impossible to imagine trains thundering through this scene of beauty, birdsong and tranquillity. South of the bridge, the northern extremity of what had once been Finmere Station and goods yard was visible. The cutting levelled out and the woodland fell back to reveal a wide, thinly grassed area where rabbits occupied themselves by grazing while their young gambolled about in the joy of youth.

The station was totally derelict with few relics of the railway to be seen. The chimney-breast of a workmen's hut, a concrete post that had once supported a loading gauge, and the overgrown goods dock were all that remained of the yard. At the site of the passenger station, sturdy trees grew from the platform – one with an eight-inch-diameter trunk. Brick rubble had been tipped into the stairway that led up from the Buckingham to Bicester road, to leave just a few lavatorial yellow and white glazed bricks visible at the top. Two steel-plate bridges, one for each running line, spanned the road between massive blue-brick and stone abutments, which had been built wide enough to support two more bridges if traffic had grown to justify quadrupling of the tracks. This was yet another example of the builder's misplaced optimism, for those original bridges bore the weight of the railway's first and last trains without the need for a second pair.

By the roadside, the station house provided someone with a good home, as did the row of what appeared to be company cottages, built at a respectful distance from the house of the Station Master, and closely

Above Going nowhere fast: BR Standard 'Britannia' Class locomotive *John Milton* is on the rollers at the Rugby Testing Station in the early 1950s. *John Click, Science and Society Picture Library*

Below Pioneer of jet flight: the prototype Gloster E 28 takes off in 1941, using a Whittle engine developed in the Rugby/Lutterworth area. *Air Ministry photograph, author's collection*

The trackbed looking south near Braunston & Willoughby station, about five miles south of Rugby, in the mid 1980s. *Author*

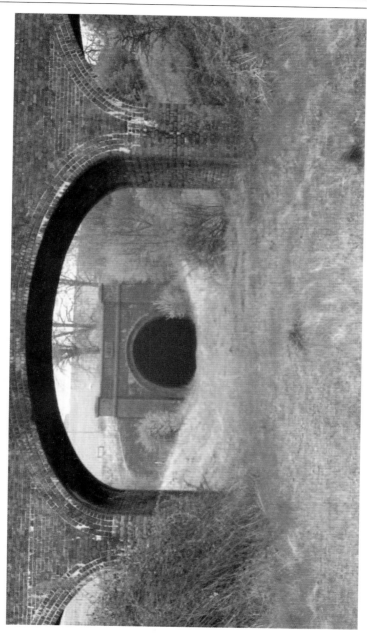

Approaching Catesby Tunnel from the north. *Author*

The loco depot at Woodford Halse, photographed from the top of the fuel oil tank by Woodford's vicar, the Rev R. H. Conway, in 1956.

Rev R. H. Conway

Above Jim Anscomb, Woodford's historian, photographed in his eighty-sixth year on the embankment above the terraced rows of railway houses. Jim was very critical of the photograph, which merged his white hair with the sky! *Author*

Below Castle Street, Woodford: architecture of the industrial north imposed on the Northamptonshire wolds. *Author*

Left On a return visit to Woodford, the author was accompanied by his father, who had been born into a railway family in the village in 1905. Here he is (right) with Jim Anscomb, retired yard foreman. *Author*

Below The pair of octogenarians tour the village. *Author*

Above Sulgrave village. *Author*

Below Sulgrave Manor, ancestral home of the Washington family. *Author*

The route of the 'Master Cutler' twenty years after closure, near Finmere (*above*) and at Twyford, and how it used to be: part of the preserved line south of Loughborough in 2008 (*right*). *All author*

Above The Buckinghamshire Railway Centre, Quainton Road, in 1985. *Author*

Below In this more recent scene at the centre, a venerable 2-4-0 tank engine, built for the London & South Western Railway in 1874 and at work on the main rail network until 1962, is fully restored and pulling passengers again. *Andrew Bratton*

Above Another recent view showing the signal gantry and signal box at Quainton Road Station. *Sheila Lobley*

Below The canal basin at Aylesbury, overlooked by the towering County Offices. *Author*

Richard Hardy as an apprentice at York in 1945, with Driver Joe Oglesby of Sheffield. Richard remembers the occasion well, for he had been allowed to fire on a Sheffield-York service, while the regular fireman rode in the train. At Selby, Driver Oglesby invited Richard to take over and the 22-year-old drove the train and its passengers to the outskirts of York. *Transport Treasury, R. H. N. Hardy*

Above As a schoolboy Richard spent many hours on Amersham Station. He took this photograph in 1940, showing Great Central 'B3' *Earl Haig* about leave for Leicester, in the hands of his good friend Driver Ted Simpson. Driver Simpson had been a fireman on the line when it opened and became a driver in 1911. Their friendship continued long after Richard joined the railway and Ted Simpson retired, in 1941. *Transport Treasury, R. H. N. Hardy*

Below In 1985 the recently retired Richard Hardy, in his role of locomotive inspector to the Buckinghamshire Railway Centre, debriefs a trainee footplate crew. *Author*

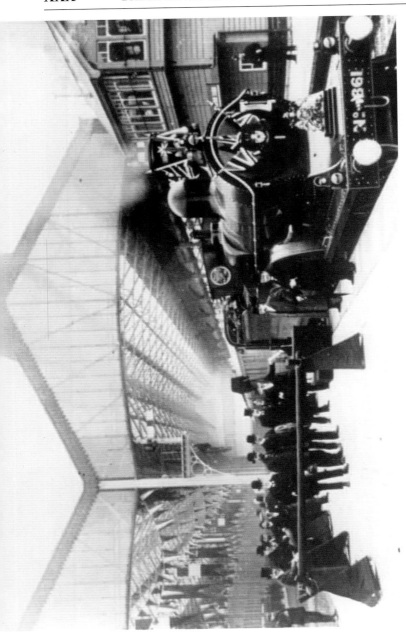

Marylebone Station, terminus of the Great Central, in 1899. The first train is about to depart. *Chiltern Railways*

Marylebone Station frontage in 1902, and the same scene a century later. The unique frontage, somehow combining the architectural style of a country house with a modest hint of metropolitan grandeur, has been tastefully restored to welcome the multitudes that pass through each day. *Chiltern Railways/Chris McKenna*

Part of the immaculately kept concourse of the thriving Marylebone station. *Chris McKenna*

resembling those at Rothley where Madge Sleath had lodged so many years before. On the track, to the south of the bridges, was one more relic: a vandalised lamp-oil tank, its heavy iron cauldron thrown to one side and the circular base of blue brick crumbling, while willow herb sought succour from the lime mortar. Ahead, that good wide trackbed continued atop its embankment, a green tree-lined avenue to the horizon.

The decision of the company to build a station here was questionable. Named Finmere for Buckingham, it stood near the hamlet of Newton Purcell, while Finmere village was two miles away and Buckingham six miles distant. A spur at Brackley, linking the Great Central with the Banbury to Buckingham line of the London & North Western Railway would have served much better. Even without that facility, Buckingham-bound passengers could transfer by changing stations at Brackley, involving a cab ride of less than a mile compared with the six between Finmere Station and Buckingham. Alternatively, they could have changed to a Metropolitan train further south, at Quainton Road, and then joined the LNWR at Verney Junction. Either route offered a service to Buckingham, but the residents of Newton Purcell were probably grateful for the presence of Finmere Station.

Away from the speeding traffic of the main road it was a pleasant little village, seeming to consist of a big house, a farm with an old single-deck tram body in use as a shed, a few thatched cottages and a diminutive church. After the self-appointed guardian of the lane, an aged and ill-tempered Labrador bitch, had been dragged away by her dungaree-clad mistress, I entered the small churchyard. Ancient trees stood within its enclosing hedges, and lichen-covered gravestones, mostly eroded by age and weather until their inscriptions were illegible, gave the place a morbid atmosphere. Other graves, marked with cast-iron crosses, had been squeezed into such a narrow gap between the church wall and a hedgerow that they seemed almost to have been deliberately hidden away. The church itself was a strange yet charming building with pebble-dashed walls, an open bell-tower at one end, a cross at the other, and a very ordinary-looking chimney set to one side in between. Yet the porch was old and ornate, with fine carving, including a bird and serpent; it had been the only part of the church to survive rebuilding in the 1870s.

The village pub, The Shellswell Inn, at the roadside near the railway, was a much more cheerful place. It was the type of building that a railway architect, who had served his apprenticeship in the office of a late-Victorian borough engineer, might have designed on returning from an Alpine holiday. A sort of Edwardian Swiss chalet in red brick, it had a hipped roof and wide eaves, supported by wooden pillars, over the ground floor, and a gable-ended roof with half-timbered dormer windows above the first. It might have been built for trade generated by the railway, but now relied on a few local people and passing motorists, although it was still residential. A doorway surmounted by a sign announcing that Ada L. Healey was licensed to sell beer, wines and spirits 'on six days only' led into the single public room. After being served, and declining the offer of the loan of a daily paper from the rosy-cheeked, greying woman who tended the bar with a brisk and pleasant manner, I sat alone, and, apart from the occasional swishing sound of a passing vehicle, in silence.

The atmosphere was of the inter-war years, brought up to the 1950s by the lavish use of cream paint, now dulled with age. All around were the pleasantly neglected ingredients of a past trendiness; even the cast-iron fireplace, adorned with patterns of grapes and Grecian women, had been painted over, while its red-brick surround had been scratched by darts players as they sharpened their points. Circular tables, with mahogany tops capping cast-iron bases, and old pine kitchen chairs with tapestry cushions littered the room in the way they used to do before antique dealers took an interest in such things. All four walls were clad to waist height in the same cream-painted tongue-and-groove boarding, which also faced the small rectangular bar, while spotlessly clean net curtains filtered and softened the sun's rays as they fell on the scene.

Soon, more customers arrived and I was joined by an elderly couple of Londoners, out for a day's drive, and for half an hour listened to their tales of life in the London Docklands in the 1920s. They told of the people, pubs, neighbourliness and community spirit, which, they said, had been swept away by industrial decline, yet their conversation was lively and optimistic, for they were active folk and not moaners.

By the time I left, the room was bustling with people and Ada L. Healey's sister, invisible in the kitchen, was producing a stream of sandwiches to feed a delivery van driver and an assorted collection of weekend motorists. I never found out whether the inn had gained much succour from the railway, but it was pleasing to see the Misses Healey caring so capably for their present-day customers.

26
FINMERE TO CALVERT

Returning to the embankment, I set off south along that broad avenue-like track in sunshine that showed the wild flowers to good effect, leaving behind the noise of the road and the more intrusive signs of human activity, although, as always, the sound of farm machinery and the occasional aeroplane was difficult to lose.

Within a mile, close to the village of Chetwode, nature had encroached strongly onto the trackbed. The hedgerows were rich in plant life, rabbits lolloped casually across the path, apparently unconcerned by my presence, and pheasants strutted about the adjacent fields. No railway artefacts remained here, except for the ever-present bridges – not a signal post or platelayers' hut had survived. Far ahead, in a cutting, two figures came into view and eventually took the shape of a man and woman with a small dog. As I gradually overhauled them, they looked repeatedly and nervously over their shoulders, anxious as to who the stranger might be. As I drew level, their manner was awkward and the man appeared grateful for the distraction offered by the ritual of tending his pipe. Neither would have spoken first but, once the ice was broken, they were friendly and told how they regularly sought solitude in this place. But, somehow, it was sad that they had brought with them the media-induced fear of strangers.

A long, low embankment that afforded a wide view across flattish fields of mixed crops replaced the cutting and curved gently eastward on its southerly journey. Wild roses bloomed in the hedges and, in the far distance, the tall chimneys of Calvert brickworks reached upward, each emitting a faint smudge of smoke into the blue sky and marking the site of journey's end for the day.

At a place where a small river marking the border between Oxfordshire and Buckinghamshire looped beneath the embankment and back again, so that I passed from Buckinghamshire into Oxfordshire and returned again within a couple of hundred yards, the way was barred. Two footpaths, clearly shown on the map to be following the river bank, did not exist and the only option was to continue forward. An excavator was digging out a section of embankment a short distance ahead and the wisest approach seemed to be the direct one – to stroll up and ask the driver's permission to walk along the line to Calvert. At a distance of a hundred and fifty yards he still had not seen me and continued with his work, but, within a few moments, my problem escalated from a doubt about the legal niceties of my position to a predicament with spine-chilling possibilities. The first shadowy glimpse was numbing. Amongst the trackside undergrowth the dark and ugly form of a massive dog silently took shape. Broad-headed, pug-faced, powerful-chested, the Rottweiler joined the path some twenty yards to my rear. Almost immediately, canine friends and relatives congregated around him – a fellow Rottweiler, a sullen-looking Labrador and a yapping Jack Russell terrier – and none doubted that the embankment was his property.

The Rottweilers lumbered along, steadily gaining on me, with lips curled back to reveal menacing fangs, while the Jack Russell snapped and snarled as only his breed can. Unexpectedly, the Labrador posed the most immediate threat, making repeated close passes, his jaws snapping together, crocodile-like, within an inch or two of my right hip. If anything was going to provoke my downfall that afternoon, it was that black beast. No escape route existed, there were no trees to climb, just the uninviting alternatives of a pathetically unequal race or some sort of inter-species diplomacy, and I chose the latter. A meeting with the digger driver was now a top priority rather than the chore it had seemed a minute previously; after all, he probably had power over these creatures and was unlikely to view trespass as a capital offence. Bravery can be born, of necessity, out of hopelessness, and once I had resolved to accept that whatever was to come should come with dignity, I was able to stroll along with apparent confidence. This amazed me and puzzled the bad-tempered Labrador. His provocations ignored, he fell back to rejoin his fellows, the Jack Russell's yapping subsided to a barely audible chuntering, and the Rotweillers ceased their growling, but still kept their lips curled as they brought up the rear, still hoping for an excuse to fight.

It was a strange and motley procession that arrived alongside the excavator. The driver stopped the machine and climbed down, his features betraying mild amusement as he expressed surprise that the Labrador had not 'ripped the arse' out of my trousers. There had been a time, a few seconds previously, when I would have gladly sacrificed the arse of a thousand trousers in exchange for safe passage, but that had all changed now and my tormentors were lounging placidly in the grass, unbelievably transformed.

Once convinced that I had no destructive intentions against his property, the digger driver's reproach for my trespassing was mild. He turned out to be a local farmer and, as the track ahead was blocked, helpfully suggested an alternative route across his fields. It proved to be a pleasant walk, criss-crossing a young river on rickety footbridges until a well-used path appeared and led into Twyford, a picturesque village, almost idyllic on that sunny afternoon, and certain to be described as a very desirable location by any estate agent with an eye to a sale. But the few ranch-style houses on the outskirts, with double garages for the Mercedes of the nouveau riche, did not overwhelm the village and it was an enjoyable stroll along the road to the churchyard. This was an ideal place to rest, alone beneath great trees, and to look at the handsome church. The building is noted for its Norman entrance, 13th-century woodwork and a monument with the figure of a knight in chainmail armour, while the graveyard contained iron headstones similar to the ones I had seen at Newton Purcell. Across the lane, in a cul-de-sac leading to the vicarage and close by the disused railway, stood the Red Lion Inn. Simple in style, whitewashed and surrounded by gardens, it was as much part of the English country scene as the neighbouring church. Sadly, the equally English licensing hours of those days made an interior inspection impossible.

To the rear of Twyford church the Great Central's trackbed was being utilised by a pig farmer, and two friendly youths, who were repairing a sty, readily gave permission for me to walk through the farm. The callous way in which most pigs in England are treated is a scandal against decency – intelligent creatures grown as an indoor crop. Born onto a floor of steel-mesh, to a mother imprisoned in a stall too narrow to allow her to turn or lay down, allowed to suckle only without comfort or bodily contact until moved to battery cages for fattening, their only glimpse of the world they were born to inhabit was a fleeting one on the way to the slaughter house. But here the pigs were confined only by a single-wire electric fence and seemed content. Each sow had a shelter, space in which to root around, and most had families of healthy looking piglets. These were clean and joyous little creatures that ran under the wire with impunity and raced up to me like excited puppies, before rushing off to join another game, gambolling around, sometimes locked, stag-like, in mock combat.

After passing under the Charndon to Steeple Claydon road, the track became overgrown with mounds of brambles six or seven feet high, but a narrow path wound its way to a gap in the embankment, where a bridge had once crossed the Buckingham road. With the Oxford to Cambridge line of the London & North Western Railway blocking the way ahead, the road, which offered the only bridge across those tracks, was now the best option. From the bridge over the Oxbridge line, there were commanding views in both directions of a twin-track railway, dead straight, with one set of rails burnished bright by regular use, and the other set rusted. To the west the rusted track had been partially lifted; to the east, the ends of the Great Central's severed embankment were visible and beyond was Claydon Junction, where a spur diverged southward from the Oxbridge line to join the still operational section of the Great Central main line.

Soon the roadway passed between two huge flooded claypits, partly hidden behind tall hawthorn hedges; one was being used by a sailing club and the other had become a nature reserve. Looking across this rough terrain, as the land fell away to the south-east, the distant shape of a Great Central Railway station house was visible in the early evening light. Half a mile further on a left turn led down to the village of Calvert. Strangely, those high brickyard chimneys, which dominated the landscape for so many miles around, were masked by trees and vegetation and barely visible now. Strange, too, that there was no background noise of machinery, as there had been in the fields, only birdsong and the calls of geese on the flooded claypit.

Calvert did not truly seem to be a village – I saw neither church, public house nor school – but the approach was pleasant. One side of the main street was graced by a terrace of Edwardian houses, rather similar to those that had housed Woodford's railway workers, but totally unspoilt. No disfiguring rash of stone-cladding scarred the attractive local brickwork and their sash windows were unaltered and well cared for. Across the road stood a bus shelter, built in a style perhaps best described as grandiose-vernacular. Brick-fronted, as might be expected in a village surrounded by brickworks, it had a neatly built arched doorway leading through the brick façade into a shed of curved corrugated asbestos sheeting – a rare, if incongruous, combination of solid municipal and makeshift agricultural architecture.

Alongside the one-time house of the Station Master, which had a juggernaut lorry parked in the garden, lay the remains of the station. A road bridge spanned the site, which was in a cutting with the village side rather higher than country one, but there were no buildings surviving and, with the passage of time, even the bricked-up entrance was no longer visible in the bridge parapet. Railway tracks ran on both sides of the platform, the eastern one being the running line linking Bletchley with Aylesbury and Marylebone, the other a siding to accommodate trains that brought the rubbish of London and Bristol to be dumped in Calvert's disused claypits. Further to the east lay the old and overgrown goods yard, in the process of being colonised by a lot of rabbits and a little rubbish. A few hundred yards to the south were the huge gantries used for unloading containers from the refuse trains, and the double tracks gave the appearance of a working railway. And it was a working railway. This village may have consisted of little more than a terrace or workers' houses, a few council-style dwellings and a smattering of private ones, all huddled beneath the brickworks chimneys, but it was the end of the path I had followed from Annesley and the beginning of a working railway. For the fifty miles from here to Marylebone Station in London, the Great Central remained an operational line. But no scheduled passenger trains travelled its metals to the north of Aylesbury, so it was one of the infrequent local buses that transported me to that town.

27
AYLESBURY

The bus hurried along Buckingham Street, which showed all the signs of leading into an interesting little town, before passing quickly through the Market Square, largely unspoilt on three sides, and diving into a monstrous car park and shopping centre that ruined the appearance of the fourth. In the labyrinthine concrete cavern below this awful building those who arrived by bus were decanted. Squalid, fume-laden, unbearably noisy and artificially lit on the brightest of summer days, its bunker-like environment formed an unwelcoming entrance to an attractive town. They knew well what they were doing, those property developers and their architectural servants, placing money-spinning shops, offices and cars above, while consigning the bus-using underclass to the basement. We did our best to be cheerful, though, we who were socially disadvantaged by the lack of a motor car, and no one could have failed to admire the tenacity of the cleaner who laboured hard and ineffectively against overwhelming odds, with only a mop and bucket to fight the inbuilt grubbiness.

Aylesbury presented a happier image the following morning, walking in from the guest house on Tring Road where I had enjoyed a night's sleep and a breakfast that, in fairness, was perfectly satisfactory but suffered from the inevitable comparison with the feast provided by Mrs Cherry at Sulgrave. For a couple of days the town was to become my base, being convenient for the Buckinghamshire Railway Centre, where enthusiasts run a museum adjacent to the old main line, and Bletchley, from where I could ride back to Aylesbury along Great Central Railway metals on a train normally barred to passengers.

That first morning was sunny and, despite the traffic, the walk pleasant along a fairly nondescript road flanked on one side by the cast-iron railings of a cemetery. But it was nearer the town centre, where the road bridged a canal, that Aylesbury first won my affection. Not that the towpath offered a conventionally pretty scene, but it suited me to swap a road for a canal and to follow a path down below street level, secluded from the town's bustle.

The Aylesbury arm of the Grand Union Canal, which linked the town with the main cut some six miles away, was opened in 1814 and still retained its narrow locks. Well populated by ducks, it was now a placid stretch of water that passed by factory backs, builders' yards and attractive terraces of houses, en route to its terminus at Walton Street basin. At the basin old and new met, not unpleasantly, and aesthetically the old held its own. There were traditionally painted narrow-boats by the score. One held a sickly looking woman, who stood shakily by the aft cabin door in a crumpled satin dressing gown, breathing the morning air and cigarette smoke deeply, apparently unaware of the body of a long-haired cat that floated near the rudder. Possibly both had been victims of similar excesses the previous evening.

A boatyard and a sawmill flourished next to the water, which reflected their image, and yet all was overlooked by modern office blocks. One was conventional, of brick and concrete, another was clad in silver-green glass and had a rhomboidal side elevation that gave it the appearance of having been partly pushed over, while the tower of the County Offices dominated from a distance. A heavy-handed tower of grey concrete, angularly oppressive like the outsize keep of a Norman castle, and as alien to the town's tradition as the Conqueror's fortifications must have been to old England.

A newish road skirted the town centre and passed by the railway station, a far more welcoming place than that provided for visitors arriving by bus. The northern terminus of rail services from Marylebone was surprisingly large and well-kept, although that was probably due more to the efforts of its staff than recent investment. Despite the generous length of the platforms, the buildings were relatively modest and of a neat 1920s style, although an attractive buffet building that still bore the initials of the Great Western Railway, the former joint owner, was probably older. It was an unusually well-kept station, considerably enhanced by flower beds, roses on platforms one and two, sunflowers on three and four. Three platforms had originally been provided for through traffic, while the fourth was a dead-end. A tall traditional-style timber signal box stood to the south, controlling the junction with the line from Princes Risborough, and an abundance of semaphore signals contributed to a scene reminiscent of the days prior to the British Railways Modernisation Plan of the 1950s.

Other traditions survived here too. Near the buffet was a newly restored bench, its freshly varnished woodwork joined to cast-iron ends formed of the letters 'GWR', and the back inscribed 'In Memory of R. Coombes'. It had been provided by the station staff as a memorial to a driver who had begun his career on the Western Region of British Railways, but who always spoke of himself as a 'Great Western man' even though he had been born too late to have worked for that company. He had recently died while on duty at Aylesbury and his memorial was a tell-tale sign of the survival of community spirit and the brotherhood among railway people.

Aylesbury's present station was not the town's first. That distinction had belonged to one built off the High Street and now submerged beneath modern development with only the names of Railway Street and Station Street remaining as physical evidence that it had ever existed. That station's origins went back to the 1830s, when the decision was taken to build the London & Birmingham Railway along a route that passed some seven miles to the east of the town; the local business community, determined not to be by-passed, formed a company to build a single-track branch from the main line at Cheddington. Despite the need to change trains at the junction, the venture was an immediate success, the two hours taken to reach London being only half the time needed to make the same journey by coach. Traders benefited too, especially the breeders of the town's famous ducklings. It was reported that in 1750 four cartloads were transported to London each week, while within a decade of its opening the Cheddington branch was transporting as much as a ton of ducklings each day.

Competition arrived in 1863 when the Wycombe Railway opened a branch from the Great Western main line at Princes Risborough, which offered Aylesbury's residents a route to Paddington – albeit a circuitous one requiring a change of trains. Shortly afterwards, in 1868, the Aylesbury & Buckingham Railway began operations northwards from the town to Verney Junction, on the Oxford to Bletchley line. This company operated from a small station owned jointly with the Great Western, which had just absorbed the Wycombe company, situated on the present site. Within a few weeks the Great Western converted its track into the town from broad to standard gauge, allowing its

Aylesbury trains to continue northward beyond the town and marking an early defeat for the proponents of Brunel's seven-foot gauge.

The London & North Western Railway, by this time operating the Cheddington branch, answered this competition by improving services and rebuilding its station. However, the arrival of the Metropolitan Railway in 1892, with a direct route to its London terminus at Baker Street, was a severe blow to the existing operators. With cheaper fares and a schedule that virtually halved the time previously taken to reach the metropolis, it soon became dominant in the area. Within a few years it was to take over the Aylesbury & Buckingham Company, a struggling little enterprise that never paid a dividend, and would thus provide the Great Central with a route into London.

With the arrival of the Metropolitan Railway, the Cheddington branch suffered stagnation and decline, eventually losing its passenger service in 1953, although a desultory goods traffic lingered for a further ten years. As Aylesbury's first railway foundered, its rivals thrived and, in 1894, the joint station was extended to accommodate the Metropolitan's trains. The requirements of the Great Central, which began using the station in 1899, led to further improvements and work to eliminate a notoriously vicious curve in the track. Ownership became very complicated in 1907, when the Metropolitan & Great Central Railways Joint Committee was formed to administer the line from London to Verney Junction, and control of the old Wycombe line was taken over by the Great Western & Great Central Railways Joint Committee, resulting in Aylesbury Joint Station achieving the unusual distinction of being managed jointly by two joint committees!

In the mid-1920s further improvements were made and the station gained its present appearance. Although it has lost its passenger trains to the north, Aylesbury retains a frequent service to Marylebone, mostly over the Metropolitan route, with considerably fewer services using the former Great Central & Great Western Joint line through Princes Risborough and High Wycombe.

The station stood just outside the town centre, with a stream meandering by the frontage, and on that day, in a neglected spot by the steps of a footbridge, two black cats lay on its bank to sunbathe and watch the ducks. Meanwhile, across the way, modern Aylesbury rose skyward: that inescapable County Office tower, a multi-storey car park and the ugly backside of the Friar's Square development. Mercifully, the roughcast concrete and curtain walls of vertical concrete slats were partially softened by trees, saved at the time of redevelopment, perhaps betraying the designer's knowledge that his work was unfit to stand alone. Through this maze of concrete crudity and tawdriness, a footpath led to the Market Square. A market no longer – that had been moved to the concrete shopping centre – it seemed to lack purpose except, perhaps, as a viewing point of surrounding architecture. Possibly the square would be a happier place if the market was to return and bring human activity with it. But, in fairness, it was superior to many town squares, with its cobbled central area set about with trees, statues of local worthies, recumbent lions, and a tall Victorian-Gothic clock tower with a once-useful appendage thoughtfully provided at its base by the Metropolitan Drinking Fountain & Cattle Trough Association.

Overlooking the square from the south was the 18th-century County Hall, built of brick and stone, with three arches of the old Corn Exchange on one side leading through to the cattle market and a new Civic Centre. The building still housed the Crown Court and meetings of the County Council, the courtroom having been painstakingly restored after a fire in 1970 – by the same architect's department that designed the dreadful County Office block! There were other fine buildings too: a Georgian public house with a fine iron balcony, an 18th-century creeper-clad house now used as a bank and, up a cobbled alleyway in the north-west corner, the medieval King's Head coaching inn. Behind this corner of the square lay the remaining part of the old town, a fascinating maze of narrow streets and ancient buildings on the gentle slope leading to St Mary's church. In Temple Square, an intimate place where five streets meet, an old ash tree shaded 18th-century buildings and a popular public house. The unspoilt frontage, lacking any sign of gentrification, made the pub irresistible. Sadly, the interior had been modernised, with reasonable taste but leaving little character. Still, the customers made up for that: a ruddy-faced man of bucolic appearance, clad in a shabby gabardine raincoat and ancient trilby, nursed his beer and belched quietly amidst sharp-suited young men and bright-eyed office girls with their chilli con carne, while a few punk rockers gathered round a constantly, if quietly, bleeping video game. Busy as he was, the landlord found time for a few words about the weather, the beer he served, and how the Aylesbury Brewery Company was now part of a combine and its beer had not been brewed in the town for forty-odd years.

Castle Street, with its pavement raised a good five feet above road level, was a place where the abuse of old Aylesbury could almost be forgotten. Time, however, had not stood still – and quite rightly so – a picturesque row of cottages having recently been given a new lease of life as flats, but with their exteriors unspoilt. Round a corner, Parson's Fee, again with raised pavements, led uphill towards the church. Timber-framed houses graced the street and near the top, close to the churchyard, a fine arched gateway led to the house among great trees where John Wilkes, the town's radical 18th-century MP, once lived.

St Mary's, set in its extensive and well-kept churchyard, was the tranquil centre of Aylesbury's old town. A solid, substantial building of grey stone with a squat, massive-looking central tower giving rise to an equally squat lead-sheathed spire, the church had charm without elegance. From its gateway, the view past the County Museum and down Church Street was of timber-framed houses, leaning at conflicting angles with a haphazard harmony. To the left the narrow, cobbled Pebble Lane, with its old water pump and expensive restaurants, led down into Kingsbury, site of the town's first market and a stone's throw from the present-day Market Square.

Regrettable though it was that redevelopment was not used to preserve and, perhaps, enhance the character of the Market Square, it was encouraging to see that lessons had been learned. Almost hidden down a narrow street on the east side stood the Hale Leys Shopping Centre. In comparison with most other new buildings in the town, it was both modern and imaginative and blended with its surroundings. A circular red-brick corner tower was supported on a central pillar, with a hexagonal slate-covered awning fanning out over the entrance in a pattern repeated above by the steeply sloping conical roof, which complimented an interesting slate roofscape beyond. This was not timid architecture. And neither, in the days when property speculators had power akin to that of medieval barons, was it a timid decision to preserve the pattern of the old streets and to offer no visible concession to concrete or motor cars. It was good to see a modern building that did not challenge its neighbours, but stood among them with a confident individuality; one that did not need foliage to conceal its ugly lines, yet met the needs of present-day commerce.

Looking around at the activity and bustle, it was difficult to imagine the little town of five thousand souls that had first welcomed the railway. The population had since grown more than tenfold and was set to reach sixty thousand by 1990, but not all that growth had been due to the railway. The doubling of the populace between 1960 and 1980 occurred when the railway was in decline and was the result of a decision to house London's overspill in the town. But Aylesbury has much to thank the railway for; the earlier lines not only helped the struggling duck-rearers, but laid an industrial base and provided good communication with the capital, while the arrival of the Great Central Railway took the town out of a backwater and placed it squarely on a main line.

It was the ease of communication between this area of rich diary farming and the nation's major cities that attracted the English

Condensed Milk Company in 1870. The company's plant soon prospered and, only a decade later, was using the milk of some two thousand cows. When I visited the town, the factory had long since passed into the ownership of a multi-national group, but remained one of the principal employers, producing vast quantities of dehydrated foodstuff and soup. Other businesses provided the people of the town with a variety of occupations; they staffed a large printing works, manufactured office equipment, put drinks into bottles and produced chemical potions to disguise the true colour of the hair of the vainer ones amongst us.

My brief stay in Aylesbury was enjoyable. Its old quarter still had a country-town feel, except during the lunchtime invasion of office workers. It was a fair town and, it must be conceded, some of its modern architecture was imaginative, but my fondest memories are of the quiet canalside and narrow streets. And that memorial seat on the railway station, a modest reminder that, despite all the frantic activity of this modern town, a caring community survived.

28
THE BUCKINGHAMSHIRE RAILWAY CENTRE

By the late 1980s, two railway preservation societies had established themselves on the Great Central's route to London. On the northern section the group based at Loughborough was running a well-known working railway each weekend of the year while, at the southern end, six miles north of Aylesbury, another scheme was flourishing under the auspices of the Buckinghamshire Railway Society. It may be a more modest operation than its northern counterpart, possessing a very short running line and opening its gates to visitors only during the summer months, but its exhibits are impressive and location charming. Centred on the old Metropolitan & Great Central station at Quainton Road, less than a half mile south of the junction where the two companies' tracks joined, it captured that elusive feel of the country junction station, isolated yet purposeful.

The scene appeared much as it must have done half a century previously, with only the splendid expresses and heavy freight trains of the main line absent from view. Certainly the countryside had not changed a great deal; the neat little station remained surrounded by the Vale of Aylesbury's green fields, overlooked from rising ground to east and west by the attractive villages of Quainton and Waddesdon. Different in style, each village reflected its past. At Waddesdon the opulence of the Rothschild family, who were Lords of the Manor for three-quarters of a century, was evident, while Quainton retained its simple charm, in many ways probably little changed since the 18th-century agricultural labourer, Joseph Mayett, wrote the story of his life in these parts.

The atmosphere is especially pleasant on summer Sundays, when visitors flock to savour the air of a country railway and watch the society's well-kept engines haul their trains along the demonstration tracks.

Quainton Road Station was itself good-looking – perhaps not the prettiest in the land, but charming and typical of Metropolitan Railway architecture in the area. On the up platform a building of brownish brick, with tall chimneys and a simple white-painted awning, housed the ticket office, waiting room, porters' room and toilets. The opposite platform, reached by a lattice footbridge, had only a wooden, awningless waiting room that resembled a grounded goods van and was currently the home of a well-stocked railway bookshop. This platform was triangular, having been built to serve both the main line and a branch that once meandered to the village of Brill, some six miles to the west. The station had a thriving appearance, neatly kept with well-tended flower beds, period advertisements on the diagonal palings of the platform fences and plenty of rolling stock in the goods yards that flanked the main line, although that main line was now a single freight-only track and some of the stock in the yard was in urgent need of attention by the society's restoration workers.

Having walked the course of the London Extension, perhaps proving that I had more than a passing interest in the railway, the society provided me with a guide in the person of Trevor Davey, a member of the executive committee. We sat out in the sun, at a picnic table near the goods yard entrance, eating the sort of ploughman's lunch that Joseph Mayett would probably have offered his right arm for, if only the women who staffed the society's catering coach had been there in his time, while Trevor told me a lot about the railway and a little about himself. Trevor and his wife travelled from their home in Potters Bar to Quainton each weekend to tackle the many jobs that needed to be done, building up an invaluable store of practical experience and background knowledge in the process. On weekdays he was a design engineer, at weekends a qualified engine driver and Chairman of the Society's engineering committee. With his everyday job being restricted to light engineering, he viewed his hand-dirtying trips to Quainton as a refreshing change. But, if I know too little of Trevor, it is to my shame that I know even less about his wife, a quiet girl who volunteered to work that day despite being in pain from a badly burned foot and who exchanged a few words before limping away to work unobtrusively among the crowds.

Our lunch break provided a useful opportunity for Trevor to explain the history of the site, which proved interesting for an unexceptional-looking station. What was now the main line had belonged originally to the Aylesbury & Buckingham Railway, which opened a station here, a little to the north of the present one, in 1868. The Aylesbury & Buckingham had been a single-track railway, which meandered through the countryside to link Aylesbury's Great Western station to the London & North Western Railway at Verney Junction, where another branch had diverged from that company's Bletchley to Oxford line to provide a route onward to Buckingham. In 1891 the Metropolitan Railway had taken over the Aylesbury & Buckingham as a means of extending its own line, which was due to reach Aylesbury the following year, northward to Verney Junction. But it was to be much more than a modest extension into northern Buckinghamshire, because it brought the Metropolitan closer to another railway that Sir Edward Watkin chaired, the Manchester, Sheffield & Lincolnshire, and hastened the fulfilment of his dream of a route to London and beyond. In preparation for this new role, the track was doubled and new stations built, including that at Quainton Road. At this new station, a junction was formed with the Wotton Tramway, previously an isolated and rustic line owned by the Duke of Buckingham, which ran westward to Brill. Later, trains using the Great Central's London Extension were to join the Metropolitan tracks at a junction about half a mile north of Quainton Road Station.

Following the opening of the Great Central's route, and after an acrimonious period in its relationship with the Metropolitan, the two companies formed a joint committee to administer the system between Verney Junction and the point where their tracks again diverged outside their London termini. This committee managed Quainton Road Station and the branch to Brill, so the junction to the north of the station became the meeting point of the Great Central and the Joint lines.

These complexities of ownership were to continue for many years. Even when the 1923 grouping of railway companies brought the Great Central into the ambit of the London & North Eastern Railway, the Metropolitan remained independent, only losing its autonomy when absorbed into London Transport a decade later. Soon afterwards, in 1935, Quainton Road lost its branch to Brill, followed by the passenger service to Verney Junction the next year, although freight trains continued to use the latter route until 1947. Yet the scene at Quainton remained a busy on; slow trains still called, expresses hurried through and the two sizeable goods yards handled considerable traffic.

Trevor Davey was able to speak of wartime activity here – not that he was old enough to have witnessed it – but some of the more senior members had. Additional sidings were laid so that oil could be off-loaded from tanker trains into road vehicles in the relative safety of the countryside where, if the worst happened, a Nazi bomb might have destroyed a train without devastating a surrounding town. About that time, a locomotive inspection and servicing pit was installed, but Quainton Road was never honoured by the presence of an engine shed during its working life. There was constant activity as well, with the arrival of Great Central freight trains, which often laid up in the goods yard to await a path into the Metropolitan section. Some coal trains were so long that they had to be divided into sections at this point because the station loops, sidings and signalling block lengths on the Metropolitan were too short to accommodate them.

Following the end of the war goods services to Verney Junction ceased and the track was lifted a few years later, but main-line traffic continued to pound through Quainton Road until the final decline and closure of the Great Central route. The line north of Aylesbury then became the domain of Freightliner trains, carrying London's refuse to the worked-out claypits at Calvert, empty workings of Marylebone-based diesel multiple units on their way to be serviced at Bletchley, and the occasional load of domestic coal, or even a tanker of French wine heading for a bottling plant at Aylesbury.

According to Trevor Davey, the London Railway Preservation Society, which began the project at Quainton Road, had no special interest in either the Great Central or Metropolitan Railways and chose the site purely for the opportunities it offered. The Society, which had been acquiring rolling stock for preservation since the early 'sixties, desperately needed a permanent base where exhibits could be housed and renovated. Eventually the various sites were reduced to a short list, the strongest contenders being Buntingford, near Royston, and Quainton. Buntingford had the advantage of being on a branch line, but was threatened by a road scheme. Quainton Road was a spacious site, essential for a large collection of locomotives and rolling stock, and stood adjacent to a line that appeared ripe for closure. Although none of the members would have wished to see another railway close, they were well aware of the advantage of being on hand if the Metropolitan & Great Central line met its expected fate and, mindful of the eventual possibility of running a service to Aylesbury, they moved onto the site in 1969.

While the dream of running steam trains to Aylesbury remained one of the group's ambitions, this had proved impossible due to British Rail's continued use of the line. For a number of years British Rail even seemed to be deliberately unhelpful, insisting on the removal of the connections between the goods yards and the running line and so isolating the Society's activities in the two yards from the main line and each other. Happily, the situation at the time of my visit had improved and the future was looking hopeful. The Buckinghamshire Railway Society, which was then running the site, was regularly chartering a British Rail train to shuttle visitors to and from Aylesbury, and was negotiating to be allowed to use its own steam locomotives to do the work.

In the early days, the Society had begun by purchasing the old down yard, but soon found it necessary to expand into the up yard as well, buying part of it and leasing the remainder and the station buildings from British Rail. While we sat at the picnic table, I remarked how well-kept and attractive the station looked. Trevor hoped that it would soon look even better, with flower beds on the public approach to further brighten things up. As we strolled into the up yard, much of it grassed over and with boundary hedges growing tall, visitors were arriving in large numbers and Trevor explained that four or five hundred was a normal attendance on a Sunday afternoon when engines were in steam. On bank holidays a thousand was usual, and six thousand visitors over a bank holiday was not unknown, although attendances did tend to be 'weather dependant', he added ruefully.

On that particular day everything was right; the sun shone, birds sang and an engine puffed quietly up and down. It was a splendid machine, a Great Western Railway pannier tank engine of 1930, immaculate in dark green with gleaming brass and copperwork. For those intent on a train ride, it hauled a solitary coach a couple of hundred yards through the goods yard, while grown men watched entranced. Trevor explained how the engine had been kept in good condition by London Transport, which took it over from British Railways in the 1960s for use on works trains, and mused whether it had ever shared a siding with the old Metropolitan engine working in the down yard.

Several organisations had their bases in the yard, where they stored and repaired locomotives. In Trevor's view the principal one was the 6024 Locomotive Preservation Society, which had already made significant progress with locomotive number 6024 *King Edward I*. This once handsome machine had travelled more that one and a half million miles during the thirty-two years it spent hauling crack expresses for the Great Western Railway and British Railways' Western Region, before being withdrawn in 1962. In a sense it had been cut down in its prime to make way for new diesel engines, never having been put out to grass on light work before being dispatched to the scrapyard at Barry Island where so many relics of the steam age languished. She was a massive machine, weighing in at all of 136 tons, and a massive job of restoration. But the volunteers who had rescued her hulk, rusting and decayed after eleven years of neglect in the damp, salt-laden air of the scrapyard on the South Wales coast, had already stripped her down, repaired her component parts and begun the process of reassembling her into the splendid machine she had once been.

Also situated in the up yard were the locomotives of the Ivatt Trust. H. G. Ivatt was the Chief Locomotive Engineer of the London Midland

& Scottish Railway from the end of the Second World War until nationalisation and his best-known work was probably to design some fine little 2-6-0 engines for light mixed-traffic duties. Two of the remaining four examples of the tank engine version were owned by the Trust, as was an example of the tender version. They were definitely creatures of the post-war era, designed for ease of maintenance while possessing the latest refinements. They had enclosed cabs to protect their crews from the weather and specially shaped coal bunkers to give a clear view when running in reverse but, with their tall chimneys, high domes and slim, elegantly tapered boilers, they conformed to almost everyone's idea of what a steam engine should look like. In the words of Trevor Davey, 'They possess real charm.'

Perhaps the unlikeliest resident of the site was a three-coach London Underground train of the 1930s. It was unlikely ever to run at the Centre, but had carried millions of folk around the capital and was of a type familiar to Londoners and visitors from all quarters of the globe, until replaced in the early 1980s. So it was worth preserving for that reason alone and perhaps, one day, might be restored to good enough order to make special runs on London Transport tracks.

The most unusual, if not the most visually exciting, engines on the site belonged to the Sentinel Trust, a society that had made it its business to collect examples of the locomotives produced by the Sentinel Wagon Works of Shrewsbury. The Trust had five exhibits at Quainton, four industrial shunting engines and a three-coach railcar unit, none of which could be thought of as resembling a steam locomotive in any way, but they represented a type once commonplace in Britain and abroad. The Sentinel company was probably best known as a manufacturer of steam lorries, tractors and even buses but, between 1923 and being taken over by Rolls-Royce in 1956, they also produced an unusual and advanced range of rail vehicles. Their power unit, derived from that fitted to the road vehicles, was supplied with high-pressure steam from a vertical boiler and connected to the driving axle by chains. Most also had a gearbox, which made them very rare creatures indeed among steam locomotives. This transmission system made the characteristic driving wheels and connecting rods of the traditional locomotive unnecessary, allowing the chassis of a Sentinel locomotive to resemble that of a four-wheeled truck. Technically fascinating machines they may have been, but the examples of Sentinel shunters at Quainton looked distinctly uninspiring, the oldest resembling a rectangular water tank on wheels, while its younger sisters looked like diesel shunters.

On the other hand, the steam railcars produced by the company possessed rather more in the way of style. The engine was enclosed within one end of a passenger coach, driving the wheels of one of the bogies and producing a useful vehicle for lightly used services. The London & North Eastern Railway, among others, operated a large fleet and similar vehicles were exported to Europe and the Empire. Sadly, none of the English vehicles survived, but the enthusiasts at Quainton had recently imported one of the most advanced examples ever built. It stood in a siding, alien in appearance, its grey paintwork peeling, yet this acquisition had the potential to become one of the most exciting steam restoration projects in Britain. Exported new to Egypt in 1951, the three-car unit was capable of whisking its 186 passengers along at more than 60mph. The vehicle was entirely British, with mechanical parts made by Sentinel and coachwork by Metro-Cammell, but somehow, with a large headlamp set in the cab roof and cowcatcher-like skirts shrouding the front end below the buffer beam, it resembled an American streamlined diesel train of the 1940s. A pair of six-cylinder steam engines, hidden beneath the floor of one of the coaches and supplied with steam by an oil-fired boiler, provided the power. And, just like the diesels that superseded it, the unit could be driven from a cab at either end.

Inside one of the coaches, members of the Sentinel Steam Trust were replacing panelling and fittings lost during its period of out-of-use storage in Egypt. Skeletal heaps of tubular steel seats told a strange tale; their plywood seats and backs had been purloined by Egyptians, who prized anything wooden because it could so easily be reused. Conversely, valuable metal items, routinely stolen in Britain, lay untouched. According to Trevor Davey, the vehicle had been in remarkably good condition on arrival, the dry heat of the desert providing a far friendlier environment for railway relics than the damp, salt-laden air of a scrapyard on the South Wales coast. In little more than six months, since the train arrived at Quainton Road, the restoration group had made rapid progress; windows had been glazed, carriage roofs re-felted and the engines turned over.

The station footbridge provided an ideal vantage point for viewing the site and for a while we stood there talking. Apparently, the bridge owed its survival to the Society, and Trevor, in his role with the Engineering Committee, had played a leading part. The problem had been that the lower part of the structure had become badly corroded and British Rail, concerned about the danger to its freight trains as they passed beneath, had ruled that it must be taken down. The prospect of demolition had appalled the Society, which would not only have lost an authentic feature in the station scene, but also the physical link between the two sites, which would then have been isolated on either side of an operational railway. Fortunately, co-operation with British

Rail proved possible and the bridge was shored up until the end of the operating season. Then the volunteers set to work. First, the rivets securing the bridge to its supports were removed and a crane, standing on the British Rail track, lifted it onto one of the station platforms. Next, the remaining rivets were taken out, the lattice sections dismantled, new girders made to replace the rusted ones and the span reassembled at ground level before being lifted back into position. The result – a bridge that few would recognise as anything other than original, the vital link between the two sides of the site maintained and the station scene preserved.

The footbridge led into the down yard, where the Society had first begun its work. Locomotives preserved on this site were smaller, though no less historic, than those in the up yard, many having been built for industrial users – power stations, collieries, chemical plants, paper mills and quarries. There was also an interesting collection of carriages and wagons, some used regularly on a vintage train.

Soon after taking over the site, Society members had erected a large concrete engine and carriage shed to protect themselves and their vehicles from the weather. Spanning three lines, on what had been the trackbed of the Brill branch, the shed housed many fine exhibits including historic coaching stock and small locomotives. Probably the most eye-catching was an old London & North Western Railway coach. Mounted on six-wheeled bogies, its long clerestory-roofed body, with end doors set in recesses, was reminiscent of a 19th-century American carriage, but it could not have been more British. Built at Wolverton Carriage Works in 1901, it was first used as a dining car on Scottish expresses on the West Coast Main Line. Trevor Davey explained a little more of its unusual history and how it had been acquired, almost by chance, from British Rail.

'The story goes back to one of our very early open days, in the late 'sixties, when a gentleman who worked at Wolverton was visiting the site and mentioned that they had an old LNWR saloon coach in the works for breaking. He thought it a shame to smash up such a beautiful vehicle and asked if we could take it.'

Funds were raised to purchase the coach for the Society and its future looked secure, then an unexpected problem arose to threaten the project. Higher authorities had suddenly realised that it was no ordinary coach, but one that had recently been retired after fifty years of service on the Royal Train. Tradition stipulated that Royal Train vehicles must not be sold and, in Trevor's words, 'they became very cagey about releasing it'.

Fortunately the authorities were persuaded to disregard tradition, although they insisted on painting the coach white, to obliterate its

Royal Train livery, before delivery to Quainton Road. On arrival it was restored to its original London & North Western Railway colours, brownish-maroon bodywork with the roof, window surrounds and a stripe along the waistline in an off-white colour, a combination known among the fraternity as 'plum and spilt milk'. Although a similar coach exists in the National Railway Museum, the people at Quainton view theirs as unique, because its luxurious interior remained unaltered. Except for the fitting of a couple of antique-looking electric fans, it remained as it was when used as a staff coach by the Royal servants, with richly carved woodwork, tapestry-covered seats with leather armrests, a wine rack adjacent to each table and, between the two saloons, a kitchen equipped with a massive and ancient gas stove.

Other items of rolling stock in the building included a London & North Eastern Railway compartment coach. Built in 1938 to a design by Sir Nigel Gresley, it was rescued from dereliction and virtually rebuilt at Quainton before being lovingly restored to its original livery of varnished teak. Goods vehicles had not been forgotten either; there was one designed to carry fruit and flowers, another for milk churns, and various others made redundant when their payloads vanished from the railway. My guide viewed the paucity of preserved goods vehicles as a tragedy, remarking that few preservation schemes would be able to capture the atmosphere of a freight railway.

'To have seen one of those enormously long, loose-coupled coal trains being hauled by a steam engine was an incredible sight and, sadly, it is something we will never witness again.'

Outside in the yard were yet more locomotives, including some early diesel shunters and what seemed a multitude of industrial steam engines. Built by once-familiar firms that existed no more, their appearances ranged from the mundane to the remarkable. One of the more unusual types were the fireless engines, which drew their steam from a factory boiler and stored it for use in a giant 'Thermos flask' that replaced the locomotive boiler, an ideal system for use in oil refineries, chemical works and other places where engines with open fires would not have been welcome. There were other engines here too that had been designed for specific purposes. One strange little machine, affectionately referred to as 'the flying buffer-beam', and said to be the smallest standard-gauge locomotive in Britain, had been built to work the private tracks of a Rayon works alongside the Dee estuary. There had been a problem because the industrial track passed through a very low tunnel, under the Chester to Holyhead main line, so Peckett of Bristol was asked to build this special little engine. Standing about five feet high at the chimney top and scarcely visible behind its standard-size buffer-beam, it would have fitted well into the Reverend Awdry's railway stories for children.

Nearby, temporarily out of use awaiting repair, stood one of the most remarkable survivors among British railway engines, an ancient 2-4-0 well tank locomotive, built for the London & South Western Railway in 1874 and in regular commercial use until 1962. One of a class of eighty-five that began life working suburban passenger services out of Waterloo, it was already obsolete by the 1890s when eighty-two of its sisters were scrapped. The three survivors were transferred, in what must have seemed the autumn of their days, to the Wenford Bridge branch in Cornwall. There they worked for a further sixty-seven years, defying all attempts to find a suitable replacement, trundling trainloads of china clay along the poorly laid and winding track of that West Country mineral line. In their later years they became objects of pilgrimage for rail enthusiasts and, when withdrawal eventually came, two were preserved. The profile of one of them, No 0314, featured proudly on the logo of the Buckinghamshire Railway Society, a remarkable tribute to a humble piece of mid-Victorian engineering that found a niche and survived into the latter half of the 20th century.

A footpath led alongside the demonstration track to a newly erected signal box. Neither Metropolitan nor Great Central Railway in origin,

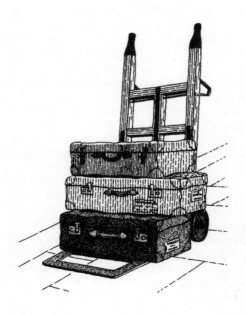

the box had been rescued from Harlington on the Midland main line, but nevertheless complimented the scene, and its gallery provided a fine view across the station to the open ground beyond. It was impossible not to admire the achievements of the volunteers who had restored a derelict station and re-created the atmosphere of a past era. Milk churns awaited collection while suitcases rested on a porter's barrow, just as he would have left them to answer a telephone call fifty years before; gardens had been planted, palings repaired, tracks laid, locomotives, coaches and wagons restored. And, every bit as important, the architects and builders of this re-created world welcomed the public to share in its delights. All of this had been achieved by a society with some six hundred members, of which, Trevor Davey told me, about ten per cent were active workers. There were all types of people from all types of background: men and women, young and old, all united in their affection for the railway. It would have been easy to think of the men as playing out their boyhood fantasies, but such hard work must have involved more than that, and what of the women? There were plenty of them, some happy to be doing traditional women's work such as serving refreshments, selling tickets and staffing the souvenir shop. But others were breaking new ground.

As Trevor and I stood on the gallery of the signal box, the old Metropolitan Railway tank engine, resplendent in red livery, pulled and pushed its train of vintage carriages up and down the demonstration track. On the footplate was a blonde girl, clad in faded blue overalls, grease-top cap and heavy boots, being passed out as a fireman by a visiting inspector. She was not the only female to crew an engine at Quainton and was certainly not a token woman, having climbed the same laborious promotional ladder as her male colleagues.

So authentic was the atmosphere that the ending of the day's activities came as a surprise. The scene had been so absorbing, the leisurely yet purposeful pace creating an atmosphere so pervasive, that it was difficult to think of the railway as an exhibit, a stage on which the curtain must inevitably fall. But that is what it was and, in the late afternoon, the performance ended. Each train drew alongside its platform and waited, each engine simmered quietly. Soon their fires would be raked out and the night would chill their bodies.

Until the next steam day this place would lie quiet and deserted, its carefully nurtured exhibits reduced to inanimate hulks of cold iron. The railway folk said their farewells before setting off for home. Each could go to bed that night well satisfied with the day's efforts, perhaps to awake as a bank clerk, gardener, general practitioner or plasterer, but in their hearts all were railwaymen.

29
RIDING WITH THE DRIVER

Riding the remnant of the Great Central Railway north of Aylesbury was difficult, but although no public passenger trains travelled the route British Rail graciously came to my assistance. The message from the Assistant Traffic Manager at Bletchley was to be on platform 8 at 16.30 hours to await the 16.40 departure for Aylesbury. This was no ordinary service for the general public, although it was a routine one for train staff. Each weekday, one of the diesel multiple units that operated between Marylebone and Aylesbury was sent to Bletchley for maintenance. So, each afternoon, a Bletchley crew would deliver a newly serviced train to Aylesbury and collect another for delivery to the maintenance depot.

The appointed time came and went, and so did the well-filled 17.15 for Bedford, yet there was no sign of my train. Eventually, a slightly built, youngish man in railway uniform appeared and introduced himself as Malcolm Simpson, my driver. As we walked alongside the tracks to the depot, he explained that the delay was due to the fitter finding an unforeseen fault, which he was then correcting. We found the six-coach multiple unit awaiting our arrival, collected our guard, climbed aboard and began the complicated series of shunting operations necessary to get us onto the Aylesbury line. First we drove back to platform 8, then alighted and walked back to the rear cab before setting off, in reverse, to the carriage sidings, while the guard hurried through the train closing windows as we approached the carriage washing plant. Once through this giant version of a car-wash, we repeated the ritual of changing ends, this time climbing down onto the ballast to walk back to the cab we had occupied originally, before moving off to begin our journey.

The first section of the route led westward, along a remnant of the London & North Western Railway's Oxford to Cambridge line. During a period of optimism, some thirty years previously, a great concrete viaduct had been built to form a flyover, carrying Oxbridge line trains high over the tracks of the West Coast Main Line at the south end of Bletchley station. Soon we were climbing the steep gradient alongside the station, then we swung round high above the town and the multiple tracks of the main line. Below, to the right, the eight platforms of Bletchley station lay beneath the tangle of overhead wires and gantries, while leftward an overgrown embankment, which had once carried a spur for northbound main line trains to join the Oxford route, closed with us. Descending to ground level as we left behind the station and viaduct, all trace of railway optimism faded as the double track merged into a single line, via a spring-loaded point (no need to pay a signalman) to be taken at a maximum speed of 15mph. All the while Driver Simpson was talking, explaining methods of working, pointing out features along the route and telling me about the job.

He was a Londoner, with dark hair that tended to fall over one eye in a loose wave, quick movements and astuteness without the smart-Alec mannerisms of the stereotype East-ender. He had not arrived on the job as the son of a railway family, previous Simpsons having laboured in the London docks, but Malcolm had spent his final years at school watching the docks close. Leaving school, he tried his hand at a number of different jobs until 1972, when he started his railway career at King's Cross and soon became 'second man' on the Cambridge run. Two years later he transferred to Euston, where he passed out as a driver and began working the electric trains of the West Coast Main Line. Marriage, to a nursing sister, brought him to Bletchley in 1979, where he mainly drove electric trains on the stopping services to and from London. Having watched the decline of the docks, he feared for the railway and, as much as he welcomed the Aylesbury run for the change of routine, he found the condition of the line a constant reminder of the threat then facing the rail system.

'Fred Karno's railway' he called it, as we trundled along at the maximum permitted speed of 25mph, slowing still further for the ungated and unmanned level crossings. We passed the site of interchange sidings near Swanbourne and rolled along past long-dead country stations that had once played a vital part in the lives of these little communities, linking their inhabitants with the market town and the district hospital, as well as with relatives and friends. Perhaps the strangest sign of those penny-pinched times that Malcolm pointed out to me was a reflective Distant signal. A recent innovation of an obscure committee, this strange device consisted of a white board with a semaphore Distant signal depicted in reflective paint. Seen at night, in the beam of a locomotive headlamp, it would appear as a disembodied signal arm set in the horizontal 'danger' position. Unfortunately, the trains on this line did not have headlamps!

As we ran through Winslow, both the driver and guard were keen to tell me of the successful 'shoppers' specials' that had recently called there. Advertised by a poster, pasted up alongside the faded notice of closure that still clung to the front of the booking hall, these privately chartered trains had loaded to full capacity and surely carried a message for those who would close yet more of our country railways. Winslow was typical of many villages and towns that had lost their passenger trains in the Beeching era, in that its population had increased greatly in recent years, thus fuelling the argument for a restored service.

Little more than a mile further on we passed Verney Junction, a few isolated cottages and a pub adjacent to the disused station. Standing at the point where the lines of the Metropolitan Railway joined those of the LNWR, this place had once enjoyed services to Aylesbury, Buckingham, London, Oxford and Cambridge. After passing the villages of Middle and Steeple Claydon, the train slowed to a walking pace as the guard leaned out to collect the staff from the signalman who occupied a small hut opposite a lofty and disused signal box. Possession of the staff authorised us to travel south to Aylesbury, along the single-track rump of the Great Central main line.

The Great Central had bridged the Oxbridge line at this point, but we approached it along a curve built during the Second World War that gradually rose to the level of the GCR embankment. Progress remained slow as Malcolm pointed out a beautiful view of the lake and nature reserve, reclaimed from one of the disused claypits, that I had passed on foot a couple of days before, and explained that our speed was limited to 15mph until we passed Calvert's overgrown platform. Half a mile or so south of Calvert, alongside the landfill site, we passed the crane that lifted containers from the rubbish trains. Inevitably these trains were colloquially known as 'shit trains', although Malcolm Simpson was anxious to explain that they only carried household refuse, 'but it might as well be shit by the time it has decomposed. The trains come up here at night and the wagons are hauled under the lifting gantries by a winch and cable, leaving the loco free to do other work elsewhere.' He pointed to an immense flock of gulls high above the tree tops and told me, 'They arrived soon after the first trains – absolutely millions of the bleeders.'

The claypits were massive, as big as the Bedfordshire ones that lie alongside the Midland main line, but well screened by trees. Tipping had started in 1980 and, at an annual rate of 680,000 cubic metres, was expected to continue until 2030. The landfill scheme had brought traffic to the railway, which was delivering a yearly total of 580,000 cubic metres from London and Bristol; an extra siding had been installed so that two trains could be accommodated, and the track had been upgraded to support their weight. Certainly it was in better condition than the Oxford to Cambridge line, and the ride was comfortable at 45mph, the track rushing towards us in the failing light as we passed milepost 158, numbered from Manchester in Great Central tradition.

At Grendon Underwood Junction, a couple of miles to the south of Calvert, we stopped. It was perfectly safe to do so; we were the only train on the line and the crew wanted to show me the electric staff apparatus, a machine housed in a trackside hut that helped ensure their confidence in our safety. In this case the purpose of the apparatus, Victorian in appearance and clearly second-hand when installed here in the late 1960s, was to allow a train to enter a branch line while maintaining safe working on the single track of the main line.

The simplest way of allowing trains to work in both directions on a single line is to issue the driver with a staff, or token, as authority to proceed; if there is only one staff for a section of track, only one train can be on the line at any one time. This safe and simple system is almost as old as single-line working itself, but it possesses an inherent limitation that caused considerable inconvenience to early railway operators. If more than one train needed to travel in the same direction through a section, none could move until the unique staff had been returned by a train travelling in the return direction. If no return train was booked, the system broke down. The problem was alleviated by a development involving the use of a staff that could be broken down into several pieces. A number of trains could then travel in the same direction along the single line, each carrying a piece of the staff, but no train would be given authority to return until the whole staff had been carried through the section. However, this system still possessed a degree of inflexibility and scope for confusion.

It was the electric staff apparatus, developed in the 1870s and very like the antique machine in the hut at Grendon Underwood, that provided the solution. Machines were placed at both ends of the single line, and were able to accommodate a number of staffs; however, if one was withdrawn to authorise travel along the line, the staff in the machine at the other end would be locked in position electrically and could not be removed. The first staff could be replaced in either machine to release the lock and permit the withdrawal of another. This method introduced both safety and flexibility to single-line working.

At Grendon Underwood the system also controlled access to a short branch line leading to a fertiliser works.

'You feed the staff into the machine, contact the signalman with the telegraph – just like tapping out a Morse code message, and he releases the points. Then you pull them over with the lever and move into the branch, resetting the points behind you. The staff remains locked in the machine, and you tell the signalman that the main line is clear and that your train is locked in the branch. And that's it – one train can run up and down the branch while others can use the main line, still with only one staff in use. To get out again, you unlock the points, after reclaiming the staff, which can only be removed from the apparatus if none of the others has been issued for the main line.'

We sat in the cab of the stationary train while Malcolm coaxed the diesel engines back to life and looked at the scene ahead. The junction was in wide open countryside, the single main line running perfectly straight and the branch curving away westward into a shallow cutting. It had not always been a truncated branch, but part of the Great Central's alternative route to London, for many years carrying some of the company's fastest trains.

The alternative route had its origin in an acrimonious period in the Great Central's relationship with the Metropolitan Railway, whose metals it needed to travel between Quainton Road, three miles south of Grendon Underwood, and Canfield Place Junction near Marylebone. The conflict had developed in the mid-1890s, when the Great Central decided to build its own London terminus instead of using the Metropolitan station at Baker Street. Not only did the Metropolitan threaten to impede the smooth running of the Great Central's services over its tracks, but the sharp curves and undulations of its line placed limitations on the speed of expresses over the last fifty miles to London. To the directors of the Great Central, the answer lay in co-operation with the Great Western Railway. Both companies had much to gain from the construction of a joint line and Parliamentary approval was given in 1899; ironically, however, by the time the line opened the dispute with the Metropolitan had been settled and Great Central trains were able to use both routes. Perhaps the Great Western gained most from the building of the new line, which provided an important stepping stone in the construction of that company's direct route between London and Birmingham.

The scheme involved the Great Western Railway constructing a line from Old Oak Common, in West London, to join an existing line at High Wycombe, which ran on to Princes Risborough. This track was brought up to main-line standards and extended to Ashendon, about six miles south-west of Grendon Underwood. The Great Western and Great Central railways administered the line jointly between Northolt and Ashendon, while the Great Central built its northern link with the new line from there to Grendon Underwood Junction and a southern one from Northolt to Neasden, where it joined the company's existing line about five miles north of Marylebone. Later, the Great Western constructed the missing link in its direct route from Paddington to Birmingham by laying track from Ashendon to Aynho, a few miles south of Banbury. At this point the line linked with the existing one to Birmingham, which had reached that point, rather circuitously, via Oxford. The Great Central's new route was used first between Neasden and Grendon Underwood by goods trains, in 1905, with passenger services commencing the following year.

As the diesel engines exploded into life and we pulled away with a deep growl, Driver Simpson reminisced about trips down the remnant of the alternative route, which now extended a mere two and a half miles to serve a fertiliser works near the site of Akeman Street Station.

'I remember one winter's day particularly – there was deep snow and we were the first train to use the branch for about four weeks. Just as we were coming out, a bunch of rail enthusiasts appeared. Apparently, they had travelled all the way from Sunderland to have a look at the branch. Just turned up on spec thinking there was a daily train, not the one a week that runs in normal circumstances and once a month at that particular time. I suppose it must have been their lucky day. Anyway, we spent a bit of time talking to them, but I'm amazed even now to think that anyone would travel all that way just to see that branch line.'

This part of the country was surprisingly sparsely populated, and Malcolm spoke of the amazingly different views to be had throughout the year.

'In the summer it's very pretty country, but it can be really bleak in winter. We came down here once with a snowplough borrowed from Buxton. It was great, charging the drifts – snow flying everywhere! But the funny part about it was that we no sooner got to Aylesbury when a message arrived from Buxton saying they were snowed in, and could they please have their snowplough back?'

Soon we passed the point where the track from Verney Junction had once joined, from the left, and rode onto Metropolitan Railway metals. Almost imperceptibly, my journey along the Great Central Railway's London Extension was over, but there was little time to muse on that. Bursting from beneath a road bridge, we were immediately in the middle of the Buckinghamshire Railway Centre at Quainton Road, saluting on our horn as we passed by. On the station a few volunteers were still at work in the gathering dusk and one, silhouetted against the light of an open doorway, returned our greeting with a wave of his hand. The scene that had been so colourful the previous day was different now. Rows of dead locomotives and carriages, elephantine and ghostly grey in the fast-fading light, lined the deserted goods yard and it was easy to sympathise with Malcolm's view that the preservation societies had taken on too much.

'Although I must confess to being pleased that some of the groups are beginning to preserve examples of early diesels, Class 25s and the like, because we did such a lot of work with them. It will be all right so long as they make a good job of preserving a couple, rather than having people running around trying to buy up everything in sight. That way you end up with a couple of really good ones, which you can use, rather than half a dozen or more which won't work. It's the same with steam. They preserve dozens of engines around the various museums, but I much prefer to see an engine on the main line, earning its grub in the way it was meant to. The sight of one of those engines that work the steam specials between Marylebone and Stratford is worth that of a hundred stuck in a museum.'

It seemed an unfair criticism of those hard-working volunteers who had achieved so much against overwhelming odds. But it was understandable in one too young to have memories of the vast range of locomotives that worked our railway system before the days of Marples and Beeching. Those same volunteers may argue in favour of saving as many types as possible for, once lost, they are gone forever, but they would also argue the case for main-line running, especially the ones I met at Quainton, who were negotiating so patiently with British Rail for permission to run steam trains into Aylesbury.

Our conversation continued, about the need to train new men in steam driving techniques, then on to the necessity for railwaymen to co-operate with each other.

'Everyone sees things from a different angle: there's us, the marketing men, the accountants and the management. And somewhere in the middle ground we ought to be able to meet but, unfortunately, the accountants hold the purse strings and their view carries the weight. Look how the economy has declined as accountants have increased their control.'

Malcolm went on to speak of the way changes in working practices had been imposed from above, and how the men were accepting new conditions because they had no choice. Unfortunately, the accountants could not measure the goodwill they were destroying, or the co-operation that was being lost. From their office windows they were unable to see that men who had lost that small degree of latitude that had existed in their work were becoming less inclined to carry out those small additional tasks, often unpaid, which helped the railway to run smoothly.

On the outskirts of Aylesbury the conversation was cut short as we braked and hooted at a group of children who were standing by the line. They waved and I remarked that everyone loved a train crew.

'It's not love when they throw bricks at you,' remarked the guard, who had rejoined us in the cab. I braced myself as we ran over a wooden pallet that had been placed across the track, but it crunched harmlessly beneath our wheels. 'You get blasé about the little –,' remarked Malcolm, but the remainder of his sentence was drowned by the hissing of our brake valves as we slowed on the approach to Aylesbury station.

I rode back with them on the other diesel unit, which was being delivered to Bletchley for servicing. It was an uneventful journey on a starlit night, which ended pleasantly with time in the train crews' mess room while Malcolm awaited his next train. That room had a strong feeling of homeliness – basic, even spartan, yet made comfortable by the friendliness of the men who used it. A few played cards, some read, while others told me of better days on the Oxbridge line or the Great Central. It was a good end to the day, drinking tea and talking with these men, and I felt honoured to be accepted by them.

30
INTO THE CHILTERNS

I returned to Aylesbury by bus, and left for London the following day. The Marylebone train, a diesel multiple unit identical to the one I had ridden from Bletchley, set off from the bay platform, rapidly leaving the station behind and passing the junction where the single track of the old Great Western route diverged towards High Wycombe. At first the land was flattish, but we were soon beginning the climb into the Chiltern Hills, interrupted after two and a half miles by a brief stop at Stoke Mandeville, a village now thought of as one of Aylesbury's suburbs, but famous in its own right for its hospital specialising in the treatment of spinal injuries.

Wendover, four miles further on, in a valley with hills rising steeply on either side, was approached over a long embankment and had a typical Metropolitan Railway station of yellowish brick. In the disused goods yard the warehouse stood empty; its heavy doors hanging forlornly from sagging hinges. As we approached Dutchlands Summit the gradient eased slightly, then steepened again for the last few yards before the train began an exhilarating run down into Great Missenden. Here the station yard was filled with commuters' cars, and a stockily built black signalman leaned on the levers in his timber-built box to watch our passing, in the manner that signalmen have done ever since there have been signal boxes.

This was beautiful undulating country, sheep pastures alternating with deciduous woodland and sunlight streaming through to illuminate and highlight leaves and flowers. Coasting down through the woods, the carriage swayed from side to side, the wind rushed past the drop-light windows and the wheels clicketty-clicked over the short lengths of track to give the feel of a train ride in the 1950s. Breaks in the foliage gave glimpses of rich green countryside and, just before the brakes were applied for Amersham, offered an extraordinary view of a field full of porkers lying on a south-facing slope, each with its belly to the sun.

Amersham station, consisting of a side platform and an island one on an embankment clinging to the edge of a steep hillside, had a simple charm. Slim cast-iron columns with ornate spandrels supported ridged canopies, the apex of each ridge sporting a wooden finial, and the eaves of every canopy were fringed with a traditional timber valance. Everything about the neat buildings, of brown brickwork with stone lintels and sills, was spick and span. The condition of the station contrasted strongly with the sad state of so many of those owned by investment-starved British Rail, and probably resulted from its ownership by London Transport, which was then controlled by the Greater London Council. Amersham was the northern outpost of the Metropolitan Line and the tracks were electrified; London Transport's silver trains alternated with British Rail's diesel services as far as Canfield Place Junction, on the approach to Marylebone, where the electric trains veered off to Baker Street and the Underground system.

A pleasant and prosperous town of some eighteen thousand people, Amersham, despite its rural setting, was industrious, too, its most famous product being radio isotopes. It was really two communities, the modern part around the railway and the old town lying at the foot of a steep hill about a mile distant. According to the local guidebook, the old town was a picturesque place with one of the finest main streets in England, much of it dating from the 16th century. But I was visiting on business and had no time to walk down Station Road in search of olde worlde charm, or to pass on the way a house of white concrete, said to be the first in England built to the ideas of Le Corbusier.

I did see a little of Amersham-on-the-Hill, the modern community near the station, where the architecture reflected the town's rapid expansion in the period between the two World Wars. There was plenty of 'twenties Tudor, which was pleasant enough if undistinguished, but not improved by pockets of 1960s development of rectangular blocks with wide open forecourts that spoiled the building line.

But the purpose for breaking my journey in Amersham was to meet a local resident, rather than explore the town.

31
MEETING MR HARDY

Richard Hardy's Volvo estate car, well-used and well-cared-for, pulled on to the forecourt of Amersham Station and the figure behind the wheel was instantly recognisable from the photographs in his books. There were several reasons for having asked to meet Richard: his vast knowledge, acquired during a lifetime of railway service, that had provided the material for his books *Steam in the Blood* and its sequel *Railways in the Blood*, and his links with the men and locomotives of the Great Central, backed by a passion for railways that had spanned the three-score years since he was a toddler. As a boy he had been befriended by some of the men who worked the line, as a London & North Eastern Railway apprentice he had worked with men and machines that had become legendary in railway circles and, through his later career in railway management, he had gained a rare insight into that aspect of the system.

An easy smile solved the mystery of how he had made the hundreds of friends mentioned in his books, and his affability became even more apparent on the short drive to his home at Chesham Bois. A bench from Northwich station, once part of his territory as British Rail's Divisional Manager for Liverpool, graced the lawn behind the laurel hedge that fronted his Edwardian Voisey-style house, but that was just a foretaste. Inside, as we settled into the comfortable living room, it became apparent that the Northwich seat was not to be equated with the nostalgic frippery, cast-iron lamp posts, wagon wheels and the like to be seen in many a fashionable garden, but part of a collection of profound importance to a man who had not deserted his roots. On one side of the mantelpiece was an old clockwork model of a Great Central 4-6-0, painted black and requiring some imagination to visualise a likeness to the original, and on the other side a professionally built model of the power car of a modern High Speed Train bearing a plaque stating that it had been 'Presented to Richard Hardy by his Friends at British Rail Engineering Ltd'. Three oil paintings of Great Central engines adorned the walls and, by the hearth were two comfortable armchairs that had begun life in a Pullman coach many years before.

A delay, caused by the dilemma of how to position my tape recorder on a chair occupied by his wife's knitting, was overcome when Richard, once boss to more that eight thousand people, decided to move the chair without disturbing the knitting and to place the recorder on the floor. Then I settled into one of the Pullman seats to hear of his life on the railway.

The Hardy family had arrived in Amersham when Richard was ten years old and it was there, during holidays from Marlborough College, that he gained some of his earliest and fondest railway memories.

'I immediately gravitated to the station and those ex-Great Central engines. There was nothing else here on the LNER at that time and there was something about their appearance and the noise they made which fascinated me – and has done ever since. And, of course, when I had been around the station for a year or so, I began to get to know people who worked on the line. Some were Metropolitan people, because Amersham had been a Metropolitan station, but I also got to know some of the LNER drivers. And my fascination for the railway – and the Great Central – grew from those days. Even more important, I began to get a working knowledge not only of the engines but of the people who worked on them – drivers and firemen from the LNER depot at Neasden and some of the Metropolitan crews. The Metropolitan men had been transferred over to the LNER by mutual agreement about 1937, when steam work on the Met became limited to permanent way trains and the occasional freight working. These people took endless trouble over me as a youngster and, although I did not realise it then, I was beginning to learn about the folk with whom I was to going to work for the rest of my life.

'It's quite amazing really, the time those men had for children. I think it still exists today actually, although the fascination can't be quite the same with the type of machine you have got now. But you still find that many men take an interest in showing children – and adults – the cab of their locomotive. When you look back, though, it's amazing that these people did take so much interest. After all, what was I? Just a boy who used to appear during the school holidays and stand at the end of the platform at certain times of the day, yet they always had time to talk to me during the short time they were at Amersham.

'Never, ever, did I ask to go on a locomotive when I was a child, or even as a young man, when I did not have a footplate pass, because the driver is captain of his ship and one realised that instinctively. But these men would say, "We'll make a cloud of steam around the cab with the injector, then hop on and we'll take you to Wendover." And off I'd go. It was quite extraordinary. Then, when I got into my middle teens and my knowledge developed, they invited me into their houses. Later, at the beginning of the war, my dear friend Ted Simpson, one of the original firemen at Neasden who actually came from Liverpool when the depot first opened, took me on the engine of the mail train from Marylebone to Aylesbury in the middle of the night. That was a tremendous thrill – something I shall never forget – but he had no need to do it. He was just interested to guide and help a young man who was interested in the railway profession.'

Years later, during his own days as a railwayman, Richard Hardy remembered the example of men like Ted Simpson and turned an occasionally blind eye to the rules, thus helping many interested people to develop their knowledge of the railway.

'When I was shedmaster at Ipswich we had two categories of visitor. One set came over the wall from the Wherstead Road, but they were not really interested in anything other than being a nuisance, and we sent them packing. However, others came along, told us they were interested, asked to have a look around and we mostly let them. If we had time we would send someone with them, not to keep them on the straight and narrow but to guide and help. There were some, of course, who looked first and asked afterwards, but, providing they behaved all right, we did not make a song and dance over it.

'I made a lot of friends that way and there are people I've known for years who I first met when they came into my depot and asked to have a look round. In later years, when I was at Stratford, there was a man called George Furby who showed innumerable people round, in official parties or not. George must have shown thousands upon thousands round Stratford; it was his life, showing people around the depot. And I must say that I never witnessed an accident, nor ever heard of one, happening to anyone visiting a loco depot.'

Richard's fascination with the railway and involvement with its people led almost inevitably to him joining the LNER as a premium apprentice at Doncaster Locomotive Works. In *Steam in the Blood* he describes graphically, yet in a matter-of-fact way, the transition in his life, an overnight transformation from public schoolboy to the clog-wearing operator of a turret lathe in a blacked-out factory in the dark days of winter in the grimmest part of the Second World War. And yet not a trace of self-pity emerges from those pages, just a line or two to show that he knows the meaning of drudgery, praise for the north country men who accepted him and his peculiar accent, and a warm affection for the many who helped him and showed him kindness.

Out of working hours he gravitated to the station, just as he had as a boy at Amersham, and was rewarded in the same manner, first being invited aboard and then taken on trips. Most trips were on the quiet, occasionally officially sanctioned, but he estimated that he covered over sixty thousand miles on the footplate during the years of his apprenticeship and learned much of the art of firing and driving.

Richard was delighted to find Great Central men and machines well represented in Yorkshire and one of the paintings of a GC engine hanging in his lounge recalled those days.

'She is No 6100, an "Immingham" Class 4-6-0. She was a Copley Hill, Leeds, engine and the chap you can see sitting in the fireman's seat is me; I did many, many, trips on that locomotive. Those engines went on to the Great Northern section about 1924 and were accepted and well-liked, which is a miracle really because GN men normally detested Great Central passenger engines. They never detested the "RODs", of course, because they were the finest freight locomotives in the country and everybody thought they were absolutely marvellous – except possibly the Great Western men. But even they ran them – and did all right with them too! Anyway, the "B4s" settled down on the Great Northern and, before the war, often ran to London with heavy excursion trains. In my time there was often one on the mail train out of Leeds, which used to load up to seventeen or eighteen coaches from Wakefield, and they would take a heavy train like that over the West Riding gradients with no trouble at all. There is no doubt they really were very good engines.'

His footplate experiences during those Doncaster years taught Richard a great respect for the engine crews and their machines. Frequently they would be using locomotives that were, in theory, too weak to haul such heavy trains so that by modern standards their achievements now seemed incredible. 'But they just got on and did the job.' And Richard's admiration of the engines used was not limited to Great Central types.

'The Great Northern "Atlantics" may have been light on their feet – they could sometimes slip persistently – but once they got a grip they had the power and did the most staggering things. Just taking the West Riding as an example, pre-war, before I was on the railway, an "Atlantic" or a "B4" would back down onto a London-Leeds express, which had been brought into Doncaster by a massive Gresley "Pacific", and whack fifteen coaches over to Wakefield in twenty-five minutes. That was twenty miles, much of it uphill!

'Heavier locomotives couldn't be used until the Aire and Calder bridges and the ninety-nine arches, at Wakefield, were strengthened. They didn't like to double-head trains in the West Riding either, for the very good reason that Leeds Central was such a poky little terminus; even with one engine and nine coaches, the rear of the train would be well off the end of the platform. So, with the length of an extra engine and tender up against the buffers, the train would have stuck out even further – cramping shunting movements at the approach to the station. The GN "Atlantics" did a wonderful job on the Great Central main line as well, because the Sheffield men really took to them. Some of the GC men at Lincoln didn't, because they never had to do any really hard work with them, but where they had to work hard they were very popular engines.'

Richard Hardy's experience of Great Central engines was wide ranging and he was able to dispel some of the myths about the last of J. G. Robinson's designs, the four-cylinder mixed-traffic 4-6-0, alleged by some to have had such a voracious appetite for coal that they were known to their crews as 'black pigs'. The last run he made over the steeply graded Sheffield-Manchester route was on such an engine, back in the summer of 1945, some years before the line was electrified.

'They were perfect for that road. The drivers understood them, always working with the regulator fully open and using expansive working wherever they could. They would pull anything; you could pull a whole town with one of those engines and they never slipped. I never had a bad trip on a Robinson four-cylinder engine – we didn't know what it was to have a bad trip! You built up a nice big fire to start and then you would fire to the chimney top: when the chimney top was clear you started again. I never found them hard work, despite the fact that, like all Central engines, the firehole door was rather high and the shovelling plate in the tender very low. The Great Northern men used to moan like hell about that, but we used to say it kept our backs supple. George Barlow, a great friend of mine who was not only the senior driver on the Romney, Hythe & Dymchurch Railway, but later on was its operating manager too, had a trip in the 'thirties on a four-cylinder – one of the last to be built. It was an excursion train from Marylebone to Nottingham and he said it was a fantastic experience – they flew through the night! Those 5ft 8in-wheeled engines were not only good at climbing, but were very fast downhill too. They were wonderful, powerful, engines – and were never known by railwaymen as "black pigs".

'Of course, George's trip was on the London Extension which, south of Nottingham, was a race track once you got off the Metropolitan. Although I suppose that going south you wouldn't have quite the race track you had in the other direction. Heading north, once you got through the tunnel at Catesby you would whizz all the way down to Braunston. Then, when you reached Shawell, after climbing from Rugby, you would whizz all the way down through Lutterworth into Leicester – that was an absolutely marvellous run. After passing

Loughborough you could do it again – down from Barnston Summit through East Leake and Ruddington into Nottingham. A wonderful line, you see.

'Those old boys before the war were fantastic on this section; they knew exactly what they could do. They'd grown up with the railway, the Fred Frances, Teddy Simpsons and all the other famous names. All of them had been firemen on the GC at the very beginning, firemen who had passed for driving quite young as the work developed and had been on expresses or the piped goods trains for years and years. They would leave Marylebone, be through Neasden in eight minutes and Harrow in thirteen. Their idea of passing Harrow, with its speed restriction, was rather different from that printed on their instructions. There were no speedometers, of course, but they knew exactly how fast they could go without being dangerous. It was the same at Rickmansworth where the limit was twenty-five, as it still is today, but nobody ever went through Rickmansworth at twenty-five. There were one or two, like old George Parks, who would sail through at about forty-five, but most would go through at about forty, then set the engine for the bank. It wouldn't be set too hard, so the speed would fall away, perhaps to thirty at the top, and they'd be just nicely on time. Next they'd let rip down to Missenden and sail over the following hill, Dutchlands Summit, before racing down to Aylesbury. They wouldn't shut off until Wendover, travelling down the 1 in 117 and doing eightyish. A touch of the brake through Aylesbury and then away they'd go – but nobody ever dared serve a meal in the dining car until the train was through Aylesbury! They really knew how to run. They were marvellous men.

'Mind you, the war killed the Great Central express trains – they never did the same downhill speeds again. If anything, the uphill work improved, but they never seemed to run in the upper eighties or the nineties. Just think what the 2.32am newspaper train out of Marylebone was like in pre-war days; that was often a four-cylinder job until the "B17s" got it regularly. What a train that was! And the 6.20pm from Marylebone was a hell of a run, usually worked by a GC "Atlantic". That used to go via Wycombe. They really had to knock hell out of the engine to keep to time. At one time they had slip coaches, then they finished with the slips in 1936 and put in extra stops, only adding about a minute for each stop, which made the job even harder.

'This meant that they had some extraordinary tight times allowed for changing engines on some of the trains at Leicester. I always believed it was two or three minutes although, in actual fact, I think they were allowed four, but it was an absolute delight to watch and it was often done in two minutes. The train would run into Leicester Central and stop well back, just short of a slip road that was controlled by a signal. Many drivers used a trick that avoided having to reverse to ease up after the train came to a stand, so that the couplings would be loose ready for the shunter to unhook. As they drew up they kept their left hand on the engine's steam brake and their right hand on the vacuum brake. Then they brought the vacuum handle down to nought just a second before stopping. Because they were pushing the engine brake in, that brake did not go on in combination with the vacuum brake. So the engine recoiled onto the train. In a flash they let the steam brake handle go – and they'd eased up without having to bother reversing. Next, the shunter hopped down from the platform, whipped off the pipes, unhooked, and off the engine went, without the driver having had to waste time going into back gear and then fore gear again. The signalman pulled off for the replacement engine, which then backed up. The shunter went down again, hooked up as a really skilled man could – in half a minute – while the driver blew up the vacuum brake and they were ready for off – in two minutes!'

Such efficiency in their work earned the men of the old Great Central and, later, the GC Section of the London & North Eastern Railway, an enviable reputation as skilled and diligent railwaymen. Many observers of the railway scene have commented on the loyalty and self-respect of these men, perhaps an unusual quality in a company with a reputation for not being particularly strong financially. Richard Hardy had worked with many former GC men in his time.

'They moved all over the Southern Area of the LNER, and wherever GC men went they left their mark. Many of the crack drivers at King's Cross in the 1940s and 1950s were Great Central men. Several of the famous names from the period were from the GC: Hoole, Marrable and Dynes had all come across to the Great Northern section as firemen in the 'twenties, and Ted Hailestone, who originated from Gorton, came from Bradford in 1950. When I was at Ipswich, two or three of the Norwich-based inspectors were ex-Great Central. Years later, the situation there was still the same with two of the three, Eric Wilkinson and Frank Rhodes, having come off the GC section – although they were too young to have worked for the company itself. At King's Cross, the Chief Inspector and fifty per cent of the total originated from the Great Central. Chief Inspector Whitehead, at Colwick, was another and he really was an outstanding railwayman!'

There are numerous theories why Great Central men were such a successful breed. Possibly their success could be attributed to good management, or careful selection at the recruitment stage. The company certainly practised both, and Richard Hardy remembered two stories that threw some light on the mystery.

'Harold Whitehead had worked at Stockport on the Cheshire Lines, which really was the Great Central of course, when he was a very young fireman, so we are talking of the period around 1908. He told me of the time he worked an old Sacre hand-brake-only saddle tank locomotive, which had originally been a Manchester, Sheffield & Lincolnshire Railway engine, into an interchange yard with the Lancashire & Yorkshire. Well, one of the L&Y's big new eight-wheel coupled freight engines came up and stopped alongside. Now, the Lanky engine had only just been built and its crew started taking the mickey out of the GC men. Harold's driver was a very old man who smoked a short clay pipe; he was probably seventy years old or so and one of the old school. And one of the L&Y men asked sarcastically, "What's she blow off at, mate?' Well, the old driver didn't say anything straight away and there was silence for a quarter of a minute or so. Then, looking steadily at the L&Y man, he slowly took his pipe out of his mouth and replied, "She blows off at three half-crowns, mate." That was the end of the conversation. And it shut the L&Y crew up properly, because Great Central drivers at that time were paid three half-crowns a day – 7s 6d – while the L&Y and everyone else in Manchester only got 6s 6d. Harold used to say that was one of the reasons why the company got quality men and, providing that it was combined with a good standard of selection, I see no reason why it should not have been.

'Now Bill Collins, who died in 1981, and was one of the men who used to take me on his engine as a boy, was another who could tell a good story. We kept up our friendship over all those years and he was a grand chap who I'm very proud to have known.'

One of the stories Bill told illustrated not only the physical requirements of the GC when recruiting men to train as drivers, but the autocratic practices of the management of another famous railway company.

'He first went to Neasden for a job about 1902 and then, being too small for the GC, which demanded that firemen be at least five foot six tall, went to Westbourne Park and got a job on the Great Western where that rule did not apply. After a year or so he was sent to Swindon to be passed out as a fireman, and at the medical the doctor told him that he was going to take out some of his teeth! Anyway, Bill was having none of that and replied, "Indeed you're not, sir – I'm off to join the Central!" Those were the very words he used and that is exactly what he did. Off he went back to Neasden, where his two brothers already worked, put newspaper in his shoes to gain a little more height, and passed the GC medical.'

Richard's position as a premium apprentice, coupled with his enthusiasm and good luck, brought him into contact with a particularly important railwayman during his days at Doncaster. It was after one of his spare-time clandestine footplate rides that he climbed down from a locomotive on Wakefield Westgate Station one murky afternoon in 1942 to be confronted on the platform by a tall well-dressed figure. Edward Thompson, newly promoted to the post of Chief Mechanical Engineer of the LNER, had, in his previous role of Chief Mechanical Engineer (Doncaster), interviewed Richard for his job on the railway and recognised him immediately. He beckoned the hapless apprentice with the words, 'Come here, sonny.' In the best public school tradition Richard decided to take the initiative and own up first.

'I'm afraid you've caught me out, sir – I've been travelling on the engine without a pass.'

Thompson's words were reassuring. 'That's all right, sonny. I'm delighted you're interested.'

Within a few minutes the Chief Engineer had invited Richard to join him for the journey back to Doncaster.

'I remember being rather overawed. There we were, sitting in this old and none-too-clean excursion coach, when he would normally have gone first class, but he was kindness itself. I can't remember the whole conversation, but he did talk about his new "B1" Class locomotive, which was due out that year. I remember also that he considered the ex-Great Central "Pom Pom", or "J11" Class mixed-traffic, and the "O4" heavy freight locomotives to be basically very sound engines on which to base an effective rebuild.

'He did go on to make alterations to those locomotives and history speaks for itself. The "Pom Poms", already good engines, were further improved by fitting long-travel piston valves. Later, when I was at Woodford, we had several and they were exceptionally good engines. Admittedly, they did not do much passenger work there but, in other areas, they were used very successfully on passenger trains. They really were very, very good.

'Then, of course, the old GC "O4" heavy freight engines as rebuilt by Thompson as the "O1" Class were outstanding locomotives. And that was proved time and time again on the "Annesley Runners", carrying coal from Annesley to Woodford at considerable speed. They had all the good points of an "O4" plus a modern front-end and a very fine steaming boiler that was also easy to maintain, which it needed to be at Annesley with the terrible water there.'

Edward Thompson was a controversial figure in railway circles, viewed as a realist by some for facing up to the reduced circumstances in which the railways found themselves during and after the Second

World War, and condemned by others who considered that his designs lacked lustre when compared to the spectacular successes of his predecessor, Sir Nigel Gresley. Richard Hardy prefaced his assessment with the observation that he was only a boy at the time and perhaps less qualified to judge Thompson than others had been, but he opted for a favourable verdict.

'Thompson was a realist and I think his work speaks for itself. He produced some very fine locomotives; the "B1s" and "O1s". And the "K1s" were really his engines. As for the "L1s", well, I suppose they could have been a lot better. But he seems to be remembered for his mistakes, while Gresley is remembered for his successes. Gresley made plenty of mistakes – and he didn't always learn from them! The time that Thompson took over was a very difficult period, when he couldn't do the things he wanted to do. Had he become Chief in the mid-1930s he would probably have produced some very outstanding locomotives, but only one set of things can happen in the circumstances. And that's it.'

Before they parted at the end of that journey to Doncaster, Edward Thompson offered to provide Richard with a footplate pass whenever he wanted to ride on a locomotive. Unfortunately, it was almost impossible to reach Thompson to collect the pass.

'There was I, in the Works, and to get the pass meant entering the holy of holies. There were thick-pile carpets and all that sort of thing, and when I went in there, wearing my clogs, the Chief Clerk took a very dim view of it. I can see and hear him now, a stiff little Londoner. I wouldn't call him a Cockney, even though he came from Stratford, and a typical Chief Clerk too – full of his own importance. I don't think that I would ever have got my pass if it had not been for Ivy Shingler, Edward Thompson's secretary, who managed to get me one about once every three months; on those occasions I would work right round the clock to make the best of it. But, of course, I still filled in the time between!'

On the completion of his apprenticeship in 1945 Richard Hardy began the rounds assigned to young men selected for higher management positions. First he went to Stratford depot in East London as a progressman; still remaining on the old Great Eastern Section his next move was to Kings Lynn with the designation of trainee foreman and shedmaster, followed by a transfer across the town to the old Midland & Great Northern Joint Railway depot at South Lynn, this time as acting shedmaster. Later he moved to March to supervise trials with an oil-burning locomotive, then to Liverpool Street as a technical assistant; in 1949 he became shedmaster at Woodford Halse, on the same line that he had observed so enthusiastically when he was a boy at Amersham.

In his first book, *Steam in the Blood*, he wrote fondly of that period: his re-acquaintance with the old Great Central, the thrill of taking charge of his own depot, of problems solved and the joy of settling down with his wife Gwenda after so much wandering and separation. He considered Woodford to be a very good depot at the time of his arrival. Its main task was to supply locomotives to haul heavy freight from the marshalling yards, although there were a few passenger jobs involving runs to Marylebone, Nottingham, Banbury and Sheffield. A collection of some forty-five engines was based there, some medium-sized ex-Great Central designs for the lighter freight work, a few ex-LNER 'Footballer' 4-6-0s for passenger work, and wartime-built 'Austerity' 2-8-0s for the coal trains to Neasden.

Both the 'Footballers' and the 'Austerities' had their problems, those with the former being solved by replacing them with Edward Thompson's new 'B1' Class and those with the latter by Richard's efforts. The trouble was that the 'Austerities' that had recently passed through the workshops at Darlington were unable to produce sufficient steam to keep time on heavy coal trains and Richard decided that prompt remedial action was necessary. A number of details were attended to, but the most important was the fitting of a device he had first come across in his days as an apprentice, which had the effect of sharpening the exhaust blast and so drawing the fire more effectively. It was an unauthorised modification, officially frowned upon, but the performance of the engines improved dramatically.

There were other problems at Woodford too, like the terrible water, which choked locomotive boilers with scale so solid that, every so often, the tubes had to be laboriously removed and the scale shovelled out and wheeled away by the barrowload. And the conditions in the enginemen's hostel proved to be more than even Richard could resolve. However, the seemingly intractable problem of the shortage of tools, which had bedevilled the depot and caused problems for the men, was dealt with in a manner notable for its simplicity. Richard gave instructions that a full set of equipment was to be allocated to each locomotive and stamped with its number. The toolman was put in charge of a rigid enforcement policy, and the new shedmaster let it be known that he gave the scheme a high priority. Soon the enginemen were jealously guarding their equipment, while the humble toolman acquired a new status and purpose in life. As was to be the case on several occasions, his superiors decided to move him just at the time he felt happy with his situation and achievements. In 1950 he was sent, much against his will, to Ipswich, but he never allowed himself to lose touch with the friends he had made in that strange little Northamptonshire village.

Richard's career saw him serve on three Regions of British Railways. After two years as shedmaster at Ipswich he spent another two and a half years in command of Stewart's Lane depot on the Southern Region, before moving to Stratford, in East London, as Assistant District Motive Power Superintendent, striving to hold up morale during the dying days of steam. In 1959 he was promoted to District Motive Power Superintendent at Liverpool Street during the hectic days of the changeover to diesel traction and, in 1963, was again in the midst of change as District Manager for Lincoln, following the British Railways Board's instruction to get rid of the Grimsby fish traffic and close down much of Lincolnshire's rail system. In 1964 he began a four-year spell as Manager of the King's Cross Division of the Eastern Region, followed by close on six more based at Liverpool on the London Midland Region.

His last job was at British Rail Headquarters, supervising the recruitment and training of young engineers entering at professional level, as well as the career development of all professional engineers throughout the system. 'One could be dealing with the problems of a graduate one minute and the appointment of a head of department the next.' It was this posting that brought him and his family back to Amersham and daily contact with the line that had fascinated him as a boy. However, the scene had changed considerably; silver-coloured electric trains of the London Underground had replaced the old Metropolitan workings, while the locomotive-hauled services of the Great Central section had been replaced by near-characterless diesel multiple units, which shuttled between Marylebone and Aylesbury. But Amersham Station, except for the loss of its goods yard and traditional-style signal box, remained much as he remembered it.

Retirement, in 1982, presented an opportunity to become more involved with railway preservation. Since 1977 he had been a director of the Ffestiniog Railway Company, finding time not only to negotiate procedural agreements with the National Union of Railwaymen but also to occasionally act as fireman on the tiny narrow-gauge locomotives as they battled through the mountains of North Wales. A wide circle of railway friends, and a willingness to help those who sought advice, ensured involvement with a number of other preserved railways, if to a lesser degree than with the Ffestiniog. At the Quainton Railway Centre he acted as an examiner of prospective drivers and fireman.

'I got that job through a dear friend called Terry Miller, who was my boss when I first went to King's Lynn in 1946 and then again when I was at Stratford, as Assistant Motive Power Superintendent, and he finished up as the Chief Mechanical & Electrical Engineer of British

Rail. Somehow or other, the Quainton Road people got Terry to come and pass out their drivers. Well, Terry lived right the other side of London and I suppose the time came when he'd had enough of it – and he asked me if I would take over. They are very nice people there and it's a job I thoroughly enjoy, although it's not like passing people out on British Rail, of course. You have to see they can do the job from a practical point of view and that they have got the basics right, but then I take the view that they can always build up the experience afterwards.'

Always welcomed by the volunteer-run railways, Richard mentioned an active season of work.

'I like to do the job I was brought up to do and there is nothing I enjoy more than firing to a good driver. This year I've had a day on the Severn Valley, three days on the Bluebell, and two on the North Yorkshire Moors firing to Keith Gayes, an ex-British Rail man a lot younger than me. I've had four days on the Ffestiniog firing to Paul Ingham, a lab technician at Leicester University. Although Paul is only half my age, he is a beautiful engineman and it is a delight to work with him, because he approaches the job in the same way as the men I grew up with. On our last day up there we had an engine named *Blanche* – an oil-burner – and we had been hauling nine coaches. But on the last trip we only had seven and were seven minutes late leaving Portmadoc – yet only half a minute down on arrival at Blaenau Ffestiniog. Both of us did our job to perfection and I was able to give him every ounce of steam he needed. I remember going through the loop at Rhiw Goch and exchanging the tablet without Paul easing up a great deal. I had the blower on for him to ease a shade and the oil controls and injector set so that, as we cleared the loop, the engine still had its full 150lb of steam ready for the work ahead. I had to tell Paul to open her up just a few yards early, so that the engine did not blow off. Now that is what I call firing and driving! Working together really well, that's the pleasure.

'I've had a couple of trips on the main line too this year. One, with the ex-LMS "Pacific" *Duchess of Hamilton*, was on the day of the Lord's test match. We left Marylebone at 10.15 to go to Bicester. After a quick change I was back sitting in the Lord's pavilion at 2.30 with one of my sons. She's a remarkable engine and the journey was an unforgettable experience. We passed through Wycombe at about 20mph, then accelerated a five-hundred-ton train uphill for five miles to pass Saunderton at 70mph. A staggering performance but, with the coal we had, it was a two-fireman job. Dick Rogers fired from one side and I from the other – as soon as his shovel came out of the firebox mine went in. The problem was that the coal did not have much body, and it just disappeared like chaff when the engine was working hard. If those engines had been fitted with a mechanical stoker they could have been class ten, never mind the eight they were officially rated at. They were very powerful engines indeed, but although I'd never been on an engine like that in this country, it burned that small coal like chaff – needed a colliery tied behind it!'

Another marvellous firing trip was on the streamlined 'Pacific' *Sir Nigel Gresley* of Richard's 'own' railway, the LNER, up the notorious 'Long Drag' between Appleby and Ais Gill on the Settle to Carlisle line.

'It was a perfect trip, steam pressure was at 230-240lb all the way but, after twenty-eight minutes going uphill, I was just about cooked at the top. It was steady firing all the way, only about half a minute to rest between sessions, and I think it might well be the last time I do that particular trip as a fireman.'

But he still felt happy at the prospect of firing on other main-line turns, quoting his old friend Driver Hailstone's view of work: 'It won't hurt your body if it don't hurt your mind.' And, by anyone's standards, sixty-one has to be a respectable age at which to hand over the shovel to a younger man, especially on the Long Drag.

There can be few industries that hold the affection of their workers and ex-workers in the way the railway does. Richard Hardy spent his working life with railwaymen and is unsurprised by the phenomenon.

'Railway work was such a wonderful job and it totally absorbed the people involved. A lot moaned and groaned but realised, deep down, that they were doing a job that had them body and soul. When you retire you can't just drop all that and, when you get near a railway, you can't help being fascinated by it, especially if a steam locomotive is involved. You need other interests or course, and I have plenty, but when I get in the company of railwaymen we are as one. Wherever we come from, whatever our grade, we have a common bond. It's the same with the old timers whenever they get near a steam engine.

'During my day on the Bluebell Railway last summer, a couple of my old firemen from Stewart's Lane came to see me. I was doing the driving as one of them stood behind me and I suggested he take over. Now, he had not handled a steam engine since 1955 and, when we reached Horsted Keynes, he told me it had been absolutely fantastic – absolutely marvellous. And there it is – you just can't leave it alone.'

When the time came for me to leave the Hardy home, Richard drove me back to Amersham Station and waited with me for the Marylebone train, saw me aboard and waved farewell. Clearly a contented man, happy in a busy retirement.

32
INTO MARYLEBONE

Twenty-five miles and forty minutes remained of my Great Central journey, and they were to pass quickly. From Amersham it was downhill all of the seven miles to Rickmansworth, passing the junction for Chesham, then calling at Chalfont & Latimer and Chorleywood on the way. Leaving Rickmansworth by that sharp curve, with its 25mph speed limit that must have been cursed by many a steam engine driver hurrying to gain time on the last stage of his run, we crossed the River Chess, the Colne and the Grand Union Canal before calling at Moor Park. From there the lineside scene was built up and remained so to the end of the journey.

Hurrying through North West London's sprawl, the train passed Northwood, Pinner and North Harrow before calling at Harrow-on-the-Hill, a place so aptly named that even its station sits astride a summit. No more stops now, just fifteen minutes to Marylebone, rushing by the old Metropolitan stations on our exclusive through lines. At Neasden the tracks of the alternative route, which had carried trains from Grendon Underwood Junction over the joint line with the Great Western, rejoined us from the west after passing alongside the concrete hulk of the old Wembley Stadium, which stood about a mile distant.

During the time of the stadium's building, for the British Empire Exhibition of 1924, the Great Central laid a circular loop off the Neasden to Wycombe line, complete with its own station to serve the exhibition. Although the company had been absorbed into the LNER four months prior to the Wembley Loop receiving its first real test, on Cup Final day in April 1923, it was the Great Central's forward planning that made possible a two-minute-interval service of trains from Marylebone. This was a remarkable achievement for steam haulage, especially with the need to change engines at Marylebone to allow each train to reverse out of the terminus, and for trains using the single-track loop to stop, disgorge up to a thousand passengers, and pull away quickly enough to avoid delaying the following one. The station saw its last train on 18 May 1968, the loop being closed officially in September of the following year. Since that time visitors to the stadium have used Wembley Complex Station, situated on the main line and known in Great Central days as Wembley Hill.

When the Great Central Railway arrived at Neasden the Metropolitan already had a works and a depot to the east of the main line and it was on a green-field site to the west that the newcomer established itself. Goods yards were built in the vee of the junction, and south of it were carriage sidings and wagon repair shops, while further south, reached by a single line passing under what is now London's North Circular Road, the company built its only major engine shed south of Woodford. Nearby, adjacent to an isolation hospital, were two streets of employees' houses, home to about a hundred families and clustered round a corrugated-iron C of E church.

A visit showed that Neasden, near to the station, had become an untidy shambles, mainly due to being cut through by the North Circular Road. A huge and gaudy hypermarket, vast car and lorry parks, tinkers' camps, wire-mesh fences and commercial buildings so incongruous with their neighbours as to imply that incompatibility had been part of their design brief, conspired with roaring traffic to create an unfriendly environment for humans. Gone were the carriage works and sidings, while the site of the engine shed was covered by a coal distribution depot, although this was still served by the same track on which Great Central engines had once travelled to their work.

The railway estate in Gresham Road and Woodhayes Road survived as a peaceful enclave, its neatly kept houses showing none of the signs of a community lacking either identity or cohesion, a fate not uncommon when the original reason for existence has passed. In Gresham Road I met a lifelong resident so content with her lot that she could not stress enough how happy she was with her neighbours, by now mostly West Indians, and how she had no desire to live anywhere else. Few houses had been spoiled by ill-advised improvements, although there was one exception so hideously hung with multicoloured reconstituted stone that it may as well have been faced with the leftovers of a stone-cladder's sample box. True, a few of the new windows would have looked better elsewhere and perhaps there was a little too much painted brickwork, but the place had the look of a self-respecting little estate. Most of the front gardens were small and well-kept, graced by hydrangeas, dwarf conifers, roses and fuchsias, while sweet peas, geraniums and other flowers cascaded from hanging baskets or sprouted from window boxes.

A few children played around the streets and alleyways, as they had done for generations, and to me it seemed a contented community. Except for the occasional motor car these streets probably looked much the same as they always had, even if the little corrugated-iron church had made way for a curious-looking Catholic shrine. A plaque recorded that it had been erected by the Holy Mother's Irish sons and daughters, apparently from an equal mix of granite road setts and cement! Around the back of Woodhayes Road the shallow, clear waters of a canal feeder channel were spanned by a simple footbridge leading to well-tended allotment gardens where a few men were working. The scene must have looked very similar to the young Richard Hardy, almost fifty years and a World War previously, when he had waited there for his heroes to trudge that path after signing off at the engine shed.

By train there were five more miles to Marylebone, flashing past more London Transport stations – Dollis Hill, Willesden Green, Kilburn – until, after a fleeting but fine view of the West London rooftops, we passed West Hampstead, veered away from the Metropolitan lines and, with a blast on the horn, dived underground. Hampstead Tunnel is the first of a series on the approach to Marylebone and we emerged only momentarily into daylight to pass over the West Coast Main Line where it appeared from the murky mouth of Primrose Hill Tunnel, before we plunged into the darkness of the 1,200-yard-long St John's Wood Tunnel. A short length of cutting followed, where the lines fanned out to form seven tracks before entering one of three short tunnels, running parallel beneath Lord's Cricket Ground, then emerging into the open for the final approach to the terminus.

Where lines had diverged westward to serve Marylebone Goods Station and the extensive area of wharves and coal yards adjacent to the Regents Canal, which we crossed on a bridge giving a sudden, colourful glimpse of brightly painted canal boats, concrete blocks of flats now stood. Nearer the running lines, a turntable survived from the steam age, one of only a handful remaining in the country. For the two decades in which diesel power had monopolised the station, it had evaded the scrapman's torch only because the power-cars of diesel multiple units sometimes arrived back from overhaul facing in the wrong direction and needed to be turned. In 1985 it was renovated for a new life, turning the locomotives of steam trains that were used on a special Sunday service to Stratford-upon-Avon. From the opposite window a steam engine was visible, ignominiously stored alongside the old milk dock – cold, dead, shorn of life and steam's magic while awaiting its weekly starring role on its run to Stratford. Seconds later, after passing beneath a massive steel road bridge, the train drew slowly to a halt at the end of the Great Central's London Extension.

The strangely tranquil atmosphere of Marylebone station, long interpreted as a portent of impending doom, was not absent on that day as passengers and staff went about their business in an unhurried manner quite foreign to London's other railway termini. Yet there was no great shortage of folk. True, the 15,500 passengers who used the station each day hardly placed it in the first division, but they did add up to around five million each year, which is not insignificant – and there was another reason for the apparent tranquillity. Marylebone's architects had tempered optimism with realism. Anticipating heavy traffic in the future they had built the station frontage and concourse wide enough to serve eight platforms but, in deference to financial constraints and a recognition that business would take time to develop, only built four of them. Custom never did grow sufficiently to justify the planned expansion and the station remained forever half-built, leaving passengers and pigeons an extraordinary amount of space in which to promenade. Additionally, with a modesty quite untypical of its owners, the station was placed on a site secluded from the noise and bustle of Marylebone Road, its approaches concealed behind the massive and splendid edifice of the Hotel Great Central. So, even before the demise of main-line train services to the north, the principal sounds here were of the railway, with few of the rude intrusions associated with road transport.

Having endured its umpteenth year of neglect and just survived a determined attempt at closure, Marylebone had an air of down-at-heel gentility. The paint on girders and stanchions had faded to drabness years previously and pigeons had established squatters' rights in the booking hall. Ornate architectural features clashed with incongruously plain British Rail corporate signboards and shabbily painted brick at the austere entrance to the underground.

How much of a shadow of its former self the station had become was obvious from a visit to Marylebone Library, just over the road from the Hotel Great Central. Helpful staff brought armfuls of information into the reading room: track plans, maps, piles of photographs, files of press cuttings, vast scrapbooks about the station and the binges and banquets that had accompanied the cutting of the first sod for the railway's building. Those scrapbooks, actually great heavy albums, were fascinating. Among their yellowing pages were ornately decorated invitations to the occasion at St John's Wood when Lady Wharncliffe, wife of the Company Chairman, ceremonially commenced the work on the new line, in November 1894, by digging out a shovelful of earth and placing it in a wheelbarrow. Lengthy details of the ornately worked spade and barrow, both made of English oak and solid silver, followed. Contemporary press cuttings gave other insights: the *Nottingham Daily*

Express mentioned somewhere within a mass of words 'that although the large space for invited guests at Alpha Road was dense, the number later assembled at the Holborn Restaurant was dense in comparison' – forever the case with invited dignitaries! There were photographs of the five-hundred-seat restaurant, seating plans and menus, followed by wordy descriptions of the line and the aims of its promoters.

Next came information about the laying of track into the borough; photographs of the new railway being covered over so that fresh turf could be laid where it cut through Lord's cricket ground; the Regents Canal being widened to accommodate barges using the Great Central's wharves; and the skeletal frameworks of the goods and passenger stations taking shape.

More followed in connection with the station's official opening on 9 March 1899, by the Rt Hon C. T. Ritchie, President of the Board of Trade. Yet more invitations and seating plans, this time for the seven hundred and thirty-four guests who banqueted in a sort of canvas hall erected on the concourse. There was even a copy of a 'Short Description of the Line and Country Through which it Passes and Other Matters of Interest', an unpromisingly lengthy title for a short pamphlet. But it was interesting to read of places that I had walked through along the route and some of the ambitions nurtured for them almost ninety years previously. Of Woodford Halse it boasted that 'Inns are being built and also an hotel for hunting men by the enterprising proprietor of the Charwelton Brickworks'. If only they had known that one was to become a down-at-heel pub, the other a working men's club and the village abandoned by the railway.

Fulsome descriptions of the new station were carried in the company's handouts and repeated, almost slavishly, by the press. The Hotel Great Central attracted more than a little interest and there was much approval of its facilities: the covered way linking it with the station, and the central courtyard surrounded by a colonnade that constituted 'an agreeable promenade or lounge and forming what is practically a winter garden'. The hotel drawing room, overlooking the station, was said to be magnificent and luxuriously furnished in Italian style. The banqueting room was claimed to be one of the most superb in London, graced by columns and walls of Norwegian marble, and able to cater for six hundred guests. Unfortunately, this opulent environment was not ready until July 1899, thus unavailable to the assemblage that celebrated the station's opening.

But the real business of running a railway was not forgotten in the adulation of luxury. There were details of the goods warehouse, boasting an area of three acres on each of its three floors and basement, and of the travelling cranes, an electrically driven twenty-five-tonner for the goods yard and a hydraulically powered twenty-ton version for the canal wharf. Completing the picture of the area was a photograph of the Wharncliffe Gardens Estate, six blocks of five-storey tenements accommodating almost 2,700 of the three thousand 'persons of the labouring class' who had been displaced by the demolition of more than five hundred houses on the site.

In the years following its grand opening Marylebone seemed to attract little in the way of media attention, although Volume Three of George Dow's book *Great Central* records some events and innovations. In 1905 the company moved its head office from Manchester London Road to the new station; in 1906 the number of passengers doubled when the Wycombe line, owned jointly with the Great Western, opened; and in 1915 Britain's first battery-powered platform trucks made their debut here. Otherwise the station went remarkably quietly about the business of winning the affection of its users, from Buckinghamshire commuters to Sheffield cutlers, from Nottingham working men rushing home for a few hours on a Sunday excursion to north country wool merchants eating good meals in solidly furnished dining cars.

But the media men were back in 1941, recording how Hitler's bombs had reduced part of the warehouse to a twisted mass of contorted girders. But while the battle-scarred goods station emerged from the war years to resume its normal role, a different fate befell the Hotel Great Central. Commandeered by the Government, as in the First World War, it was destined for post-war conversion to offices. Initially occupied by staff of the London & North Eastern Railway, it later enjoyed a period as headquarters of the British Transport Commission, until the nationally integrated transport system, created by the Attlee Government in the late 1940s, was dismantled by a subsequent Conservative administration and the hotel became the head office of the British Railways Board.

Interest in Marylebone was aroused again towards the end of the 1960s, when the scent of closure hung heavily in the air. The station had lost its goods depot, and its passenger services only served the suburban rump of the old Great Central. Beeching's influence still dominated British Rail's thinking and the new Chairman, Richard Marsh, was a man who had declared that 'there is no romance in railways' and betrayed little affection for his new charge. In 1968 the *Evening News* columnist Ivor Herbert wrote, 'Like the White Cliffs of Dover, the red and cream façade of Marylebone Station lingers on.' He went on to quote Charlie Smith, a porter nearing retirement, as saying, 'It'll be dead in a couple of years at this rate – I'd like to see it out.'

Two years later the ornate iron gates were removed from the

forecourt to provide a better turning area for buses. Lord Sudeley, who lived nearby, complained bitterly to the local paper that, 'This latest piece of vandalism has quite destroyed my affair with Marylebone Station.' A philistinic British Rail spokesperson replied that there were plenty more gates like them around London and added for good measure that 'they have probably been carted off by a scrap merchant to be broken up.' In fact the gates were eventually taken into care by the National Tramway Museum and now form a splendid entrance to its site in the Derbyshire Peak District.

In 1972 a sigh of relief was breathed by friends of Marylebone, when the Government vetoed a scheme to starve the station by diverting Wycombe-line trains into Paddington, but the threat did not recede very far. Marylebone survived on desultory traffic and occasional starring roles on film and television, even then usually masquerading as somewhere else. Filmgoers saw it in Disney's *One of Our Dinosaurs is Missing* and again in *Young Winston*, while for television's *Upstairs, Downstairs* it was disguised as Charing Cross, with crowds of extras cluttering the platforms to play the role of First World War soldiers being ministered to by pretty, upper-class young ladies.

Throughout the 'seventies talk was of closure and redevelopment of the site. Stakes were high, and articles appeared in the Fleet Street heavies explaining the bonanza that awaited property developers. In 1976 *The Times* mentioned 'the new township of Lisson Green' – the estate of multi-storey flats that had replaced the goods station, wharves and coalyard. By 1982 well-informed reports of proposals for closure and the diversion of trains into Paddington and Baker Street had begun to appear.

Fortunately, by this time organisations such as Transport 2000 and the Railway Development Society had emerged to join forces with passengers to make positive suggestions for improving services, while further closures had become difficult to justify and politically unpopular. When the proposal to close Marylebone was formally announced in 1984 it awoke a nest of serpents, for if British Rail's defeatist officials could see no future for the station, more imaginative minds could, including those advocating schemes to convert railways into roads. The National Bus Company's proposal for the conversion of Marylebone to a coach station, linked to London's orbital motorway by a dedicated bus route laid over the Great Central trackbed, with a guidance system to steer coaches through the tunnels, received considerable support in the face of British Rail's lame assertion that development for a non-transport use would be preferable.

Others could see scope for development too; some of the station's defenders argued for an extension of services, pointing to towns such as Winslow, connected to Marylebone by a freight-only track yet having experienced a population growth of three hundred per cent since its station closed. Other towns cited as likely sources of custom included Bicester, where the population had increased by two hundred per cent in twenty years, and the new town of Milton Keynes, by then attracting commuters from along the route of the GC and the freight-only Oxford-Bletchley line, yet scarcely born when Beeching's spirit had stalked the railway.

Perhaps British Rail was convinced by these arguments, or surprised and shamed by the audacity of its principal competitor, but when it withdrew the closure proposal in April 1986, its volte-face was attributed to Baker Street Station having insufficient capacity to handle the diverted trains – due to London Regional Transport having successfully promoted its own rail system. Additionally, studies had established that the diversion of the High Wycombe trains to Paddington would not have resulted in significant savings. Immediately a new optimism arose and the Area Manager, Steven Hawks, who was quoted in *Modern Railways* magazine comparing the jubilant atmosphere on the station to that witnessed on VE Day, went on to speak of a positive future for the station and its services.

Later, he told me of the plans and explained that, initially, they would not be dramatic, the first sign to passengers being a long overdue coat of paint for Marylebone and the other neglected stations on the line. Timetable improvements would soon follow, aimed particularly at speeding up the High Wycombe service, while reducing the amount of rolling stock needed to operate it. Further accelerations were anticipated with the introduction of 'Sprinter' trains, when the maintenance depot was equipped to handle them and track improvements made it possible to take advantage of their superior performance. Old semaphore signals were to be replaced by modern colour-light systems and the track layout at some of the stations, designed for the needs of the steam age, rationalised.

Marylebone Station, too, was to be the subject of more rationalisation and Steven Hawkes wrote, 'We will seek to reduce the amount of this most valuable site required for railway operation.'

Travellers with an affection for the station and knowledge of the British Rail Property Board's activities might have felt uneasy at such a statement, even with the rider that the emphasis 'would be on justifiable improvements rather than pure cost-cutting'.

Rationalisation was a process that had already affected the railway around Marylebone for many years. The extensive goods and coal yards had been replaced by the huge concrete blocks of the Lisson Green Estate, which flanked Lisson Grove. All that remained of the railway's seventy-year tenure of that area was a blue-brick boundary wall fronting Rossmore Road and the bridge that had carried Lisson Grove over the line linking the two yards. When this estate was built there had been little sympathy for railway heritage – and precious little for people. Large blocks of flats, built in the discredited deck-access style, dominated the scene, although their occupants seemed to be making a better job of living in them than their counterparts in many other areas. Some ground-floor flats had well-tended, unvandalised gardens and one displayed a strikingly colourful array of hollyhocks backed by a wall-climbing vine.

The tenement blocks provided to house residents displaced by the building of the railway had also been replaced, thankfully in a style presenting a welcome contrast to the goods yard development. Built within a decade of their soulless neighbours, at a time when the consequences of the grand plans of the 1960s were becoming apparent and the public was getting pig-sick of concrete, their design demonstrated that people could influence planners. A pleasing mix of three- and four-storey blocks, of brick with slate roofs and walled gardens with well-established greenery, they at least looked like real homes. Another modest victory for tradition was evident here as well: the name of Wharncliffe Gardens, bestowed upon the original estate by the Great Central, had been retained, while Hucknall, Rothley and Brackley Courts maintained a link with the railway and the towns it had served.

Apart from a group of temporary offices, planted at the end of the widest platform and spoiling the nostalgic aura surrounding the successful steam service to Stratford-upon-Avon, the station itself had survived the years with little visual damage. And there was every hope that, in an era when the Chairman of British Rail had recently spoken of the railway's historic environment being able to give rail travel a quality unmatched by air or road transport, the philistines of the Property Board might have been tamed and there was just a chance that Marylebone's modernisation might be undertaken sympathetically. It certainly deserved to be, and that unique frontage, somehow combining the architectural style of a country house with a modest hint of metropolitan grandeur, would have begun to look very sad if restoration was not commenced shortly. The red-brick walls and cream terracotta window surrounds were dull and dirty, while on rainy days water dripped from the deteriorating glass and ironwork of the covered way that crossed the forecourt to the former hotel. But the frontage retained much of its original charm, assisted by attractive wrought- and cast-iron gates, railings and lamp supports that had survived wartime scrap-drives and the subsequent age of vandalism. Perhaps British Rail's improvements would include the removal of the modern clutter from that handsome frontage, such as the galvanised-steel air extraction duct that reached from the basement to the eaves.

But there was one part of Marylebone that needed no improvement, for even a lick of paint could not have enhanced the splendid buffet. Named the Victoria and Albert Bar, it occupied a room with dark mahogany fittings, panelled walls and an ornately moulded ceiling with gilt detailing. Great Central Railway posters, station scenes from the early years and pictures of the company's trains adorned the walls, helping to create the right sort of atmosphere in which to enjoy the hand-pumped beer. It was a good place to end the journey and ponder its lessons – one being how people's attitudes had changed little on my trek from north to south, for those I had met were mainly railway folk bound by a common interest and membership of what old Jim Anscomb had called 'the family of railwaymen'. In this case it was a linear family, spread along the line of the old Great Central, a family with time-honoured values that crossed boundaries of regions and class in a nation divided by both. It was also a place to sit and observe my fellow customers and to wonder whether they knew of Marylebone's significance as a memorial to those far-sighted north country men who had viewed their railway to the capital not as an end in itself, but a stopover on their uncompleted journey to Europe.

POSTSCRIPT

Since the 1980s there have been many changes along the path I trod. Perhaps the most significant was the destruction of the coal industry. In a few short years the Leen Valley, in common with other once rich mining areas, saw the ending of its main industry so that now only the occasional winding wheel, mounted on a concrete plinth, the grassed-over slag heaps and struggling communities remain as memorials to an industry that helped build Britain. Almost all of the towns and cities on the route have seen major changes as the industries that characterised them – whether Nottingham's bicycles and lace or Leicester's hosiery – have died or been exported to the Far East.

In Nottingham there is now little visual evidence of the tunnels that pass beneath the city, while most of the viaducts that carried the railway above the rooftops of Leicester have disappeared. And change in the countryside has been no less significant. Saplings that were beginning to grow from the trackbed in the 1980s have become mature trees. In other places, the building of houses or industrial units has obliterated the trackbed and, here and there, landscaping has removed the traces of a once proud railway. Yet, in some parts, the trend has been in the opposite direction.

The Nottingham Transport Heritage Centre, featuring historic rail vehicles, buses and a fine miniature railway, is developing on the site of the Ruddington Ordnance Depot and sends trains along the former main line almost as far as Loughborough, where it is separated from the other section of the preserved Great Central Railway by a tantalisingly narrow gap – through which runs the main railway line from the East Midlands to London. The volunteers at Ruddington have also brought part of the line back into commercial use, to form a link between the national rail system and the gypsum works at East Leake. Now, heavy freight trains regularly use the once neglected line to deliver gypsum, a by-product of the desulphurisation of emissions from coal-fired power stations.

South of Loughborough, the preserved railway has extended to the outskirts of Leicester. Part of it is now double-tracked, making it the only volunteer-run railway in Britain where the impressive sight of two speeding steam trains passing in opposite directions may be witnessed. And if the volunteers at Ruddington and those at Loughborough were able to bridge the half-mile gap that separates them, the preserved railway would stretch from the southern outskirts of Nottingham to the northern environs of Leicester, an outcome that would elevate to prophetic the suggestion made by George Chambers back in 1967, when speaking to the press after driving the last passenger train from Nottingham's Victoria Station. Further south still, the Buckinghamshire Railway Centre at Quainton has developed its status from that described in the 1980s. A major change here has been the rebuilding of the disused Oxford Rewley Road Station – a historic structure containing cast-iron components common to some used in the Crystal Palace – as an event and exhibition hall.

In London, Marylebone Station, which at the time of writing had only just survived an attempt at closure, has been beautifully restored and is now the terminus of a thriving rail service run by the go-ahead Chiltern Railway Company, linking the capital with Aylesbury, Stratford-upon-Avon, Birmingham and Kidderminster. In the years since the book was written, patronage has increased from 15,500 to 40,000 passengers each day, and the station built more than a century ago by the visionaries of the Great Central Railway now has a secure future. And, of course, the other vision of those same great Victorians, the Channel Tunnel, is now a thriving and essential part of the European transport system.

Finally, something very satisfying and unexpected has happened in that strange little Northamptonshire village of Woodford. Not only is the vast expanse of land once occupied by the marshalling yard now thickly wooded, but of the numerous streets of new houses that have appeared in recent years, one has been named in memory of Jim Anscomb, my knowledgeable, modest and very hospitable guide to the village.

INDEX